The Disneyization of Society

The Disneyization of Society

Alan Bryman

SAGE Publishers
London • Thousand Oaks • New Delhi

First Published 2004

Reprinted 2005, 2006

SAGE Publications Ltd
1 Oliver's Yard
55 City Road
London EC1Y 1SP

SAGE Publications Inc.
2455 Teller Road
Thousand Oaks, California 91320

SAGE Publications India Pvt Ltd
B-42, Panchsheel Enclave
Post Box 4109
New Delhi 110 017

British Library Cataloguing in Publication data

A catalogue record for this book is available
from the British Library

ISBN-10 0-7619-6764-8   ISBN-13 978-0-7619-6764-4
ISBN-10 0-7619-6765-6 (pbk) ISBN-13 978-0-7619-6765-1 (pbk)

Library of Congress Control Number available

Typeset by C&M Digitals (P) Ltd., Chennai, India
Printed and bound in Great Britain by TJ International Ltd, Padstow, Cornwall

Contents

Preface

In this book, I seek to make a case that more and more aspects of our society are exhibiting features that are associated with the Disney theme parks. The idea of Disneyization springs from a conviction that there are changes to our social world that the Disney theme parks exemplify. Disneyization thus becomes a lens through which the nature of modern society can be viewed, as well as a way of thinking about issues to do with consumption and globalization.

I am by no means the first person to suggest that modern society is increasingly taking on the characteristics of the Disney theme parks, but I discuss this issue in a systematic way rather than make general allusions to the influence of the Disney theme parks. In addition to drawing attention to ways in which the Disney parks may have been influential on a variety of social institutions and practices, I also argue that they exemplify certain developments that were in train before the first park opened (Disneyland in 1955). In other words, the Disney theme parks are emblematic of certain trends that I identify in this book while simultaneously having been influential in their own right.

In attempting to adopt a more systematic approach than merely making general mention of the way in which many social institutions and practices increasingly resemble the Disney theme parks, I outline four aspects or dimensions of what I call 'Disneyization'. Following a general introduction to the idea of Disneyization in Chapter 1, I then outline these four dimensions – theming, hybrid consumption, merchandising, and performative labour – in the succeeding four chapters. In these chapters, I show how each aspect of Disneyization operates in the Disney theme parks and the ways in which it can be discerned beyond the parks' environs in our wider society. In Chapter 6, I suggest that crucial to the successful operation of Disneyization are control and surveillance and I outline the ways in which these are salient to the Disney theme parks and to Disneyized institutions and practices more generally. In the final chapter, I link Disneyization to wider issues to do with consumption and globalization. Here, I raise the question of whether Disneyization should be viewed as a homogenizing trend that creates a standardized world. I coin the idea of a *systemscape* to help deal with this issue. Disneyization is treated as a systemscape in the sense of a set of underlying principles that are diffusing throughout the economy, culture and society, but which allow considerable variation in how they are implemented. Consequently, the forms that Disneyized institutions take on are likely to vary considerably. In this final chapter, I also seek to inject a more critical tone than is usually apparent in the other chapters, by asking how far Disneyization has adverse consequences and implications.

While writing the book, I have drawn very occasionally on material that I have written elsewhere. I am grateful to: Blackwell Publishers for permission to use material from 'The Disneyization of society', *The Sociological Review*, 47 (1), 1999, 25–47; SAGE Publications Ltd. for permission to use material from 'The wild animal in late modernity: the case of the Disneyization of zoos', *Tourism Studies*, 1 (1), 2001, 83–104, written with Alan Beardsworth to whom I am further grateful for permission to use material from our joint work; and SAGE Publications, Inc. for permission to use material from 'McDonald's as a Disneyized institution', *American Behavioral Scientist*, 41 (2), 154–67.

In this book, I have slightly changed the way in which I conceptualize the dimensions of Disneyization from the ways in which they were presented in these three articles. Hybrid consumption was formerly called 'dedifferentiation of consumption'. In addition, performative labour is employed rather than 'emotional labour', which was the term employed in these three earlier publications, because I felt that a slightly less specific term was needed to capture trends in the area of work that I felt could be linked to the Disney theme parks.

In addition, I would like to thank: Alan Beardsworth and Janet Wasko for constructive and helpful comments on drafts of the book; Chris Rojek and Kay Bridger of SAGE for their patience in the late delivery of my book, for helping me at all stages in getting it to publication, and for their unfailing support of my work; George Ritzer for giving us the idea of McDonaldization, which stimulated the concept of Disneyization, and for putting the idea of writing on McDonald's into my head; an anonymous reviewer for his or her comments; and Sue, Sarah and Darren for continuing to support my intrepid fieldwork in uncovering the extent to which our world is becoming Disneyized.

Chapter One
Disneyization

In this book, I make the case that more and more sectors of society and the economy are being infiltrated by a process I call Disneyization. By Disneyization I mean simply:

> the process by which *the principles* of the Disney theme parks are coming to dominate more and more sectors of American society as well as the rest of the world.

I see the principles that are described in this book as infiltrating many and a growing number of areas of social, cultural, and economic life. Others have drawn attention to the way in which many areas of modern life are coming to take on the manifestations of a theme park, such as when a *Times* journalist referred to Canary Wharf in London as 'theme park city'.[1] In this book I go beyond such general allusions to the growing influence of the Disney theme parks on social life by delineating, in more precise terms, the specific theme park principles that I see seeping through our society. In other words, the project with which this book is concerned is a more analytic assessment of the manifestation of Disney theme parks' principles than is typically undertaken. At the same time, I will emphasize that we cannot attribute the dispersion of these principles solely to the rise of the Disney theme parks, since they clearly predate the parks themselves. The Disney theme park principles may well have leaked into our social institutions and practices without the aid of the parks themselves. However, it is also likely that the high profile of the parks and the frequency with which they are held up as models in a variety of areas – for theming, for their architecture, for their transformation of shopping into play, for their smiling ever-helpful employees, and so on – have contributed greatly to the circulation of the underlying principles described in this book.

Disneyization is portrayed as a globalizing force. In other words, the principles with which it is associated are gradually spreading throughout the globe. The issue of the global diffusion of Disneyizing principles in relation to globalization is discussed in Chapter 7. I recognize that globalization has become simultaneously fashionable and unfashionable: fashionable in the sense that it is a frequently discussed topic in the literature on modern societies; unfashionable in the sense that there has been a sharp reaction to the notion of a world-embracing trend that rides roughshod over local cultures and practices. The issues involved in these considerations are also addressed in Chapter 7.

Chapters 2 to 5 explore the dimensions of Disneyization. These are:

- *theming* – clothing institutions or objects in a narrative that is largely unrelated to the institution or object to which it is applied, such as a casino or restaurant with a Wild West narrative;

- *hybrid consumption* – a general trend whereby the forms of consumption associated with different institutional spheres become interlocked with each other and increasingly difficult to distinguish;[2]

- *merchandising* – the promotion and sale of goods in the form of or bearing copyright images and/or logos, including such products made under licence;

- *performative labour* – the growing tendency for frontline service work to be viewed as a performance, especially one in which the deliberate display of a certain mood is seen as part of the labour involved in service work.[3]

I see these four dimensions as emblematic of the Disney theme parks but also as constituting principles that are pervading many spheres of modern life.

In discussing each dimension, the following issues will be addressed:

- The ways in which that aspect of Disneyization is evident in the Disney theme parks themselves.

- Evidence of the existence of that aspect of Disneyization before the opening of the first Disney theme park – Disneyland in Anaheim, California, in 1955 (see Box 1.1).

- Evidence of the diffusion of that aspect of Disneyization beyond the Disney theme parks.

The second of these three issues is presented to remind us that it is not being suggested that the Disney theme parks were the first context to manifest each of the four aspects of Disneyization. Instead, it is suggested that the Disney theme parks are emblems of the four trends that are discussed. It is almost certainly the case that there has been a process of emulation of the Disney theme park principles due to the immense success, prominence and popularity of the parks. Where appropriate, these processes of imitation will be noted. However, the central point is that the parks exemplify and symbolize the four aspects of Disneyization. In

Box 1.1 The Disney theme parks

Since some readers may not be familiar with the parks, this box contains a listing of all the major Disney theme parks. The parks are organized nowadays as 'resorts', so that Walt Disney World in Orlando, for example, is not a theme park as such but a resort that contains theme parks, as well as many other Disney venues: three water parks, a nightclub area (Pleasure Island), many hotels, restaurants and shops other than those in the parks, and so on. Consequently, the listing that follows is organized by resort and then by year of opening.

Disneyland Resort, Anaheim, California

Magic Kingdom (opened 1955) The original theme park was organized into lands, the main ones being: Adventureland, Frontierland, Tomorrowland, and Fantasyland. Main Street USA is the artery that leads the visitor inexorably towards the lands. As with all Disney theme parks, a land provides the background narrative to the attractions within it.

California Adventure (opened 2001) Divided into lands, themed in terms of California, such as: Pacific Wharf, Bountiful Valley Farm, Condor Flats, and Hollywood Pictures Backlot.

Walt Disney World Resort, Orlando, Florida

Magic Kingdom (opened 1971) More or less identical to the Magic Kingdom in Disneyland (see above).

Epcot Center (opened 1982) This theme park has changed its name slightly on a number of occasions and is now just called Epcot, which stands for Experimental Prototype Community of Tomorrow. It has two main areas: Future World, containing pavilions dedicated to aspects of science and nature and World Showcase, containing representations of a variety of nations.

Disney-MGM Studios (opened 1989) Divided into lands, themed in terms of the movies and Hollywood, including Sunset Boulevard, Hollywood Boulevard, Studio Courtyard, and the Backlot.

Disney's Animal Kingdom (opened 1998) Divided into lands, themed in terms of animals and their locations, both past and present, including: Africa, Asia, Safari Village, Oasis, and Dinoland, USA.

Tokyo Disney Resort, Japan

Tokyo Disneyland (opened in 1983) More or less identical to the Magic Kingdom in Disneyland (see above), but Frontierland is called Westernland and Main Street USA is called World Bazaar.

(Box 1.1 Continued)

Disney Sea (opened in 2001) Divided into lands with nautical themes, including: Port Discovery, American Waterfront, Mermaid Lagoon, Mysterious Island, and Mediterranean Harbor.

Disneyland Resort Paris, France

Disneyland Park (opened in 1992) More or less identical to the Magic Kingdom in Disneyland (see above), but Tomorrowland is called Discoveryland.
   Walt Disney Studios (opened in 2002) Divided into lands, themed in terms of the movies and Hollywood, including: Frontlot, Backlot, Production Courtyard, and Animation Courtyard.

Hong Kong Disneyland

Phase 1 is due to open in 2005. See://www.info.gov.hk/disneyland/eng.htm

much the same way that Walt Disney did not invent modern animation,[4] he did not did not invent Disneyization through the Disney theme parks. (Hereafter, Walt Disney will be referred to simply as 'Walt' following common practice to distinguish the man from the company he founded and nurtured. 'Disney' will refer to the company.)

Disneyization parallels Ritzer's[5] notion of McDonaldization, which was concerned with the diffusion of the principles associated with the fast-food restaurant. Indeed, the definition of Disneyization offered above is meant to be a slightly ironic but nevertheless serious adaptation of Ritzer's definition of McDonaldization. 'Disneyization' is meant to draw attention to the spread of *principles* exemplified by the Disney theme parks.

In a sense, Disneyization takes up where McDonaldization leaves off. McDonaldization is frequently accused of creating a world of homogeneity and sameness. One of the main foundations for Disneyization is that of increasing the appeal of goods and services and the settings in which they are purveyed in the increasingly homogenized environments that are the products of McDonaldization. In essence, Disneyization is about consumption. Consumption and, in particular, increasing the inclination to consume, is Disneyization's driving force. Disneyization seeks to create variety and difference, where McDonaldization wreaks likeness and similarity. It exchanges the mundane blandness of homogenized consumption experiences with frequently spectacular experiences. In addition, Disneyization seeks to remove consumers' need for the prosaic fulfilling of basic needs and to entice them into consumption beyond mere necessity. To take a simple and somewhat stereotyped illustration: eating in a standard McDonald's or Burger King may have the advantage of filling a basic need (hunger) cheaply and in a predictable environment,[6] but Disneyized restaurants are likely to provide an experience that gives the impression of being different and even a sense of the dramatic while being in a location that perhaps increases the likelihood that the consumer will engage in other types of consumption, such as pur- chasing merchandise or participating in other activities in a hybrid consumption setting. Hybrid cons- umption environments themselves frequently take on the characteristics of the spectacular because of the sheer variety of consumption opportunities they offer and especially when accompanied by theming. To a significant extent, then, Disneyization connects with a post-Fordist world of variety and choice in which consumers reign supreme.

Disneyization not Disneyfication

The term 'Disneyization' is a slightly clumsy one and is also somewhat unusual given the preference of many writers and commentators to prefer the more commonly used 'Disneyfication'. My reason for preferring the alternative term is that Disneyfication is typically associated with a statement about the cultural products of the Disney company. To Disneyfy means to translate or transform an object into something superficial and even simplistic. Schickel's portrayal of Disneyfication is one of the most comprehensive, as well as being representative of the kinds of meaning typically attributed to it:

> …that shameless process by which everything the Studio later touched, no matter how unique the vision of the original from which the Studio worked, was reduced to the limited terms Disney and his people could understand. Magic, mystery, individuality … were consistently destroyed when a literary work passed through this machine that had been taught there was only one correct way to draw.[7]

Walz draws attention to similar components in his rendition of Disneyfication: 'Often used pejoratively, [Disneyfication] denotes the company's bowdlerization of literature, myth, and/or history in a simplified, sentimentalized, program-matic way.'[8] Similarly, Ross writes about Disneyfication in terms of 'a process of sanitizing culture or history',[9] while Wasko[10] associates it with sanitization and Americanization.

For writers like these, the process of Disneyfication is one of rendering the material being worked upon (a fairy tale, a novel, a historical event) into a stan-dardized format that is almost instantly recognizable as being from the Disney stable. In actual fact, this is not strictly true. So successful is the Disney company at what it does, namely applying a distinctive template to stories and legends, par-ticularly when making cartoon feature films that will then be marketed along with a raft of merchandise, that its style is frequently copied. As a result, audiences are sometimes unsure about what is and is not a Disney film or indeed what is or is not a Disney theme park (a particularly common mistake among Orlando visitors). However, that possibility should not detract from the fact that Disneyfication is widely perceived in terms similar to those outlined above by Schickel, Walz, and other writers.

Trivialization and sanitization

It is the association of Disneyfication with trivialization and sanitization that is often behind the critiques that are launched against the company and its products. This association lies behind the frequent critiques of Disney's treatments of fairy tales and other stories. A critique by Frances Clarke Sayers provides an example of the kind of concern expressed. She accused Walt of: leaving 'nothing to the imagination of the child';[11] sweetening fairy tales and thereby ruining their effect and purpose; falsifying what life is like, for example, by eliminating conflict; and having scant regard for authors. Similarly, *Pocahontas* has been berated for its colonialist narrative, which they suggest legitimates 'a cultural framework rooted in racism, anti-miscegenation, patriarchy, and capitalism',[12] although not all commentators have interpreted issues of race and gender in the film in this negative light, even though they have been aware of the impact of traditional Disney themes on the story.[13] O'Brien argues that in both *Cinderella* and *The Little Mermaid* the fairy tales on which they are based are distorted to provide a patriarchal reading that is designed to serve corporate marketing goals.[14]

However, it is not just the treatment of fairy tales and children's literature that comes in for such criticism. Haas also writes about Disneyfication, but in the context of the gangster novel in the form of the Disney version of E.L. Doctorow's novel *Billy Bathgate*, which was filmed by Touchstone Pictures, a division of Disney. For Haas, the novel underwent Disneyfication in the sense that the Disney version of the story was 'sanitized' and 'clean and civilized'.[15] Disneyfication is also evident in the themes of patriarchy and innocence that are overlaid on Doctorow's story. Haas argues that the movie was a critical and box office failure because in its Disneyfication, it went against the grain of the conventions of the gangster film. Audiences that were familiar with contemporary gangster films such as *The Untouchables* and *Goodfellas* were unprepared for and dismissive of the alternative template that Disney had imposed.

Walz also discusses Disneyfication in the context of his examination of the work of a former Disney animator, Charlie Thorson who, in 1938, moved from MGM to Warner Bros., leaving two years later.[16] Walz argues that during the period Thorson worked at Warner and indeed during the immediate aftermath following his departure, the Warner Bros. cartoons underwent a temporary Disneyfication. During the period of Thorson's tenure, Bugs Bunny emerged as a clearly different character from the streetwise, sharp-talking rabbit that was to spring from the pen of later Warner animators like Chuck Jones. In particular, the characters during this phase of temporary Disneyfication are cuter and more sentimentalized than those of the period before Thorson's arrival and after the immediate period following his departure. Walz observes that during this period traditional Disney themes of the kind that will be encountered in later chapters, such as nostalgic yearnings, were in evidence.

A second assault on the world of Disney from the point of view of its trivialization and sanitization of culture can be seen in the controversy surrounding Disney's abortive attempt to launch a new theme park called Disney's America. In 1993, Disney proposed a theme park dedicated to American history to be built at Haymarket, close to the Bull Run/Manassas battlefields in Virginia. The location would also have been 35 miles from Washington, DC. Disney's proposals were subjected to a torrent of criticism from historians and environmentalists. In spite of posturing that it was determined to go ahead even in the face of opposition, the company pulled out of the proposal the following year. While the term Disneyfication was not necessarily employed by contributors to this debate, the kinds of points that were made about the likely impact of the park and its representation of history were more or less exactly the same as those of authors who inveigh against the spread of Disneyfication.

Two factors lay behind historians' opposition to the plan. One was that the proposed park was to be located on almost sacred ground, an area of immense symbolic significance for the American people. The other, which is more salient to the present discussion, was to do with doubts about Disney's ability to get across American history in anything other than a trivialized and sanitized way. As Synnott notes, Disney's treatment of American history in theme park attractions such as *American Adventure* in Epcot and *Hall of Presidents* in the Magic Kingdom (both in Walt Disney World, Orlando – hereafter referred to simply as Disney World), which was widely viewed among historians as banal, was very much associated with this lack of faith in Disney versions of history.[17] Even Michael Eisner, Disney's chief executive, acknowledged in his autobiography that historians believed that the company 'couldn't be trusted to depict American history in ways that were sufficiently complex, subtle, and inclusive.'[18] Fears about the handling of such complex and sensitive issues as the treatment of Native Americans and of slavery, which had been the subject of considerable criticism in *American Adventure* in particular, loomed especially large. For Giroux, Disney's capitulation was evidence that the 'Disnification of American culture' could be resisted and challenged.[19]

A further example of this kind of unwanted historical portrayal can be seen in Colonial Williamsburg, the living history museum that celebrates the lives of upper-class Virginians of the colonial period. Prior to the revision of the museum in the 1970s by 'new historians', Colonial Williamsburg was frequently criticized for its omission of conflicts and inequalities, in much the same way that Disney representations of history tend to be criticised for the omission of inequality and tensions. As Handler and Gable note, the museum of this period was frequently depicted as too much like a theme park. Indeed, as one commentator put it, Colonial Williamsburg was 'a too-cute, too-contrived Disneyesque re-creation of what was once the capital of the British colony of Virginia. A historical theme park'.[20] The new historians sought to inject a heavy dose of realism and authenticity into the museum. However, Handler and Gable, as well as other commentators such as Huxtable,[21] still point to systematic omissions from its presentation of history, which is typically regarded as having been purged of undesirable features of the time.

For present purposes, the crucial point is that the kind of history presented at Colonial Williamsburg was precisely the kind of history that was deemed undesirable – one that lacked a sense of the diverse and conflictful nature of the period, a history that was too influenced by a Disney view of how American history should be presented to the masses. Thus, even though Disney's influence on the representation of history was merely that it provided the inspiration prior to the incursions of the new historians, it was widely seen as symbolizing the kind of history that was not wanted. The historians and others fighting Disney's America theme park took the earlier phases of Colonial Williamsburg as their image of the kind of historical havoc that Disney might wreak, even though the company was merely a symbol of sanitized history rather than its manufacturer.

What we see here is a tendency for Disneyfication to be applied to the cultural realm in the form of stories and the depiction of history. Sometimes, authors attribute Disneyfication to other kinds of phenomena. Thus, Ross writes that when he left New York City to live for a year in Disney's new town, Celebration in Florida, he was conscious of the fact that he 'left behind a town frothing with offense at the Disneyfication of Times Square.'[22] Giroux similarly writes of the 'Disnification' of this area of the city.[23] These are direct references to the transformation that Disney has wrought on the area through its location of a flagship Disney Store and its refurbishment of the New Amsterdam Theater in which shows based on Disney feature films (*Beauty and the Beast* and *The Lion King*) are shown. Prior to Disney's arrival, Times Square had become a tawdry and dangerous area replete with sex shops, prostitution and drug transactions. It had become an area that many New Yorkers chose to avoid unless they were looking for the less than salubrious trade that was rife there. Disney's arrival and its colonization of the area cleansed Times Square and encouraged a host of restaurants and retail outlets to open. It became a tourist and consumer enclave within the city. While Giroux acknowledges that the transformation may have had benefits in terms of bringing a wider range of entertainment opportunities to the area for native New Yorkers and tourists alike, he also sees it as evidence of Disney's proclivities for sanitization. In addition, he argues that the regenerated Times Square provides the company with a further opportunity to promote its image and to roll out further its homogenizing view of the world and the corporation's licensed wares.

The tone of such accounts is almost relentlessly negative. Even Walz's account, which recognizes the quality of much of Thorson's cartoon work, also acknowledges that the cartoons of his Warner period are considerably tamer and less sharply perceptive than the animation that took place in the years after Thorson's departure when his influence on the studio had begun to diminish.[24] However, it is precisely the negative tone that is the problem, because Disneyfication has become a synonym for depthless products. It has become difficult to discuss the impacts of Walt Disney and his company in a neutral tone when employing Disneyfication as shorthand for discussing the nature of those impacts. Moreover, the emphasis tends to be upon cultural products like stories and historical representations rather than upon wider changes in culture and the economy. The mention of the Disneyfication (or Disnification) of Times Square by writers like Ross and Giroux calls attention to the influence of Disney in the area but does little more than that. There is even a vagueness about the term. The focus in Walz's definition of Disneyfication as involving sentimentalization, simplification and a programmed way of doing things is only partly followed through in the analysis of the Warner cartoons, where the emphasis is on such features as the cuteness of the characters, which have only a loose connection with the definition.

In other words, the problem for a social scientist confronting a discussion of the wider impact of the Disney company and the emblematic aspects of its operations is that the term with the widest currency – Disneyfication – has become tainted with a largely negative view of the company and its influence. Moreover, Disneyfication has largely become associated with a particular stance on that impact, namely that it is mainly to do with sanitization and trivialization. Even then, the brief coverage of a few definitions suggests that it does not have a singular meaning and is not necessarily applied in a consistent or rigorous way.

There are exceptions to this last point. Warren writes about the Disneyfication of the metropolis and as such is concerned with the way in which the Disney parks have been taken to represent 'a whole approach to urban planning'.[25] Disneyfication is not explicitly defined, but can be inferred from the components of the Disney city. First, it is a social order which is controlled by an all-powerful organization. Second, we find a breach between production and consumption which is achieved 'through the visual removal of all hint of production and the blanketing of consumption with layers of fantasy so that residents are blinkered from seeing the actual labor processes that condition and define their lives'.[26] Third, it is only residents' capacity to consume that is viewed as, in any sense, significant or important. Warren shows that in addition to the emulation of planning principles that can be discerned in the Disney theme parks, Disney representatives have sometimes acted as urban planning consultants, as in the case of the redesign of Seattle's civic centre. She demonstrates how the Disneyfication of Seattle was resisted by locals in this particular instance.

This is an interesting analysis that is somewhat different from the other treatments of Disneyfication, most notably in its less negative tone and in its application of the idea to the built environment in a more systematic way than was seen in the brief allusions above to the Disneyfication of Times Square. However, I have opted not to use the term Disneyfication in this book because I wanted one that was not accompanied by negative baggage and also one that had not been employed in other contexts and would allow me to generate a discussion of the spread of the principles associated with the Disney theme parks.

Reflections on Disneyization

Disneyization seems to fit the requirements outlined in the previous paragraph, in spite of its inelegance. I cannot claim that it has never been used before. For example, in a news article on Las Vegas, Warren Bates, a journalist, has written: 'Distributors of adult materials on the Las Vegas strip have accused local legislators who have sought to stem their activities of attempting to further the "Disneyization of Las Vegas"'.[27] This reference draws attention to the practice on the famous Las Vegas 'strip' (the main thoroughfare in Las Vegas where most of the city's more famous casino-hotels are located) of distributing leaflets that advertise outlets for sex shows and similar 'attractions'. However, as will be discussed in later chapters, since the late 1980s Las Vegas hotels have sought to reposition themselves as playgrounds, not just for adults but also for children by including theme park attractions. This is what Bates is referring to as the 'Disneyization of Las Vegas'. Thrusting leaflets advertising pornography and sex shows into bypassers' hands is inconsistent with this reorientation. Las Vegas has often been referred to as an adult Disneyland, but for the author of this news item, Disneyization means making it appropriate to children as well as adults.

Another use of the term is in an article on 'Disneyitis' in *The New Yorker* by Brendan Gill in which he argues that architecture in the US is increasingly becoming 'Disneyized'. He draws attention to several examples such as Helmut Jahn's State of Illinois Center in Chicago. For Gill, the Center is part of the trend whereby 'public buildings as well as private ones bear the stamp of toyland'.[28] Indeed, he argues that the use of a term like 'Center' rather than 'state office building' is meant to be redolent of pleasure in contrast to the grim realities of bureaucratic routine and humdrumness that are likely to take place in a state office building. In a sense, Gill misses a further Disney-related point here: the use of a term that is meant to say what something is, while simultaneously saying something else about it, is typical of Disney-speak, that special language of 'cast members' (workers) and 'guests' (paying visitors) that will be a topic for later discussion (Box 1.2). Using terms in this way may be yet a further way in which Disney influences our perceptions.

Box 1.2 Disney language

The Disney theme parks are very much associated with the generation of a distinctive language to describe (some would say mask) different groups and activities. Many of the terms can be seen in terms of a performance metaphor, an observation that has important links with the issues addressed in Chapter 5. Here are some common Disney terms and their equivalents:

Everyday term	Disney-speak
theme park visitor/customer	guest
employee	cast member
frontline employee	host or hostess
public areas	onstage
restricted areas	backstage
theme park ride or show	attraction
hiring for a job	casting
job	role
foreman	lead
uniform	costume
job interview	audition
crowd	audience
accident	incident
queue/line	pre-entertainment area
attraction designer	imagineer
talking robot	audio-animatronic figure

Sources: Bryman (1995: 108); Disney Institute (2001: 81); Koenig (1994)

Nor should we be surprised at writers pointing out the influence of Disney. Edward Ball, writing in *Village Voice*, has called Disney 'America's urban laboratory, the clinic whose concoctions are exported around the world.'[29] In a sense, it is not the company as such that is the laboratory but its theme parks. It is these which have had such a profound influence and have led architects to enthuse about their design.[30] However we should not get too carried away with talk of Disney and the influence of the company and its theme parks. It is crucial to remember that Disneyization is not about the influence of Disney but about the spread of the principles that its theme parks exemplify. The four dimensions of Disneyization can be shown to predate Disneyland – hence my insistence on presenting in each chapter, evidence of Disneyization that precedes the opening of this first Disney theme park.

In spite of the occasional use of the term in contexts like the Las Vegas leaflet, Disneyization seemed to be a term that had fewer connotations and implications than Disneyfication. It therefore appeared more like a *tabula rasa* onto which my particular spin, that is, to depict the term as concerned with the spread of the principles with which the Disney theme parks are associated, could be etched. Moreover, although Warren[31] is a rare exception, expositions of Disneyfication rarely explore the principles underlying the features that they expose and are not usually concerned with wider issues to do with Disney's influence in the wider culture (as opposed to its impact on particular texts like fairy tales). In this book, I seek to show that Disneyization is to do with the four underlying principles that were briefly outlined above. Disneyization is therefore to do with the myriad ways in which features associated with the Disney theme parks seep into the economy and into the consumer culture of our times.

What some of these allusions also suggest is that Disney and its theme parks are often treated as reference points. When Wolf observes that everyone wants their brand to be like Disney's,[32] or when commentators express admiration for its product synergies, what we are seeing is a clear notion that Disney, and its theme parks in particular, provide a highly sought after template for the service sector. Thus, while some of the time in this book I will draw attention to the way in which Walt capitalized upon pre-existing trends or features in planning Disneyland, it is also undoubtedly the case that the Disney theme parks are themselves much copied.

A distinction may usefully be drawn between *structural* and *transferred Disneyization*.[33] The former is to do with a collection of underlying changes that are merely exemplified by the Disney theme parks. Transferred Disneyization occurs when the principles associated with the Disney theme parks are reassigned to another sphere, such as a shopping mall. Thus, two separate sets of processes may be at work in the spread of Disneyization: the first set concerns the fact that there are several changes in society of which the Disney theme parks are exemplars; the second set recognizes the success of the Disney theme parks and the likelihood that many of their ingredients can be (and often are) copied and relocated. A similar distinction could be relevant to McDonaldization too in terms of its underlying principles, but that is beyond the scope of this book. In practice, it is likely to be difficult to distinguish between concrete cases of Disneyization in terms of which process – structural or transferred – has taken place, but the distinction is instructive in that it reminds us that the Disney theme parks are much copied.

Conclusion

In this introductory chapter, I have set out what I mean by Disneyization in very general terms. Disneyization is meant to be distinguishable from Disneyfication, which has come to be seen as a distinctive approach to literature and history that entails a crude simplification that also cleanses the object being Disneyfied of unpleasantness. While 'Disneyization' suffers from the fact that it has also been used by some writers, and from being a somewhat awkward term, it is encumbered with less baggage, hence my preference for it over Disneyfication. The key point to remember about the term is that it is to do with spread of principles associated with the Disney theme parks, which predate the opening of the first park in 1955. Undoubtedly, the principles that are described in the next four chapters are directly copied some of the time. Indeed, Disney is sometimes complicit in this copying because it offers courses in which managers are introduced to the way things are done in the parks, the reasons for doing them in particular ways, and how best to implement them.[34] When Disney theme park principles are learned and directly implemented into other spheres in this way, we can see this process as an example of explicit *transferred* Disneyization.

Inevitably, readers familiar with Ritzer's influential work on McDonaldization[35] will draw comparisons with his concept, especially since, as noted above, the definition of Disneyization is an adaptation of his definition. In fact, Disneyization and McDonaldization can be thought of as parallel processes rather than as in any sense competing. They both provide viable accounts of some of the changes occurring in modern society. Neither provides a complete account but each is meant to offer a springboard for understanding some of the processes that are going on around us and to present capsule accounts of those processes. In this chapter, Disneyization has been painted as a set of principles that address a consumerist world in which McDonaldization has wrought homogeneity and in its place projects an ambience of choice, difference, and frequently the spectacular. Both Disneyization and McDonaldization are concerned with consumption, but whereas McDonaldization is rooted in rationalization and its associations with Fordism, scientific management and bureaucracy, Disneyization's affinities are with a post-Fordist world of variety and consumer choice. These issues will be returned to in the final chapter.

Notes

1 Dyckhoff (2003).
2 In earlier publications on Disneyization, I referred to this dimension as *dedifferentiation of consumption* but have decided to employ the somewhat less opaque term, *hybrid consumption*.
3 In earlier publications on Disneyization I referred to this dimension as *emotional labour*. My use of the term *performative labour* is meant to be slightly broader and to include *emotional labour*. In other words, I now see emotional labour as indicative of performative labour but take the view that the latter refers to a slightly wider range of forms of service work in particular.
4 Bryman (1997).
5 Ritzer (1993).
6 Small international differences notwithstanding, a point that will be returned to in Chapter 7.
7 Schickel (1986: 225).
8 Walz (1998: 51).
9 Ross (1999: 134).

14

10 Wasko (2001: 113).
11 Sayers (1965: 604).
12 Buescher and Ono (1996: 151).
13 See Edgerton and Jackson (1996) for a review of reactions to the film.
14 O'Brien (1996).
15 Haas (1995: 74, 79).
16 Walz (1998).
17 Synnott (1995).
18 Eisner (1998: 330).
19 Giroux (1999: 118).
20 Quoted in Handler and Gable (1997: 6).
21 Huxtable (1997).
22 Ross (1999: 6).
23 Giroux (1999: 157).
24 Walz (1998).
25 Warren (1994: 90).
26 Warren (1994: 92).
27 Bates (1997).
28 Gill (1991: 97).
29 Ball (1991: 81).
30 For example, Goldberger (1972).
31 Warren (1994).
32 Wolf (1999: 224).
33 Beardsworth and Bryman (2001).
34 Eisman (1993).
35 Ritzer (1993).

Chapter Two
Theming

Theming is probably the most obvious dimension of Disneyization. Since the term is to do with the diffusion of the principles of the Disney *theme* parks, and since the notion of *theme* is by definition a part of the process, it is inevitable that it would be an important component of the analysis. But what is theming? Theming consists of the application of a narrative to institutions or locations. Typically, the source of the theme is external to the institution or object to which it is applied. This externality is usually revealed as being external in terms of space, time, sphere or any combination of these sources.

Theming provides a veneer of meaning and symbolism to the objects to which it is applied. It is meant to give them a meaning that transcends or at the very least is in addition to what they actually *are*. In infusing objects with meaning through theming, they are deemed to be made more attractive and interesting than they would otherwise be. The rationale for theming will be examined in greater detail below, but to anticipate some of the motives that will be addressed, we can look at the issue from the point of view of the supplier of the themed environment and the consumer of it.

Why Theme?

From the point of view of the consumer of the themed environment, theming offers the opportunity to be entertained and to enjoy novel experiences. It is sometimes suggested that we live in an entertainment economy[1] in which the constant exposure to forms of entertainment – most notably through television, the movies, and computer games – leads us to expect that we will be entertained even when entertainment is not the main focus of the activity. Relatedly, when so much of the consumer's landscape is made up of homogenized, standardized fare – near identical malls, shops, restaurants – entertainment provides an additional level of enjoyment that adds a layer of charm to, and helps to differentiate, the same and the similar. Ritzer, for example, argues that theming and similar strategies help to enchant sites of consumption in an increasingly McDonaldized and hence standardized world.[2]

As the balance of many people's consumption has shifted from goods to services, they begin to seek more from those services. However, it is well known that consumers' enjoyment and dislike of a service is only partly conditioned by the objective quality of the service itself. The *servicescape* is crucial to the consumer's response.[3] The servicescape is made up of a host of features in addition to the service itself (though in practical terms, it may be difficult to remove the service from the context within which it is embedded). The servicescape will involve cues to the consumer concerning the enjoyment of the service. The most notable of these components of the servicescape is the physical environment within which the service is delivered and the manner in which it is delivered.[4] Theming forms an important component of a servicescape.

Clearly, services that entertain are more likely to be enjoyed than those which not, particularly among consumers who are well primed with the appropriate cultural capital to produce positive – perhaps even ecstatic – impressions. Services that entertain and that are memorable – that provide fun – are the kinds of experience that are increasingly becoming expected features. Developments like theme parks may bear some responsibility for this inflation in expectations of the provision of services, resulting in services in the form of shopping and eating that take place in themed and thereby entertaining environments. The service-cum-theme principle pervades these locations and generates experiences that are more likely to be memorable to consumers, especially when they return to blander servicescapes. Increasingly, then, we live in an *experience economy* in which consumers seek out services that will be provided in an entertaining way and will result in a memorable experience.[5]

From the point of view of the service suppliers, they know that many consumers are increasingly bored with the standardized services and settings with which they are typically confronted. Theming helps to differentiate one service or context from another. Thus, providing an entertaining environment that excites the senses may be a mechanism for distinguishing a service from that of its competitors even though the actual services may otherwise be more or less identical. This proposition is an extension of the principle that we have all known for a long time, namely, that people do not consume on the basis of use value alone. As any student of Coca-Cola advertisements will have noticed, the company rarely seeks to sell its well-known beverage on the basis of flavour; instead, it positions itself as a purveyor of identities and lifestyles. The same kind of formula operates in connection with many areas of service provision: the themed environment in affording an engaging location for consumption, becomes a major component of the service and how it is responded to. Indeed, the nature of the themed environment may even connect with the consumer's identity and lifestyle projects.

However, theming presents several problems for service providers. Two points can be usefully noted at this stage, in anticipation of some of the points to be made below. First, it is costly. Theming requires substantial investments without any certainty that the theme and the way it is presented will be sufficiently absorbing to warrant the expenditures involved. The costs are likely to revolve around the expenses associated with supplying the physical embodiment of the theme in terms of visual, auditory and even tactile stimuli and the costs of training staff to behave in ways consonant with the theme and other aspects of desirable service provision. On top of this, no matter how well the theme is physically implemented, it may simply be unappealing to consumers. Second, and relatedly, expectations of themed environments probably operate like a ratchet screwdriver, in that people's expectations are constantly increasing. For new entrants to themed service provision, this means that costs are constantly likely to increase as the theming stakes grow. For existing providers, they have to face the fact that what is innovative and exciting today may be hackneyed and dull tomorrow as new entrants enter the field with more compelling ideas and ever more engaging ways of implementing them. As we will see, the world of theming is littered with high-profile casualties, alongside some spectacular successes.

Sources of Themes

The sources of themes are many and varied but modern culture, along with its distinctive takes on other cultures and epochs, provides a rich source of themes on which to draw. Referring to built environments in the United States, Gottdiener[6] has identified nine prominent themes: status; tropical paradise; wild west; classical civilization; nostalgia; Arabian fantasy; urban motif; fortress architecture and surveillance; and modernism and progress. Essentially, we can see here the implication that geography, history, and social organization provide rich repositories of narratives on which the architects of theming can draw. However, Gottdiener's list is by no means comprehensive and omits three of the most renowned sources of theming, each of which will be covered in this chapter and elsewhere: music and in particular rock music; sport; and Hollywood and the movies more generally. Schmitt and Simonson suggest five 'cultural domains' that are the source of themes: the physical world; philosophical and psychological concepts; religion, politics and history; the arts; and fashion and popular culture.[7] While they use somewhat broader categories than Gottdiener, they are more prone to overlap. For example, does Hollywood as a theme fall into the arts or popular culture? Nonetheless, this review of two influential taxonomies of sources of theming gets across the rich reservoir of sources that the architects of theming can draw upon.

- Place – nations, cities or even planets.
- Time – past, present and future. Images of the past are mined particularly for the sense of *nostalgia* they are frequently designed to evoke.
- Sport – sport generally, as well as individual sports.
- Music – rock music and genres, such as Motown or country and western.
- Cinema – the movies generally, as well as particular genres or influential figures.
- Fashion – clothes and models.
- Commodities – such as cars and motorbikes.
- Architecture – iconic buildings.
- Natural world – symbolic natural environments, such as the rainforest and savannah, as well as volcanoes.
- Literature – well known literary figures, such as Sherlock Holmes, Jekyll and Hyde, as well as fairy tales.
- Morality or philosophy – such as notions of conservation.

Very often, a theme may contain more than one of these ingredients. For example, the theme of the wild west, which has been a very popular thematic motif that was particularly influential in the early days of the theming of Las Vegas's casinos and hotels,[8] contains elements of place (the United States), time (a period in the past), the cinema (in that it is invariably a cinematic version of the wild west that is presented), and possibly the natural world (with the use of well-known landscaped features such as John Ford's use of Monument Valley).

The list has omitted one further source of theming:

- The company and its logo.

Many company brands and logos become so distinctive that they become themes in themselves. They do not fit the definition of theming offered above when it was suggested that typically, the source of the theme is external to the institution or object to which it is applied. Company logos and brands are exceptions to the externality of a theme and account for the use of the hedging term 'typically'. Beardsworth and

Bryman refer to such theming as *reflexive theming*, whereby the theme and the brand and its expression become coterminous. With reflexive theming, the organization does not draw upon external devices for its narratives; instead, the thematic elements are internally generated and then continuously reproduced. With such theming, the 'themed setting refers reflexively to itself and to the population of clones which reflect it and are reflected by it'.[9] Schmitt and Simonson also recognize that corporate brands and logos can act as themes when they write: 'Themes refer to the content, the meaning, the projected image of an identity. Corporate and brand themes are cultural signs and symbols created ... to express corporate and brand characteristics'.[10] Such theming is essentially self-referential and refers to those relatively rare instances in which a brand provides its own theme.

These 12 sources of theming are meant to form a backdrop to the analysis that follows. Moreover, the different sources or types of theme frequently overlap. A theme may, for example, combine a sense of both place and time for its inspiration. Thus, contemporary merchants and corporations have a rich repository of ideas to draw upon in veiling commerce in themes, as did Walt Disney when he began his plans for Disneyland.

Theming in Disney Theme Parks

It could be argued that theming in the Disney theme parks operates at several levels. First, each theme park is itself themed in the sense of having an overarching narrative unity. Disneyland was given the overall theme of celebrating America and its achievements and also as a magical place in which people can leave the harsh realities of the outside world behind them.

Second, each Disney theme park is divided into 'lands' which are themed and have their own thematic coherence and integrity. The Magic Kingdoms are divided into the following main lands each with its own theme: Adventureland; Frontierland; Tomorrowland (or Discoveryland); and Fantasyland. Each of the Magic Kingdoms also has other lands or regions (like New Orleans Square and Mickey's Toontime in Disneyland), as well as Main Street USA, the main thoroughfare from which the lands can be reached. However, these four lands are common to all the Magic Kingdoms. The theme of each land or region is expressed in architecture, decoration, ambience, clothing of cast members (employees), sound, and food and goods for sale. The attractions – the rides and shows – are similarly tailored to the land in which they are located. Thus, Big Thunder Mountain Railroad (basically a runaway mine train) in Frontierland, is themed through: its name; the garb of the cast members; the music (country and western); posters; wood cabin structures; lots of red rock and cacti; audioanimatronic figures that speak in western drawl and are dressed in cowboy outfits; and so on. It is unmistakably the Wild West. When Mickey or any of the other Disney characters appear as costumed cast members, they too are clothed in the appropriate uniform. Thus, Donald Duck has a rakish beret when posing for photographs in 'France' in Epcot's World Showcase.

The aim of such theming is described as follows in the share prospectus issued in October 1989 for Euro Disneyland (now Disneyland Paris):

> Rather than presenting a random collection of roller coasters, merry-go-rounds and Ferris wheels in a carnival atmosphere, these parks are divided into distinct areas called 'lands' in which a selected theme (such as exotic adventures, childhood fairy tales or the frontier life of the nineteenth century American West) is presented through architecture, landscaping, costuming, music, live entertainment, attractions, merchandise and food and beverages. Within a particular land, intrusions and distractions from the theme are minimised so that the visitor becomes immersed in its atmosphere. ... Restaurants and retail stores at Disney theme parks are designed to entertain guests and support the theme.[11]

Distractions are further kept to a minimum in the Magic Kingdom theme parks through a physical separation that is designed to ensure that, as far as possible, thematic discontinuities are minimized by shielding the lands from each other. This insistence seems to have been relaxed to a considerable extent in the other Disney theme parks in that the different components are visible from each other. Thus, for example, World Showcase in Epcot can be seen across the lake from Future World and vice versa, and the different pavilions within each of these areas are invariably visible from each other.

The third level of theming at the Disney theme parks is the Disney company itself. Disney can call upon and deploy its reputation for providing magical experiences, especially those that are aimed at children, and the well-known stable of characters it has created and popularized throughout the globe. In a sense this is a form of reflexive theming but it is a much richer one than most organizations involved in such theming can enjoy, in that it extends beyond corporate logos and stylized architecture. For Disney, this additional layer of theming can be embodied in the costumed Mickeys, Snow Whites, and Buzz Lightyears that populate the parks for photography and autograph sessions.

It is the second of the three senses of theming in the Disney theme parks that is probably the most significant and is the most copied. The idea is to immerse the visitor (or 'guest' in Disney language) in another world. One of the main reasons for theming was that Walt felt that it would differentiate his theme park idea from traditional amusement parks and as a consequence make it more attractive to adults. Walt disliked traditional amusement parks because he felt that they were often dirty, contained dull and unimaginative rides, and were seedy and tawdry. The sense of seediness was particularly a result of the atmosphere in which owners of rides or stalls would bark out loudly and often uncouthly to passersby. He detested the atmosphere and often mentioned in his reflections how uncomfortable he felt when he used to take his two daughters (Diane and Sharon) to them. Another tale that is often told is that when he first mentioned his intention to build an amusement park to his wife, Lillian, she proclaimed her disappointment saying they were such horrible places. Walt is supposed to have retorted that his park would not be like those parks. Thus, Walt's antipathy towards amusement parks was borne of his own experience of being a reluctant visitor to them and a feeling that not only could they be so much better but they would actually appeal to adults. He also noticed that many parents were like him in that they only frequented these parks to appease their children.[12]

Disneyland was conceived as a celebration of America's past and as a paean to progress, or as Walt put it: 'the older generation can recapture the nostalgia of days gone by, and the younger generation can savour the challenge of the future.'[13] The former element allowed Walt to lace many of the attractions and environments with heavy doses of nostalgia that he felt would have a direct appeal to adults. Main Street USA, the thoroughfare to the attractions, exemplifies this sentiment with its unashamed harking back to turn-of-the-century middle America with which many American adults could nostalgically associate themselves. Similarly, Frontierland recalls the era of the Wild West but in a very cinematic mould and was designed to provide a set of images to which adults could easily relate. The very process of theming was central to this product differentiation strategy, since most pre-Disneyland amusement parks were loose assemblages of rides of various degrees of thrill.

Walt's genius in this connection was to turn adults from reluctant into enthusiastic visitors to such venues. There is little doubt that he was successful in this connection, since the ratio of adults to children who visit the parks is usually put at 4:1.[14] The fact that in the American Disney parks, many visitors are returnees is a further testament to his success in attracting adults and to the significance of forging a connection with an adult audience.

Theming accomplished at least two things. First, it established coherence in the various rides and attractions in Disneyland and the environments in which they were located. Second, in the design of rides and attractions, the accent was placed on their theming rather than on the thrill factor, which was the emphasis in traditional amusement parks. Indeed, Walt initially did not plan for roller coaster rides in order to set his park apart from the amusement parks he loathed so much. Gradually, such rides have been incorporated as a result of pressure from younger visitors who found Disney fare too tame. However, when such rides were built they were in heavily themed form, for example, Big Thunder Mountain Railroad (themed on prospecting in the Wild West), Space Mountain (space travel) and Splash Mountain (*Song of the South*). By establishing coherence to rides and by placing an emphasis on the theme rather than on thrills, Walt was able to differentiate Disneyland from the traditional amusement parks that he so disliked.

Precursors of Theming

It would be a mistake to think of Disneyland as the progenitor of theming. It may have (and almost certainly has) acted as a high profile spur to a realization of the significance and possibilities of theming, but its basic principles can be discerned in a number of forerunners. Two types of precursor stand out. One is amusement parks that had incorporated elementary theming features at an early stage. Coney Island's Luna Park and Dreamland Park provide examples of this, in that attractions were clothed in exotic and sometimes erotic motifs. In Luna Park, attractions such as recreations of the Johnstown flood of 1889, the eruption of Mount Vesuvius and the subsequent fall of Pompeii, and a Trip to the Moon provided the rudiments of theming, as did attractions relating to cultural, geographical and historical themes.[15] Regarding the latter, Kasson writes:

> For its opening season Luna [Park] boasted a Venetian city complete with gondoliers, a Japanese garden, an Irish village, an Eskimo village, a Dutch windmill, and a Chinese theater. The following year, the park added a reproduction of the Durbar of Delhi and attempted to re-create its splendor.[16]

A journalist proclaimed that this last exhibit 'was such as to make those who witnessed it imagine they were in a genuine Oriental city'.[17] The use of indigenous people from the areas concerned, encouraged the sense of the realism and exoticism of these areas of the park.

It is not known whether Coney Island influenced Walt's thinking in the design of Disneyland. In fact, both Luna Park (in 1946) and Dreamland (in 1911), with its Lilliputian village of dwarves and ethnographic villages, had burned to the ground by the time Walt was looking around for ideas for the park that was germinating in his mind. Moreover, the Coney Island amusement parks represented for him the kinds of tasteless venue that he was seeking to avoid. He did send a team to the area for ideas, though primarily, they identified features to avoid rather than to include.[18] Instead, Walt tended to gain inspiration from parks like the Tivoli Gardens in Copenhagen for the kind of environment he was seeking. This park merged rides and other attractions with carefully and gently landscaped gardens. Walt was impressed by its cleanliness, its family atmosphere, the use of music, the quality of its restaurants, and the courtesy of its employees.[19]

A second type of forerunner is the exposition or world's fair which acted as a means of displaying modernity's wares by suffusing them with a sense of continuing scientific and technological progress and with utopianism. A number of writers have drawn attention to the continuities between the Disney theme parks and expositions and world's fairs.[20] Kasson, for example, notes how the Midway of the Columbian Exposition in Chicago in 1893 contained many themed elements that almost certainly would have had an impact on the Coney Island parks:

> Fairgoers threaded their way on foot or in hired chairs among a hurly-burly of exotic attractions: mosques and pagodas, Viennese streets and Turkish bazaars, South Sea Island huts, Irish and German castles, and Indian tepees.[21]

A later example of this kind of theming was at the New York World's Fair (1939–40), which contained representations of Shakespeare's England and New York City at the end of the nineteenth century.[22] Marling has suggested that the Chicago Railroad Fair of 1948 was a particular inspiration for Disneyland. The Fair was designed to celebrate the centenary of the first train to enter the city. It showcased many futuristic trains and an even greater number of trains of the past. It therefore combined the celebration of the past with visions of the future, which would be a feature of Disneyland. Furthermore, the rolling stock was surrounded by carefully re-created models and settings. According to Marling these included: a model dude ranch; a mechanical representation of Yellowstone Park's Old Faithful geyser; a French Quarter; an Indian Quarter; and an area modelled on the beaches of Florida's Gulf Coast. There were also numerous shows including re-enactments of historical events. Marling writes that at each venue 'the illusion of being there was sustained by workers in appropriate garb and by restaurants with matching cuisine'.[23]

Marling argues that what was significant was not the originality of these ideas, many of which could be seen in the Century of Progress Exposition in Chicago in 1933; instead, the significance lay in the 'coherence and concentration of the experience'.[24] It was this aspect of the Fair, in particular, that she regards as a major inspiration for the form that Disneyland assumed. Disneyland's originality lies in the combination of the transformation of themed *attractions* into one of themed environments with the transformation of the world's fair/exposition concept into a *permanent* site.

Other precursors of theming can be pointed to, many of them involving quite low levels of theming. The early Las Vegas institutions often employed Wild West theming,[25] while bars and restaurants have frequently loosely themed themselves on such motifs as sport or the movies. Between 1890 and 1910 considerable amounts of money were expended on New York restaurants so that they were renovated and transformed into exotic simulated locations. One restaurant – Roman Gardens – was designed to represent the trimmings of the ancient world with Roman gardens and imitations of Egyptian and Pompeii rooms.[26] Doss has written that before Disneyland '...California's built environment featured plenty of restaurants pretending to be Moorish castles, apartment buildings disguised as Spanish colonial missions, movie theaters designed as Chinese palaces, and a factory (the Samson Tire and Rubber Company) posed as an Assyrian temple.'[27]

The spread of theming is not something that we can attribute to Walt and his theme parks, since it is clear that there are many examples of high- and low-profile contexts in which theming was imaginatively employed. Undoubtedly, as the foregoing speculations suggest, some of these are likely to have influenced the form and content of Disneyland and its attractions. Building the park represented a massive investment for Walt, who effectively went into massive debt in order to finance it. What began as a simple idea for a small playground close to his studio exploded into something much more substantial and expensive. It is hardly surprising that he would draw on a wide variety of resources in order to work with ideas that were reasonably well tried and tested. By sending out teams to visit a wide variety of amusement parks and bringing in designers to advise him, the form of Disneyland will undoubtedly have been influenced by these forerunners of theming. Three points should be registered. First, that he may have borrowed from others' ideas does not in any way detract from the immense originality of Disneyland. The manner in which theming in the Disney theme parks plunges the visitor into a narrativized environment is far greater than in the predecessors that have been discussed. Second, Disneyland's approach to theming has undoubtedly influenced other applications, many of which will be discussed in the remainder of this chapter. Third, it is also the case that we can see vestiges of theming processes prior to the opening of Disneyland. These final reflections suggest that both structural and transferred Disneyization are involved in the spread of theming.

The Diffusion of Theming

Amusement parks

It is easy to forget that one manifestation of the spread of theming is the theme park, which is essentially an amusement park to which narratives are applied. One increasingly rarely hears about amusement parks these days. Most of them are theme parks, even if they cannot call upon the rich narratives that Disney can enjoy. Even Knott's Berry Farm, which is close to but predates Disneyland, has taken on the trappings of a theme park with the familiar layout of themed 'lands'. Knott's Berry Farm is nowadays suffused with an overall Wild West theme that is then broken down into the familiar 'lands' (Roaring 20s, Fiesta Village, Wild Water Wilderness, etc.). Busch Gardens in Tampa, Florida, has an overall theme of Africa, which then becomes the context for themed lands (Timbuktu, Serengeti Plain, Stanleyville, Nairobi, etc.). Dolly Parton's Dollywood is, like some other theme parks, themed at two or more levels. It is themed in terms of Dolly herself (her own life as a poor Appalachian girl who made good), country and western music, and Appalachian culture. Within the park, there are different lands: Country Fair, Rivertown Junction, Craftsmen's Valley, etc.

In Europe, amusement parks often tend to become theme parks too. Universal Mediterranea theme park, Port Aventura, close to Barcelona in Spain has four themed lands: Mexico, Far West, Polynesia, and China. Rides are given names that link to the land in question, for example, the stomach churning steel roller coaster with eight loops in China is called Dragon Khan. Like Universal Mediterranea, Chessington World of Adventures has little in the way of an overall theme but has several themed lands with appropriately named rides and restaurants, including: Mystic East, Forbidden Kingdom, Mexicana, Transylvania, and Beanoland (Beano is a long-standing British comic that is still published). Alton Towers, the largest theme park in the UK, has a weak overall theme but has divided the park into themed lands such as: Forbidden Valley, Gloomy Wood, Cred Street, and Katanga Canyon. Warner Brothers Movie World near Madrid in Spain is themed on the movies and has five themed areas: Hollywood Boulevard, Cartoon Village, Old West, Superheroes World, and Studios. While not themed in terms of lands, other European theme parks like Parc Asterix in France and de Efteling in Holland are no less themed overall – the former in terms of the much-loved cartoon character and his associates and the latter in terms of fairy tales. In Japan, the opening of Tokyo Disneyland in 1983 spawned a large number of theme parks. These too are typically thought of as theme rather than amusement parks because in the majority of cases they take nations as their overarching theme.

Restaurants

There is now a veritable themed restaurant industry, which draws on such well-known and accessible cultural themes as rock and other kinds of music; sport; Hollywood and the film industry more generally; geography and history.[28] These themes find their expression in chains of themed restaurants, like Hard Rock Cafe, Planet Hollywood, All Sports Cafe, Harley-Davidson Cafe, Rainforest Cafe, Fashion Cafe, as well as one-off themed eating establishments. Diners are surrounded by sounds and sights that are constitutive of the themed environment, which, although incidental to the act of eating as such, are major reasons for such restaurants being sought out. In Britain, themed pubs are increasingly prominent and popular, such as Irish pubs, while in the USA, bars themed on British pubs have become popular venues.

Essentially, with themed restaurants, the theme and the sumptuousness of its implementation become the main ways in which competitors differentiate themselves and compete with each other. Hard Rock Cafe, which began in London, became the template for many other chains of themed restaurants. These have sought to capitalize on potent themes such as:

- Rock, soul or country music – Hard Rock Cafe, Motown Cafe, Country Star, House of Blues.
- Race cars, racing and motorbikes – NASCAR Cafe, Race Rock Cafe, Harley-Davidson Cafe.
- Sport – Official All Star Cafe, ESPN Zone.
- Fashion – Fashion Cafe.
- Magic and fantasy – Copperfield's Magic Underground, Jekyll and Hyde Club, Mars 2112.
- Natural world – Rainforest Cafe, Dive!
- Movies and entertainment – Planet Hollywood, Billboard Live.
- Nostalgia – Johnny Rockets (see Figure 5.1), Dick Clark's Bandstand Grill, Ruby Tuesday, Lori's Diner chain.

In addition, there are ethnically themed restaurant chains[29] like the Olive Garden restaurants (Italian) and Ricardo's Mexican restaurants in the United States. These involve playing up and tweaking symbols of ethnicity and in particular their food-related expression. In the UK, there are standard formats for the ubiquitous Indian restaurant such as flock wallpaper, zither music, plastercast models of Indian gods, and so on. Indeed, these features have become such a cliché that there is something of a trend whereby new restaurants self-consciously differentiate themselves by *not* having them, for example, by adopting a more general, neutral restaurant ambience.

By no means all themed restaurants are part of chains. There are many independent restaurants that are loosely themed on sports as well as the ethnic theming previously referred to. Shoval mentions the Cardo Culiniaria in old Jerusalem's Jewish Quarter which advertises itself as 'a "reconstruction" of an "authentic" Roman gastronomic experience'.[30] The Cowshed Cafe advertises itself as 'New Zealand's only restaurant in a once operating dairy shed (no shit)'.[31] The CB Huntington Railroad Co. Family Fun Eatery in Bayville, New Jersey, is themed on the American railroads and contains a working model and train memorabilia.[32] Mr. Bones is a restaurant on Holmes Beach in Florida which is themed on voodoo and employs various macabre models to reinforce the theme. On entry, the diners take their chosen bottle of beer from a coffin full of ice! The House of Mao restaurant in Singapore may have Hunan cuisine as its main attraction but is heavily themed on Beijing (including real artefacts such as Mao and Communist Party memorabilia), a Great Hall that is supposed to represent the Great Hall of the People, chairs in red fabric that are supposed to refer to the collars on red army uniforms, and the toilets are supposed to be like Chinese prison cells![33]

Themed restaurants also provide a prism through which to view some of the pitfalls of theming as a differentiation strategy. After a period in which themed restaurant chains rolled out more and more outlets and newcomers arrived on the scene to participate in what was seen as an insatiable appetite for this genre of eating, around the turn of the millennium the eating public began to fall out of love with them. Planet Hollywood was probably the most high profile casualty, filing twice for bankruptcy, but there are many others too: the Fashion Cafe chain has all but disappeared; the Dive! chain of nautically themed restaurants soon closed down some of its outlets; some Official All Star Sports restaurants closed, even in themed restaurant hotspots like Las Vegas; and there have been persistent industry rumours of imminent closures and restaurants facing trouble.[34]

Several reasons have been proffered for the sudden reversal in fortunes. One is that restaurants rely a great deal on repeat business and therefore if the emphasis is placed on the experience and entertaining guests, once they have enjoyed that experience on one or two occasions they will move onto another theme or will decide not to pay what they perceive to be the mark up for the entertainment component. Second, some themes have a limited appeal or go out of fashion.

Theming in this sense is very risky and could have been worse for one themed restaurant had it materialized. It was reported in the news-journal wire services on 25 September, 2001 that plans for a disaster-themed restaurant in Baltimore with simulated airliner wreckage, video footage of train wreckage and building explosions, and explosive sound effects had been scrapped because of September 11.[35] The Crash Cafe was to include a huge DC-3 tail section over the entrance. Clearly, if the Crash Cafe had been much further on in its plans, the impact of the September 11 tragedy on its business could have been calamitous.

Third, there is a widespread view that themed restaurants were placing too much emphasis on theming at the expense of the food and that diners were voting with their feet in response to the drop in quality. As a journalist writing on Philadelphia's themed restaurant scene put it, customers are basically asking 'Forget Bruce Willis, how's the food?'.[36] This is a clear reference to the actor's Planet Hollywood chain of which he is a co-founder, which, because of its troubles around the time of the article, became a byword for much of what was wrong with the industry. He quotes the president of Mars 2112, whose restaurant chain takes diners to their tables on flying saucers, as saying that the lack of attention to the quality of food was the chief reason for the troubles at chains like Planet Hollywood and Fashion Cafe. There was a growing feeling in the industry that themed restaurant chains might be able to get away with mediocre food in prime tourist locations where there is a tradition of tourists going to such establishments, like Orlando, Las Vegas, and New York City, but in areas where repeat business is much more crucial, they would not get away with it.

A fourth reason that has been proffered is that some themed restaurants simply have not gone far enough in the implementation of theming. Karen Daroff of Daroff Design Inc., a company which has designed some of the main themed restaurant concepts, advocates: 'Don't tone it down. Turn it up. Every detail in entertainment architecture should be part of the illusion to support the overriding story'.[37] In other words, she implies that sometimes themed restaurants do not go far enough in their designs and she goes on to say:

> More than anything, what we believe and what we're seeing is the consumer wants more than a meal. They want an adventurous experience in a hyper-immersive, cinematic environment that emotionally, intellectually and physically transports them. If only for a moment, the guests leave their lives behind and become part of the story.[38]

The double bind of theming for themed restaurants is clear: whether on the one hand to choose the kind of enveloping and costly theming Daroff describes and recommends and risk sinking a large investment in a theme that may simply not enthral, or may go out of fashion; or on the other hand to opt for less elaborate and less costly themes, such as the common 'diner' narrative or ethnic theming, which may not go far enough. However, even in the case of the high concept themed restaurants, to quote Daroff again 'Food really does matter'.[39]

What this brief discussion of the tribulations faced by themed restaurants shows is that despite the enthusiasm for theming and similar devices among the advocates of the entertainment economy and the experience economy,[40] providing people with entertaining experiences is not a guarantee of success. On the other hand, it is striking that in spite of these troubles, openings of themed restaurants continue although at a less hectic pace than in their mid-1990s heyday and rumours of new themes persist.

McDonald's

In this and the next four chapters, McDonald's will be considered as a possible site of Disneyization. Such a discussion is significant in two respects. First, its restaurants are extremely widespread throughout the world, so that, if it can be shown to be a carrier of Disneyization, it would be a very important one. Second, as the primary carrier of McDonaldization, a consideration of the possibility that McDonald's is Disneyized is potentially significant, since it would imply that the two processes co-exist.

McDonald's can be viewed as themed in different ways and at different levels. First, it is themed in terms of itself and as such is reflexively themed.[41] This theme is expressed in the corporate decoration, modes of service delivery, staff clothing, and various architectural cues that are pervasive features of these establishments. Such theming is essentially self-referential and refers to those relatively rare instances in which a brand provides its own organizational narrative. McDonald's as a company is acutely aware of its self-referential theming. It portrays its eating environments as experiences. Benjamin Barber quotes Jim Cantalupo, then president of international operations, who explains how McDonald's 'is more than just price. It's the whole experience which our customers have come to expect from McDonald's. It's the drive-thrus … it's the Playlands … it's the smile at the front counter … it's all those things … the experience'.[42] When Ray Kroc, the founder of McDonald's, once observed, 'when you are in this business you are in show business',[43] he was drawing attention to the way in which the development of a brand was to do with turning the perception of it into an experience by which it becomes instantly recognizable. Certainly, Manning and Callum-Swan have drawn attention to the way in which there are theatrical or dramatic connotations to a McDonald's visit. Thus, when it is suggested by the latter writers that 'McDonald's is a brilliantly conceived dramatic production',[44] it is the brand as a unique eating experience that is crucial. As Twitchell has observed, with branding '[w]hat is being bought is place, prestige, comfort, security, confidence, purpose, meaning'.[45] Thus, McDonald's as a company is acutely aware of the significance of its brand as a provider of meaning and organizer of experiences.

There is also evidence of McDonald's becoming increasingly attracted to the use of external narratives in its restaurants. Chicago's rock 'n' roll McDonald's serves as an illustration of the use of this kind of development (see Figure 2.1). The

Figure 2.1   The Rock 'n' Roll McDonald's in Chicago

McDonald's in Disney Village at Disneyland Paris is claimed to have been inspired by Italian theatre. In 2001, an article in the *New York Times* announced that a huge McDonald's was planned for Times Square that would have the ambience of a Broadway theatre.[46] When Schlosser visited the McDonald's near Dachau concentration camp, it had a Wild West theme.[47] Yan describes a themed McDonald's in Beijing in which the restaurant was decorated like a ship and crew members wore sailor uniforms, rather than conventional McDonald's garb.[48] The narrative was one of Uncle McDonald's Adventure which is meant to entail a round-the-world trip. Also, the company has announced that it is going to refurbish some of its outlets as traditional diners,[49] thereby drawing on a motif that is an extremely popular thematic focus for American restaurant chains. A journalist reported in *The Times* that not only was Denny's remodelling some of its restaurants 'to give the nostalgic feel of traditional diners', McDonald's was doing the same and had just opened its 'first diner-style outlet in Kokomo, Indiana, and customers are lining up to eat such old-fashioned American fare as turkey steak and mashed potato'.[50] A second has since opened in another town in Indiana. It remains to be seen whether these McDonald's diners will be rolled out more widely but the fact that they are experimenting with such theming is very telling about the directions that the company is considering.

A further sign of theming is the use of ethnic theming. In the UK, for example, the company often features lines that are themed in terms of Indian or Italian cooking (both of which are very popular among the British). In Spring 2000, McDonald's launched a series of locally themed meals in France. In one month, the enthusiast could buy a burger with a different French cheese on each day of the week. The following month, 'gourmet' meals were available in the South of France. 'Gourmet' was signified by being able to eat burgers topped with ratatouille or by ice cream with a blackcurrant sauce topping.[51]

Therefore, in several ways, McDonald's restaurants can be viewed as themed. The growing use of theming that goes beyond reflexive theming may be due to a belief that, while the company does provide a certain kind of experience, as Cantalupo suggests (see above), it increasingly needs to do more in this regard. Pine and Gilmore have suggested that, with regard to the experience economy, companies increasingly need to raise consumers' experiences to new highly memorable levels.[52] While it is unlikely that McDonald's would want to turn itself into a chain of themed restaurants that become destinations in their own right, especially in view of the financial difficulties experienced by such chains in recent years, the slow move in some of its outlets to a more distinctive kind of theming may prove an interesting long-term development in terms of Disneyization.

Hotels

Hotels are increasingly being themed and it is no coincidence that two of the better known themed restaurant brands – Hard Rock Cafe and Planet Hollywood – are being deployed for such a purpose. The opening in 2001 of McDonald's Golden Arch hotel in Zurich, where the headboards on the beds are in the shape of a golden arch, is an interesting illustration of the use of a brand as a mechanism for theming.[53] However, the really striking developments in themed hotels have tended to be in hotels attached to theme parks, where the Disney theme park hotels in particular – especially those at Disney World and Disneyland Paris – have taken a clear lead, and in the Las Vegas hotel-casinos.

In the Disney theme parks, there are variations in the degree of intensity and flamboyancy in the theming of their hotels, and these features are more or less directly related to room rates. Nonetheless, all are themed. Disneyland Paris, for example, has the following hotels (in brackets are the 'headlines' for each hotel in the 2002–3 Disneyland Paris brochure):

- Disneyland Hotel – 'a lavish Victorian fantasy'
- New York Hotel – 'the excitement of New York'

- Newport Bay Club – 'set sail for New England!'

- Sequoia Lodge – 'savour the mountain atmosphere'

- Hotel Cheyenne – 'the legendary Wild West'

- Hotel Santa Fe – 'journey to the old South-West'

Each hotel has an external and interior décor that is consistent with the overarching theme and has restaurants consistent with the theme: for example, Hotel New York has the Manhattan Restaurant and the Parkside Diner, while Sequoia Lodge has the Hunter's Grill restaurant and the Beaver Creek Tavern.

Other examples of theme parks that have themed hotels linked to them are:

- Universal Resort Orlando has three themed hotels: Portofino Bay Hotel described as 'A stunning re-creation of the seaside village of Portofino, Italy, complete down to the cobblestone streets and sidewalk cafes' and as having three themed swimming pools; Hard Rock Hotel; and Royal Pacific Resort ('Sail away to a tropical paradise as swaying palm trees, exotic plants, a bamboo forest and tropical lotus lagoon transport you to the enchanted isles of the South Pacific').[54]

- Alton Towers theme park in England has two themed hotels: the Alton Towers Hotel (loosely themed on a flying machine and its travellers and having some rooms with the themes of Coca-Cola, chocolate, Peter Rabbit, Arabian Nights, and Oblivion and Nemesis, both of which are white knuckle rides at the park) and the Splash Landings Hotel, which has its own new water park – Cariba Creek – themed on a flooded creek adjacent to the theme park. The water park is for the exclusive use of hotel guests.

- Universal Mediterranea in Spain has two themed hotels: Hotel Port Aventura, themed on the Mediterranean, and Hotel El Paso which has a Mexican setting.

In Las Vegas, virtually every new hotel on the 'strip' is heavily themed. The famous strip now contains such themes as ancient Rome (Caesar's Palace), ancient Egypt (Luxor), ye olde England (Excalibur), the movies (MGM Grand), city life (New York New York), turn-of-the-century high life on the Mediterranean (Monte Carlo), the sea (Treasure Island), Paris (Paris), Venice (the Venetian), Italy and its artistic heritage (Bellagio), and so on. Here in Las Vegas we find what are probably the most extreme hotels in terms of the degree of complexity and intensity of the theming. The theming that is expressed in terms of the architecture and decoration is further underscored by the presence of attractions and restaurants that are closely linked to the master theme, an issue that will be discussed further in Chapter 3.

However, it is not just such high-profile themed hotels that provide examples of this genre. An interesting example of a themed hotel that predates their proliferation in theme parks and Las Vegas is provided by Gottdiener's (1997) discussion of the Hotel Boulderado in Boulder, Colorado. Built in 1909, it is a paean to the American West in its architecture and decoration. Gottdiener tells us:

The interior features imitation Tiffany lamps in the lobby and rooms, an impressive stained glass ceiling in the lobby, mahogany-stained furniture and wood detailing, turn-of-the-century patterned wall paper, and old-fashioned metal poster beds. Meeting rooms embellish signification further by using names that invoke the Rocky Mountain setting...as an object it is ... a sign of nostalgia and a representation of the theme of the 'Old West.'[55]

Other examples of themed hotels are:

- The Fantasyland Hotel at West Edmonton Mall, like the Madonna Inn in San Luis Obispo, California, has themed international rooms, so guests can stay in a different country on each visit. The themed rooms allow the guest to stay in places that are far away in terms of location (for example, Polynesia and Hollywood) or in terms of both time and location (for example, ancient Rome and Victorian England).[56]

- At Old Te Whaiti Jail in New Zealand, guests can stay in a jail/hotel for a distinctly different kind of overnight accommodation experience.[57]

- Shoval refers to the plans for the building of a Holiday Inn in Jerusalem that will be themed in terms of both the Old and New Testaments.[58]

- The Caboose Taupo Hotel by Lake Taupo in New Zealand is themed on the era of rail travel in Colonial Africa.[59]

- The Sherlock Holmes Hotel, Baker Street, London is themed unsurprisingly on the sleuth and his associate, Dr Watson. The theming is not intensive and mainly revolves around simulated artefacts and images.

- The House of Blues Hotel, like the Hard Rock and Planet Hollywood hotels, takes its inspiration from the themed restaurant brand that it has created. It was described by one journalist as offering 'less than an organic, subtle evocation of African-American art and music'.[60]

- A Beatles themed hotel, The Hard Day's Night Hotel, was due to open in Liverpool in 2004.

- The Madonna Inn has 108 rooms each with a distinctive theme and colour scheme with names like Espana, Indian, Irish Hills, and Old English.[61]

- The See Vue Motel on the Oregon Coast boasts a smaller but nonetheless varied range of themed rooms, such as: The Salish, Far Out East, and The Santa Fe.[62]

It seems quite likely that this penchant for themed hotels will proliferate though possibly not with the exotic façades that adorn the Las Vegas establishments.

As this brief tour suggests, themed hotels vary considerably in the intensity and range of the theming process but there can be little doubt that it is a growing trend, especially when linked to major international resorts and theme parks.

Malls

Malls are increasingly becoming themed in the sense either of having an overarching theme or of having themed areas within them. Mall of America in

Minneapolis and West Edmonton Mall in Edmonton, Alberta exemplify this feature. As Gottdiener points out, Mall of America takes America as its master theme both through its name and the outside façade which is decorated with stars and stripes.[63] In addition, areas within the mall are individually themed. Cohn, quoting it would seem from a publicity leaflet about Mall of America, notes that

> South Avenue was 'chic sophisticated … cosmopolitan shopping and flair'; North Garden 'lushly landscaped … a park-like setting with gazebos, trellises and natural skylights'; West Market 'reminiscent of a European railway station'; and East Broadway a honky tonk, all neon and chrome.[64]

Cohn also observes that the muzak changes according to which area one is in. As with all theming, the mall designers call upon accessible imagery to project the kinds of impressions they seek to convey. In West Edmonton Mall, one encounters arcades modelled on the boulevards of Paris and on Bourbon Street in New Orleans along with the conventional juxtapositions associated with North American malls.

While the Mall of America and West Edmonton Mall are unusual in their size and the numbers of visitors they attract, so that it is important not to generalize too much from them, many of the features they exhibit can be seen in much smaller malls in the United States and elsewhere. Adjacent to Caesar's Palace in Las Vegas is a mall called the Forum Shops where the largely upscale shops and restaurants are surrounded by signs of ancient Rome. This is one of the most successful malls in the United States in terms of retail sales per square foot. It has become a tourist attraction in its own right by virtue of its audio-animatronic statues and the clever ceiling, which is a sky that changes from night to day and back again. This playing with time in part adds to the attraction but can also be viewed as related to the way in which casinos like Caesar's Palace disorientate by not having clocks and windows so that visitors/players are not reminded what time of the day it is. Other examples of themed malls include the Borgata, a Scottsdale open air shopping mall 'set down in the flat Arizona desert, reinterprets the medieval Tuscan hill town of San Gimignano with piazza and scaled-down towers (made of real Italian bricks)'.[65]

The Mills Corporation has become well-known for building out-of-town malls with distinctive themes. Opry Mills in Nashville has distinct areas: 'When a Nashville consumer crosses from the "American classic" neighborhood into the more upscale "fashion" neighborhood, bright lights give way to softer lighting, top-40 tunes are replaced with classical music, the floors become carpeted, homey rocking chairs and garden benches are displaced by upholstered chairs.'[66] Arundel Mills in Baltimore features a number of 'neighbourhoods' each of which denotes different aspects of the city or the state of Maryland: Charm City, Baltimore's nickname, has simulated row houses and marble steps, the Ocean City boardwalk, and Chesapeake marshes along with turtles as seats and hovering dragonflies.

Similarly, the MetroCentre in Gateshead in the north east of England contains themed shopping areas like the Mediterranean Village.[67] When we look at the Trafford Centre just outside Manchester in the north west of England, we find what the writer of a *Times* article referred to as turning 'shopping into a Disneyesque filmic

Figure 2.2   The New Orleans Quarter in Manchester's Trafford Centre

adventure'.[68] There are areas based on the Orient, New York's Grand Central station, turn-of-the-century New Orleans, a Moroccan souk, Egypt, Venice and China. Figure 2.2 shows the Trafford Centre's New Orleans area (see also Figure 3.2 which portrays areas signifying ancient Egypt and the Aztecs).

It might be asked why theming of this kind takes place. Why, in other words, spend not inconsiderable amounts of money on simulated environments for shopping and related activities, such as eating? One reason is that theming turns the mall from a neutral and otherwise potentially uninteresting group of shops into something of interest in its own right. In other words, in addition to differentiating itself from other malls, the themed mall becomes a *destination* in itself above and beyond being a place people want to visit in order to shop. I will have more to say about this issue in Chapter 3.

The second factor has to do with the principle of *adjacent attraction*, which has implications for the discussion in the next two sections as well. This is a marketing principle that proposes that 'the most dissimilar objects lend each other mutual support when they are placed next to each other'.[69] This principle implies that placing otherwise unremarkable goods or services for sale in an environment that is interesting or conveys messages beyond those provided by the goods or services themselves renders them more attractive and hence more likely to be purchased. The shopping experience is enlivened by theming. In part, the consumer in a themed setting is consuming that setting as much as the goods or services themselves when making a purchase.

The spread of the themed mall poses problems for malls that do not have the additional layers of attractiveness and meaning. Sandicki and Holt describe a mall with a largely dull design and which, as they see it, does little to conceal its essentially commercial nature. Their study of mall users found that many complained about its 'aesthetically boring, depressive, and unexciting nature'.[70] As one shopper put it: 'It is a boring mall. It is very small and very average. You can't do much. There are only shops, and if you are not really into shopping, there is nothing else here. It looks cold'.[71] While large themed malls are still a comparative rarity, it is clear that to the extent that shoppers are familiar with them, they become yardsticks against which other malls are measured. This constitutes a problem for the mall designers who are likely to feel increasingly pushed to add expensive theming to their designs in order to provide the kinds of shopping experience many consumers are clearly coming to expect.

Heritage shopping

A context for shopping that is highly related to the themed mall is one that occurs when sites that are deemed to have heritage value are turned into locales for consumption. Very often old buildings are taken over to form the framework for shops and restaurants and are sometimes added onto in a faux design that is able to feed off the character and heritage value of the buildings and location. In much the same way that Main Street USA in the Disney theme parks acts as a themed environment for shopping that feeds off the feelings of warmth and nostalgia with which this tribute to small town middle America is associated, so areas with 'real' heritage value (or at least a heritage value that is constructed as real) have been turned into shopping locations that feed off a sense of a valued past and thus function essentially as themed malls.

This trend is invariably attributed to the festival marketplace movement that is generally regarded as having begun with the redevelopment of Boston's Faneuil Hall which resulted in its being turned into an upmarket shopping location by James Rouse, an architect who has been a big fan of the Disney theme parks as models of urban development and architecture and who has been responsible for the design of some of the company's hotels. The work of Rouse and his company has been described as 'a commercial developer that regenerates downmarket neighborhoods into Thumbelina-clean commercial strips Walt would have loved'.[72] Faneuil Hall, which opened in August 1976, is based on three restored buildings of historic significance in downtown Boston and in its second year of operation it attracted more visitors than Disneyland that year. Such developments are often seen as revitalizing downtown areas and as providing destination attractions for tourists, as well as providing locals with a safe shopping environment. The historic significance of the buildings or their locations and the constructed heritage with which they are suffused provides a themed environment which is similar to that of the themed mall.

According to the publicity surrounding Faneuil Hall, the main buildings were created by Peter Faneuil in order to provide accommodation for Boston's merchants and sellers of produce and to provide a forum for orators. It was the site of the first protests against the Sugar Act in 1764. According to the website: 'Firebrand Samuel Adams rallied the citizens of Boston to the cause of independence from Great Britain in the hallowed Hall, and George Washington toasted the nation on its first birthday'.[73]

Faneuil Hall provided a model for many other redevelopments of inner city areas or areas of cities that had formerly been important regions of economic activity that had gone into decline or even disuse. These include: Harborplace, Baltimore, Maryland; Jacksonville Landing, Jacksonville, Florida; Riverwalk Marketplace, New Orleans; South Street Seaport, New York City; Pioneer Place, Portland, Oregon; Fisherman's Wharf and Ghirardelli Square in San Francisco; Laclede's Landing in St. Louis; Cannery Row in Monterey, California; and Old Town Alexandria, Washington D.C. At least twenty-five US cities had festival marketplaces developments by the mid-1990s.[74]

Nor are such developments confined to the USA. The Rocks, a harbour front area in Sydney's Central Business District, draws on its past as a port and on the lives and the work of its labourers.[75] Harbour front locations have been popular sites for festival marketplace developments in part because of the ease with which they can be invested with an attractive maritime theme. In the case of Aloha Tower Marketplace in Honolulu, its location on the waterfront and the artefacts that are employed to suggest its exotic maritime past[76] provide a theme of transport and trade in much the same way as The Rocks and South Street Seaport in New York. In addition, The Rocks lays claim to many 'firsts': Australia's first hospital, first cemetery, as well as oldest surviving houses. These heritage features provide the backcloth to, and in a sense a rationale for, upscale shopping and dining opportunities. In 1996, it attracted 1.2 million visitors which was only half a million fewer than the nearby Opera House. Similar approaches to the development of heritage attractions-cum-shopping malls have emerged in London's Tobacco Dock, Liverpool's Albert Docks, Barcelona's Port Vaill and in Cape Town's Victoria and Albert Waterfront.

Whereas the Disney theme parks and themed malls clothe consumption in false environments in order to feed off the advantages of the adjacent attraction principle, the approach of Faneuil Hall and its emulators is to take authentic buildings and/or environments, fit them out with additional layers of heritage meaning, and attract retailers and restaurants to buy into the architectural fabric and its fabricated meanings. This heritage shopping combines cultural tourism with shopping and dining.

This apparently benign process of reinvigorating areas that have fallen on hard times, in the case of dock areas usually in response to declines in ship building or to shifts in commercial maritime activity, has been heavily criticized. An example is

New York's South Street Seaport. This former maritime and mercantile district has been redesigned as a shopping and eating area with allusions to its past. However, for commentators like Boyer, this is a filtered past that does injustice to the realities of the districts and the lives of those who lived and worked there. Artefacts, buildings, and streetscapes involving cobbled roads are used as icons of heritage but in the process lived history is obscured. It is a highly nostalgic, not to say romanticized rendition of the past. For Boyer, South Street Seaport is a way of creating a feelgood mood about the past in order to occlude the problems of the present – 'highways in disrepair, charred and abandoned tenements, the scourge of drugs, the wandering homeless, subway breakdowns and deteriorating buses, visual litter and auditory bombardment'.[77] But in this past, conflict, class and ethnic inequality, oppression, and the dangers of labour are concealed in order to project an image that is consistent with and encourages consumption. Thus, not only is this a commodified past, it is a past that contains significant omissions in the cause of consumption.

Waitt makes very similar points about Sydney's The Rocks.[78] He notes that the version of history that the Sydney Cove Redevelopment Authority devised is only one of several versions of history that might have been selected. Like Boyer's commentary on South Street Seaport, Waitt argues that the heritage diet that is offered is a sanitized one that ignores such issues as Aboriginal claims and history, the role of women as merchants or as conscripted prostitutes, conflict and the suffering of labourers. Instead, an idealized and mythical world is created, themed on a past divested of ugliness that serves as a backdrop to shopping and eating.

Interestingly, these criticisms of history at South Street Seaport and The Rocks are strikingly similar to those that are often levelled at the representation of history at Disney theme parks. In addition to projecting a highly sanitized, nostalgic view of history in the Disney theme parks, critics have observed that the company regularly omits certain areas: the problems caused by corporations; issues of class, race and gender; and conflict.[79] These are almost identical to the kinds of critique levelled against the festival marketplace environments discussed in this section, where designers are accused of cleansing the past in the cause of providing a positive and invariably nostalgic version of history that commodifies history to render it a suitable rationale and milieu for shopping in these heritage enclaves. The message is simultaneously one that conveys a sense of loss (for a past life that was simpler or more exotic than the current one) and upbeat (because it communicates a sense of the recovery of that lost era). In a sense, this is a case of triumph through nostalgia. As a strategy it is by no means a certain recipe for success: a case in point is that of Flint, Michigan, whose civic leaders attempted in the 1970s to turn the town, which had been ravaged by the closure of a General Motors plant, into a tourist attraction.[80] Massive sums of public money were raised to build a museum, which closed within six months of opening, and to help subsidize a luxury hotel. In addition, subsidies were committed to a Faneuil Hall-style festival marketplace, called Water Street Pavilion, most of whose shops closed within its first year of operation.

In addition, there are examples of commercial regions that have some of the characteristics of festival marketplaces in that they draw on heritage themes but are not based on buildings or areas of intrinsic heritage significance. An example is Burgis Junction in Singapore, which is a retail and entertainment district comprising six blocks. The designers themed the block on the country's historical trading culture using 'seaside architecture, sails, chronometers, and kindred elements' along with signs conveying information about the seafaring past to communicate the overall theme.[81]

Themed shopping

Having discussed themed malls and heritage shopping, a section on themed shopping might seem as though we are going over the same ground again. However, in introducing this notion, I am seeking to draw a distinction between on the one hand, shopping in which theming is to do with the environment within which shops, restaurants and so on are located – in other words, themed malls and heritage shopping – and the use by retailers of themed environments in their shops. In much the same way that in themed restaurants theming is often accompanied by simulation in order to project a sense of the theme – like the moving animals and tropical downpours in Rainforest Cafes – so too themed shopping is often complemented by simulation, especially in the more sumptuously themed establishments.

Two major kinds of theming can be identified in relation to themed shopping: the use of external narratives of the kind distinguished in relation to themed restaurants and the use of brand theming. These will be discussed in turn.

External narratives

Bass Pro Shops Outdoor World, REI, and Cabela's, all of which are outfitters for hunting, fishing and outdoor wear generally, are examples of the kinds of retailer that have turned themed shopping into a kind of art form. These retailers are often found in themed malls like those developed by Mills Corporation. Bass Pro Shops Outdoor World stores 'include such things as indoor waterfalls, archery ranges, shooting ranges, and outdoor decks where fly fishermen can try out their casts'.[82] The Recreational Equipment (REI) store in Seattle is described as having 'a nearly 100,000-square-foot, warehouselike structure that contains a 65-foot-high freestanding artificial rock for climbing, a glass-enclosed wet stall for testing rain gear, a vented area for testing camp stoves and an outdoor trail for mountainbiking'.[83] According to Wolf this store has become one of the main tourist attractions in Seattle with over 1.5 million visitors in its first year.[84] Stores at other locations have different experiences, which are in large part associated with the local kinds of terrain and sporting interests. Cabela's store in Owatonna, Minnesota, is described as an aesthetic experience

> centered, literally, around a thirty-five-foot high mountain with a waterfall, and featuring more than a hundred stuffed taxidermic animals ... This part of the store represents four different North American biosystems. Elsewhere, two huge dioramas depict African scenes that include the so-called Big Five big-game targets: the elephant, lion, leopard, rhinoceros, and cape buffalo. Three aquariums hold a number of varieties of prized fish, while almost seven hundred different kinds of animals in total are mounted in and around every department of the store.[85]

Other stores operating in the same sector as these three chains, like Timberland, are also themed in the sense of having an outdoors feel to them, but what distinguishes this latest phase of themed shopping is the emphasis being placed on the theming as a focus in its own right and not merely a general background. In its use of simulation in the form of such devices as dioramas and indoor waterfalls, the elaborateness of the theming is being taken several steps further, in much the same way that has happened with some of the more recent themed restaurants.

Theming can be found with varying degrees of elaborateness in other retail sectors as well. It has been suggested that the Barnes & Noble book stores have been designed to look like old world libraries.[86] Goldberger suggests that some Diesel clothes stores have been designed to give the impression of being in a trendy nightclub. The Sneaker Stadium in Paramus, New Jersey, is a massive building with tracks and basketball courts so that customers can try out their possible purchases.[87] The Nature Company shop in Universal City Walk in Los Angeles has a small rainforest.

Wallendorf et al. have provided an interesting case study of a toy and children's clothing store – Mrs. Tiggy-Winkle's – which, at the time that their research began, was located in a downtown shopping centre in Arizona and themed in order to create a sense of what the authors call 'homeyness'.[88] This was conveyed by the design of the store but also by the warm greetings and the apparently unprompted displays of favourite toys by sales personnel. This last element brings out the importance of performance work in Disneyization, an issue that will be returned to in Chapter 5. The store's homeyness appeals as much to adults attracted by the nostalgic setting as to children. During the period of the research, Mrs. Tiggy-Winkle's relocated to a much bigger store in an out-of-town strip mall three-and-a-half miles from its original location. The store's relocation also entailed a change of theming. The new store was more visually exciting and less homey than its predecessor. One way in which theming is revealed is that toys and other items are displayed in such a way as to tell a story: 'The stories told by these displays are children's dream experiences: a backyard bug safari, an afternoon with Mistress Mary tending the garden, or an imaginary swing through the trees with jungle primate friends'.[89] Items are displayed to support the story, with the result that they frequently appear in more than one place when they are used to support two or more stories. Regarding the overall tone of the store, the authors write: 'Whereas the old store animated customers through nostalgic, cozy security, the new store embeds them in a Hollywood-dream playroom permeated by energy and excitement with a sophisticated, contemporary aesthetic'.[90] The new store, like many of the lavishly themed outfitters previously mentioned, has become a destination in itself.

Sometimes, the theme can be controversial. In May 2000, the National Rifle Association in the USA announced plans for a 'total shooting sports' themed store in New York's Times Square, which would also include a themed restaurant. According to an Association's representative, the store would provide a 'total shooting sports and sporting goods experience'. However, the emphasis on guns was inconsistent with the kind of image the denizens of the cleaned-up Times Square wanted to convey and representatives of the improvement district claimed it was harking back to an environment at Times Square they had sought to eradicate.[91]

Brand narratives

Brand theming occurs when the brand forms a theme in itself. Examples of brand theming are: the Disney Stores, in which the goods for sale and the overall store are entirely themed on Disney films, characters, and theme parks; the Coca-Cola stores; Lego Imagination Center; and the Niketowns.

The Niketowns are particularly interesting and one of the stores, Niketown Chicago, has been the focus of two separate ethnographies.[92] Discussing the New York City store, Goldberger has written:

> the merchandise is secondary to the experience of being in this store, an experience that bears more than a passing resemblance to a visit to a theme park. Niketown is a fantasy environment, one part nostalgia to two parts high tech, and it exists to bedazzle the consumer, to give its merchandise sex appeal and establish Nike as the essence not just of athletic wear but also of our culture and way of life.[93]

The Niketowns are temples for the celebration of the brand. They draw upon two motifs in order to get across their brand identity: the narrative of a gymnasium[94] and of a museum.[95] Sherry quotes from a Niketown Chicago press release that among other features, the store would have 'the museum quality of the Smithsonian Institution'.[96] Indeed, the deliberate use of a museum approach to presenting merchandise, most notably by showcasing trainers and other Nike goods in display cases and interspersing these displays with exhibits of valuable sporting memorabilia, causes considerable confusion among shoppers who are often uncertain about whether they should pay an entrance fee and whether items are actually for sale. They *are* for sale, though many potential customers realize that they can purchase items more cheaply elsewhere. The Niketowns, in their adoption of a museum mode of representing their wares, are in a sense acting as showcases for Nike wear and less as stores in the traditional sense. Perhaps this is part of the reason for their names, that is, Nike*towns* rather than Nike*stores*. The gymnasium theme is evident not just in general ambience and style of the store but also in the presence of a small basketball court. This is complete with a polished wooden floor and sounds of a cheering crowd where customers could try on basketball shoes.

Different areas of each Niketown are themed. Referring to the Chicago store, Peñaloza writes:

> New age melodies permeated the sports sandals area, swatted tennis balls and cheering crowds enlivened the tennis area, and the high-pitched squeaks of sneakers on wood, the *swoosh* of a basketball passing through the hoop, and cheering crowds accentuated the basketball area and made me want to get out and play. ... In the room for the All Condition Gear (ACG), the calls of birds and crickets, and the sound of setting a climbing rope were audible. Sales associate Anthony (Latino, 20's) told me they were going to remodel it, adding a waterfall and fish to make it *more natural*.[97]

Like some other examples of theming such as the Disney theme parks themselves, the Niketowns are therefore themed at several levels: in terms of Nike and its goods; in terms of a gymnasium and a museum; and in terms of different regions of the store which function like 'lands' in the Disney theme parks. The result has been that Niketown Chicago is second only to the city's Art Institute in terms of the number of visitors.

Shopping in themed environments

Themed malls, heritage shopping and themed shopping are clearly becoming more and more prevalent. Aside from their use as strategies for differentiation, they are unlikely to become less important in the future because they constitute a major approach to combatting shopping from home in its various forms: television shopping, catalogue shopping, and above all internet shopping. Shopping in themed environments provides experiences that direct involvement in mall or store locations can most easily provide. They supply reasons for getting out of the house in order to shop. They also provide alternatives to the pile-'em-high and sell-'em-cheap strategy of discount shops and warehouses by giving the customer additional value in the form of memorable experiences and entertainment as part of the shopping transaction. Just as with themed restaurants, themed shops and the extravagant simulated environments that often accompany them are differentiation strategies. The various forms of themed shopping environments attempt to differentiate themselves not just from other malls and shops but also from the new forms of retailing that are taking their market share (home shopping, catalogue and internet shopping, and discount warehouses).

Zoos

Theming can be said to be a feature of many zoos in two major senses. First, there is evidence of growing theming within zoos, so that areas or collections are themed in a more abstract way than the conventional presentation of animals in categories such as monkey house, lion and tiger house, and so on. The second sense in which theming can be said to be occurring in relation to zoos is that, in the process of reconstructing their institutional identities, zoos are theming themselves at the corporate level. Each of these senses will now be examined.

Theming within zoos

First, an example of theming within zoos is to be found in Jungle World in Bronx Zoo which opened in 1985 and which is often regarded as an exemplar. The various components are intended to represent Asian rainforest, mangrove swamp and scrub forest.[98] Thus the zoo architecture and flora are no longer neutral but are in effect simulations of natural habitats. Another example is the Lied Jungle at Henry Doorly Zoo in Omaha which similarly places animals within a wider ecosystem context. The Ford African Rainforest in Zoo Atlanta, Amazonia in the National Zoo in Washington DC, and the Thai Elephant Forest and Rain Forest at Woodland Park Zoo in Seattle are further instances of this process. Lowry Park Zoo in Tampa, Florida, includes themed areas such as Primate World, Asian Domain, and Florida Wildlife Center which is dedicated to typical wild animals found in Florida. London Zoo's biodiversity exhibit is a yet another illustration and one which bravely seeks to present some of earth's more numerous but less celebrated creatures, especially insects. The Zoo's Director described the new exhibit in *The Times* as 'a mission statement writ large'.[99] At Adelaide Zoo, there is a nocturnal house in which night-time is simulated so that normally dormant and therefore rarely viewed nocturnal animals are on display. There is also a World of Primates in which the visitor is immersed in an apparently pristine natural environment.[100]

The whole of Busch Gardens in Tampa, Florida is themed around Africa (which, Malamud observes,[101] is a particularly popular theme in zoos) and includes a massive area containing free-roaming animals in zones like the Myombe Reserve. The Sea World theme parks are basically zoos/aquariums for various forms of marine life and their exhibits are themed in several different ways: Penguin Encounter, Tropical Rain Forest, Tropical Reef, Key West, and Pacific Point Preserve. As Davis observes in connection with the Sea World in San Diego, the theme park gradually replaced small cages and pools and tanks with 'exhibits that tried to represent whole worlds'.[102]

Disney has in a sense created its own zoo in the form of the Animal Kingdom in Walt Disney World in Florida, which opened in 1998. Initially, the bulk of the park was themed on the African Savannah (an Asian zone opened in 1999). Guests travel on a Kilimanjaro safari and visit areas like the Harambe Village. The publicity this venture has attracted and its sheer scale are likely to provide food for thought among zoo managers.

In part, theming inside the zoo is a product of public unease about the sight of captive animals in cages.[103] Placing animals in contexts in which they could roam more freely is much more consistent with modern sensibilities and attitudes to animals in captivity. However, theming was not a *necessary* accompaniment to this shift. Theming, for example in terms of an African motif, is largely extraneous to the removal of cages, since the backdrops can be, and indeed often still are, neutral in their connotations, although it could be argued that re-creating for wild animals their 'natural' habitats provides a more comfortable environment for them. The evidence that the animals somehow benefit from such environments is unclear, and some commentators suggest that they are designed to enhance the sense of well-being of the zoo visitor more than that of the animal.[104]

Theming of zoos

The second sense in which zoos are becoming themed is that they are seeking to reinvent themselves in an institutional and cultural sense, in the light of changing public sensibilities concerning the capture and caging of animals, and changing conceptions of the relationships between humans and nature.[105] This trend suggests a growing theming *of* the zoo as a corporate form. Increasingly, zoos publicize and justify themselves not as repositories of animals to be gawked at, but as agencies dedicated to education and to the preservation of rare and nearly extinct species. As Dibb notes from her examination of UK zoos and wildlife parks, as a result of changes in public opinion regarding captivity in zoos 'the role of wildlife facilities in protecting endangered species and encouraging breeding programmes is increasingly pushed to the fore'.[106] The President and General Director of the Wildlife Conservation Bureau has written that a

> developing new synthesis of zoo programming and expertise suggests that the future of zoos is to become 'conservation parks' actively contributing to nature's survival – not quiescent museums.[107]

Some zoos have adopted this conception of zoos as their mission more or less from the outset. Others have essentially themed along these lines and in the process reinvented themselves. In 1993, the New York Zoological Society rebranded the zoos under its jurisdiction as 'wildlife conservation parks',[108] while the National Zoo in Washington DC now calls itself a BioPark. Likewise, the Sea World parks place great emphasis on their role in rescuing and breeding rare marine mammals like the manatee. As Davis observes, in the 1980s science became an overarching theme for the San Diego Sea World.[109] This gave it a more acceptable face that allowed it to link with concerns about animals and their conservation.

What is more, a 1997 Busch Gardens publicity leaflet tells us that

> while entertainment is [its] most visible facet, education, conservation and research are fundamental commitments … Our award-winning programs provide opportunities for students of all ages to better appreciate the importance of diversity and the need for conservation. Our captive breeding programs have been tremendously successful in preserving rare and endangered species for generations to come.

These themes are equally prominent in zoos' websites. For example, Chester Zoo's opening page cites the following as its mission:

> The role of the zoo is to support and promote conservation by breeding threatened species, by excellent animal welfare, high quality public service, recreation, education and science.[110]

It is not surprising that conservation at this zoo is especially prominent in its web pages.

Unsurprisingly, the motifs of species conservation plus education are major components of Disney's Animal Kingdom's *raison d'être* too. Disney say that: 'inspiring a love of animals and concern for their welfare is the underlying theme, both subtle and obvious, throughout the Animal Kingdom'.[111] This remark nicely side-steps the fact that one of its lands is sponsored by McDonald's and the park itself sells vast quantities of steaks, burgers, hot dogs and nuggets and is built on former wetlands. However, its director of animal operations, who was lured from the famous San Diego Zoo, has stated that he would not have taken on the task unless he was 'sure Disney was a 100 per cent committed to conservation'.[112]

This growing unease about the use of the depiction 'zoo' and the substitution of alternative terms stressing conservation and education are in themselves components of the turn towards theming. However, it has to be acknowledged that some commentators are sceptical about the application of narratives of education, science and species conservation.[113] Nevertheless, the theming of zoos in terms of these master narratives is a continuing process, as is the internal theming of the zoo in terms of regions, species types, and so on. Of course, these two processes usually coincide. Busch Gardens in Tampa, which began life as a zoo adjacent to a brewery (owned by Anheuser-Busch, the then and current owners of the park), has been described as 'a theme park, with an African motif largely submerged into a naturalist-environmentalist theme'.[114] At many zoos, the theming of areas or attractions within their grounds has gone hand in hand with the introduction of the conservation theme.

Theming of place

This section deals with two related forms of theming. They are both concerned with the notion of place and with the role that theming plays in creating a sense of place. The emphasis will be placed primarily on the creation of place in connection with tourism. One way in which we can talk about the theming of place is in relation to the use of cultural narratives to create a sense of place. This occurs when a place is themed in terms of its association with well-known or striking cultural products or events. The second sense is a more internalist theming which takes as its starting point features that are intrinsic qualities of a place or at least are commonly regarded as such. With this second sense, the theming of place takes the form of embroidering the essential and taken-for-granted features. It is rarely obvious that a place is worthy of being visited.[115] While some places have a self-evident 'must-see' quality, the majority do not. For the latter their significance and the case for visiting them must be impressed upon potential tourists. At the same time, the visitor is being given a short course in how such places should be gazed upon.

Cultural narratives of place

As a starting point, we can take Urry's observation that

> there is an increasingly pervasive tendency to divide up countries in terms of new spatial divisions with new place names. In the north of England there is 'Last of the Summer Wine Country', 'Emmerdale Farm Country', 'James Herriot Country', 'Robin Hood Country', 'Catherine Cookson Country', 'Brontë Country' and so on. Space is divided up in terms of signs that signify particular themes...[116]

In these cases, regions are being themed in terms of well-known totems of popular culture: much-loved British television programmes (*Last of the Summer Wine* and *Emmerdale Farm*); popular novelists (Herriot, Cookson, and Brontë); and a legendary character (Robin Hood). Such theming triggers an appreciation of the kind of terrain that one is likely to encounter (rolling hills, forest, rural life) and its cultural associations. It helps to bestow a 'specific character' on the region concerned.[117] It is essentially a marketing device that helps to differentiate a region at the same time as conveying some information about the forms of tourism with which it is associated. In addition to Urry's examples, there are further illustrations of this process. Edensor notes that in the wake of the Hollywood movie, *Braveheart*, the Loch Lomond, Trossachs and Stirling Tourist Board produced an advertisement which read, 'Where the Highlands met the Lowlands, step into the echoes of Rob Roy, Robert the Bruce and William Wallace – Braveheart Country'.[118] Similarly, Beatrix Potter has been appropriated as a theme for the village of Sawrey in England's Lake District. Such an association, which revolved around Potter's farm (Hill Top) acted as a magnet for adults suffused with a nostalgia for English country life and the notion of a rural idyll.[119] Pretes shows how in 1984, the Finnish Tourist Board along with regional authorities and commercial interests started to brand Lapland as 'Santa Claus Land'. The area became Santa's home and workplace and is used as a sign of the area's cultural distinctiveness. To underscore this theming exercise, close to Rovaniemi, Lapland's capital, a Santa Claus Village and Workshop was built complete with 'Santa Claus's Post Office ... a reindeer enclosure, several restaurants, and many gift and souvenir shops'.[120]

However, this theming of place through cultural narratives is sometimes controversial. The village of Goathland in England's North Yorkshire moors and the surrounding countryside are marketed by the Yorkshire Tourist Board as Heartbeat

Country. *Heartbeat* is a popular television series based in a fictional village called Aidensfield which is in fact Goathland. The association with the television series marks the place and its inhabitants indelibly in the minds of potential visitors as having a certain cluster of characteristics. Mordue shows that whereas the villagers were not unhappy about the use of *Hearbeat* as a lure for visitors, they drew a distinction between genuine tourists visiting the village and the moors and the day trippers.[121] While the former were regarded as being prepared to appreciate the village and the region for its intrinsic characteristics, the day trippers were believed to want only superficial contact with the village and also behaved in ways that were disliked. It was felt that unrealistic and unhelpful packaged versions of a rural idyll were being created that clashed with the realities of village life. At the same time, the day trippers in buses, cars and campers were seen as causing considerable disruption to the village and its residents.

Liverpool has made use of its associations with popular music and with the Beatles in particular as a source of cultural heritage. This use of such associations can be viewed as another example of a cultural narrative of place. Urry, for example, refers to a *Discover Merseyside* brochure from 1988 that refers to 'Beatleland'.[122] However, Cohen's research shows that for many Liverpudlians the link between the city and the Beatles is unfortunate because they view the four members of the group as people who deserted the city. Thus, while she quotes one tourism official as saying that the Beatles 'are to Liverpool what the Pope is to Rome and Shakespeare to Stratford. If you can milk it then you should',[123] residents took a less enthusiastic view of this version of their city's heritage, not least because for many of them, the Beatles were perceived as having deserted the city.

Finnish Lapland's claim to being Santa Claus Land also proved to be controversial because other countries have similar claims. Pretes observes that 'The mayor of Drøbak, home of the Norwegian Santa, asked King Harald and Queen Sonja to cancel their trip, planned for March 1993, on the grounds that visiting Rovaniemi would lend support to Finland's claim'.[124] In fact, the trip did go ahead but Santa's Village was not visited. A similar kind of dispute broke out around the time of the premiere of *The Lord of the Rings* in December 2001, with three competing claims to being Tolkien Country: New Zealand, where the film was made; Moseley in Birmingham, where Tolkien grew up; and the Ribble Valley in Lancashire, where Tolkien did most of his writing.[125]

Intrinsic narratives of place

With intrinsic narratives of place, the theming takes the form of bringing out inherent features of the place in question. The features are 'there' but need to be imprinted in the consciousness of visitors and in many cases exaggerated in order to make the message clear and unambiguous.

For example, the marketing of East African safaris is permeated with a sense of being able to encounter nature in the raw.[126] This is expressed through an emphasis on animals in both the text and particularly images which show the most popular animals (lion, giraffe, elephant, rhinoceros, and hippopotamus) in natural habitats. In addition, images of the Masai are interspersed in a similar way among the images of the big five animals. The images and the text surrounding them are designed to give the impression of direct contact with raw nature and Norton's research on safari tourists in the region shows that this was the primary reason for an East African safari as a choice of holiday.

In a similar vein, Nuttall argues in connection with tourism in Alaska that:

> As in the early days of Alaskan tourism, Alaska continues to be marketed as a land of superlatives and extremes, where nature can still be experienced as raw and untouched. Tour brochures ... reproduce predictable stereotypical descriptions and images of pristine wilderness, fascinating Native culture and abundant wildlife, so that a trip to Alaska will be an unforgettable encounter with majestic scenery, gold rush history, indigenous people, and a once-in-a-lifetime opportunity to see whales, spawning salmon, bears and other animals.[127]

The references to gold rush history and Native culture in this passage suggest that intrinsic narratives are often supplemented by cultural narratives of place but the message of a pristine wilderness and its creatures seems to be the prevailing one. Similarly, Goss shows in relation to Hawaii how its intrinsic theming as an 'earthly paradise' is supplemented by references to its culture and history.[128] In order to get across this thematic element, Hawaii's urban developments and its tourist infrastructure are all but ignored to convey a sense of unfettered contact with nature and the history of the islands. Likewise, the tourist publicity for Canada's Eastern Arctic emphasizes 'nature', augmented by references to Inuit culture and similar cultural themes, and is presented in opposition to urban life.[129]

These studies show that an important component of tourist imagery and publicity entails the theming of place in terms of intrinsic narratives, which emphasize inherent qualities of regions, as well as cultural ones, which are supplemented by cultural narratives. However, in a sense the very fact that the material that forms the basis for intrinsic narratives – nature, wilderness, wild animals – undergoes a process of theming means that it too becomes a form of cultural theming. As the intrinsic qualities of regions become commodities that are projected in tourist publicity, they become a kind of cultural artefact too.

Theming of tourism and holidays

Tourism and holidays generally can be viewed as being increasingly themed. Urry refers to 'adventure tourism' in New Zealand and 'boring tours' in Sydney which can be interpreted in such terms.[130] A London firm launched a Jack the Ripper themed tour in the wake of a new movie retelling the Ripper story.[131] 'Terror tourism', organized trips to some of the world's trouble spots,[132] a genre of themed tourism that included 'axis of evil' tours to Kabul[133] can also be seen in these terms. Urry also observes that many hotel chains in the United Kingdom offer 'various themed weekends [including] arts and antiques, bridge, watercolour painting, archery, clay pigeon shooting, fly fishing, golf and pony-trekking'.[134] These themed weekends can similarly be interpreted in terms of the growing tendency for the theming of tourism. In Japan, there has been a growth in package tours themed in terms of such motifs as honeymoons, sex, gourmet cooking, urban life, and the countryside.[135]

Towns

In the United States, the rise of what is often referred to as *New Urbanism* provides a further example of the spread of the theming principle. New Urbanism is associated with neo-traditional residential developments that are designed along the lines of a nostalgic representation of small town life as it used to be. In practice, this means: restricting the influence of the automobile in public spaces; encouraging people to walk by having shops and entertainment amenities close to homes; stimulating a sense of community by having central civic amenities; and restricting the amount of variability in the external and interior design of homes so that individualist impulses are moderated. New Urbanist towns place an emphasis on the pedestrian rather than on the driver and seek to re-create the sense of a public space in which all residents have an investment as citizens.

The New Urbanism movement, which is mainly associated with the architects Andres Duany and Elizabeth Plater-Zyberk, has gradually made inroads through the design of small towns using its underlying principles, which have gradually taken root in various parts of the United States. Until fairly recently, its best known monument was Seaside in Florida, which began life in December 1981 and was was the setting for the Jim Carrey film, *The Truman Show*.

However, in 1996 an even more high-profile New Urbanist town admitted its first citizens – Celebration, which was built for Disney and is located next to Disney World in Florida (although in January 2004 it was announced that Disney had sold the downtown core to a real estate company). According to two journalists who lived in Celebration for over a year, the New Urbanist principles are apparent in the following way:

> A sense of place was reflected in the post-neotraditional planning and the attempt to create a pleasant, workable physical environment: the public parks, the easy walk to shops, the distinctive architecture, and its hoped-for front-porch culture. The intention was to provide the safe neighborhoods and opportunities for social interaction that surveys showed most people wanted.[136]

It is widely expected that the publicity and popularity of Celebration will result in further developments of this kind, even though the town has received quite a lot of adverse publicity, primarily associated with Disney's tight control over residents and their houses (about which more will be said in Chapter 6) and with criticism of the school from which a great deal had been anticipated by residents.[137] Other New Urbanist developments include: Rosemary Beach, WaterColor, and Windsor in Florida; Kentlands, Maryland; Mashpee Commons, Cape Cod; Fort Mill, South Carolina; and DuPont, Washingon. Views about New Urbanist developments vary considerably. Some see them as models of future suburban development which will give people back the sense of community and civic life that sprawling suburbs and the motor car took away. Critics see them as exclusionary because they are most likely to be accessible and appealing to the white middle class and because they essentially ignore the problems of American cities by creating enclaves that turn a blind eye to what is going on in the wider world. Still others decry the reliance on a sentimental nostalgia as the route to suburban redemption.[138]

New Urbanist towns are themed in that they are based on a narrative of nostalgia for both an era and a style of living in towns that projects a sense of otherness on the urban and suburban landscape in which most Americans live. In addition, in some cases the housing styles are themed too in the sense that a limited range of housing prototypes is specified and these draw on external narratives. At Rosemary Beach in Florida, the house style prototypes are based on Caribbean and early Spanish Florida styles. In Celebration, there are six housing styles: Classical; Victorian; Colonial Revival; Coastal; Mediterranean; and French.

Museums

Theming in museums can be seen most notably in the surge of specialist museums that can be viewed as examples of theming. In a sense, museums have always been themed, but as museums have proliferated and become increasingly specialized, they have looked more and more like themed institutions. Concerning England, Urry has written: 'Some apparently unlikely museums are the pencil museum in Keswick, a museum of the chemical industry in Widnes, various Holocaust museums, a dental museum in London, and a shoe museum in Street [in Somerset]'.[139] His list by no means ends there. Other museums include: a colour museum in Bradford in Yorkshire; a Greater Manchester Police Museum; a Guinness Museum in Dublin; the International Spy Museum in Washington DC; and the Museum of Sex in New York. In addition, as Gottdiener points out, many of the more eclectic museums have special exhibitions which draw upon general themes.[140]

It is also relevant to this discussion that as many commentators have observed, the distinction between theme parks and museums has increasingly become blurred, a trend which has contributed to the growth in the theming of museums. In Japan, the *gaikoku mura* (foreign country villages) which were built following the opening of Tokyo Disneyland have elements of both a museum and theme park. As one commentator puts it:

For countries ranging from Canada, Switzerland and Spain, to Russia, Holland and Germany, parks have been built that offer replicas and reconstructions of buildings, furniture and all manner of other artefacts. Music and crafts are performed by native experts, and there is an abundant stock of food, drink and ornaments from the area in question, often advertised as exclusive to the location. All this, domestic [i.e., Japanese] tourists can enjoy without ever leaving their own shores.[141]

In the UK and USA some museums, rather than presenting exhibits in glass cases amid respectful silence and awe, seek to immerse the visitor in an experience that draws on theme park modes of presentation and representation. The Beamish Museum near Newcastle in the north-east of England uses recreations of village life along with 'inhabitants' who operate machinery, talk about and demonstrate crafts, and interact and play out roles with visitors. This process of immersing visitors in a life that represents a different time and place in effect generates and constitutes a theme in its own right. Similarly, at Snibston Discovery Park in Leicestershire in the East Midlands, ex-miners explain the workings of coal mines and machinery at the site of one of England's many disused mines. Colonial Williamsburg in Virginia is renowned for its use of restored buildings and museum staff to recreate the world of ordinary life in the revolutionary era. The Ellis Island Immigration Museum similarly seeks to provide an immersive experience for the visitor and in the process, it 'thematizes immigration'.[142] Experiencing the past can be further intensified through simulations of extreme incidents. At the Imperial War Museum in London, there are two themed areas: one on life in the trenches in the First World War and one of living during the Blitz in the Second World War. In each case, there are simulations of the experience with recreations of a trench and a London street and bunker, along which the visitor can wander. The visual impact is underscored with sounds and other special effects (such as smoke in the aftermath of a German bomb when visitors exit the bunker). The success of such themes can often be affected by the degree to which convincing and aesthetically pleasing simulations can be contrived.

Clever recreations of settings coupled with live displays on the part of museum staff blur the lines between reality and unreality but the key point is that they are very much part of the theming process. For their part, museums vary in their attitude to such a recognition. While visitors sometimes believe that Colonial Williamsburg is in fact a theme park, the museum's representatives try to distance themselves from theme parks.[143] Others such as the Director of *Den Gamle By* (The Old Town), an open-air museum in Denmark, are more prepared to concede the influence of theme parks on their establishments.[144]

Other domains of theming

The foregoing discussion has emphasized some of the major spheres in which theming has taken place in late modern society. However, it does not exhaust all of them by any means. The following is a catalogue of others along with a brief discussion of each.

- *American criminal justice* In an article specifically concerned with Disneyization that drew on my early exposition of the concept, Robinson argues that American criminal justice is themed. However, Robinson argues that the process of theming is carried out predominantly by the mass media. He suggests that the mass media identify issues and crises in connection with crime and this process influences the issues that leaders and American citizens will be concerned about. Robinson regards this as a form of theming, one which has implications for the perceptions of the operation of the criminal justice system. He draws particular attention to corporate and white-collar crimes which are prevalent but largely ignored, in comparison to spectacular but relatively unusual crimes which receive widespread attention.[145]

- *Health clubs* One chain of British health clubs has been described by an investment magazine as 'offering customers a range of themed zones designed to create a unique environment offering fun and entertainment'.[146]

- *Health-care facilities* Baldwin describes a facility in New Canaan, Connecticut, for people with memory loss that has a reproduction Main Street 'based on the way downtown New Canaan looked 40 years ago'. Apparently, the design team worked with photographs of 1950s New Canaan, as well as of reproduced streets in shopping malls and Disney World. She goes on to write that: 'Recognizing that people who can't remember what they were doing moments before nonetheless can unearth memories of life 30 years earlier, senior care centers from Australia to Manhattan are relying on settings laden with nostalgic cues, hoping to get patients talking in what are called reminiscence groups'.[147]

- *Casinos* As the discussion of the elaborately themed hotels in Las Vegas suggests, these hotels are in fact casinos. Whether they are themed hotels with casinos or themed casinos with hotels is a moot point, though given the centrality of gambling to the city one suspects the second is the more accurate description. Nonetheless, the hotel-casinos in Las Vegas entail intricate theming in terms of the various narratives found in the hotels. Moreover, this predilection for themed casinos is spreading. Following the anticipated deregulation of gambling in Britain, Blackpool, a popular seaside destination similarly famed for its hedonism and attractions, is likely to attract a themed hotel-casino along Las Vegas lines. Several casino resorts are planned along the town's famed Golden Mile, including Pharaoh's Palace, an Egyptian themed hotel-casino complete with the usual symbols of Ancient Egypt.[148]

- *Cruise ships* Ritzer and Liska suggest that cruise ships are increasingly becoming themed[149] and Wood has argued that fantasy theming and simulation are common on many cruise ships.[150] Sometimes, the ships have an overall theme, such as Carnival's *Fascination*, which is themed in terms of Hollywood, or *Disney Magic* which is largely themed on Disney itself. In addition, there are often themed areas influenced by motifs such as nationality. *Disney Magic* has a themed Beat Street entertainment area, which has dance and comedy clubs and a piano lounge.[151]

- *Events* Club Disney playsites designed by Disney for young children, not only have themed play-areas, but also themed birthday parties, such as 101 Dalmations Bow-wow Bash and Toy Story Search Party.[152]

- *University accommodation* Ritzer notes that some American universities have introduced themed dormitories to cater for students with similar interests.[153]

- *Cookies* Schmitt and Simonson suggest that a range of cookies marketed by Pepperidge Farm in the USA are themed. There is a 'Distinctive Collection' which draws on European narratives: Milano, Geneva, Brussels, etc. They quote from the Mint Brussels packet: 'Imagine strolling down a cobblestone street to your favorite European bake shop. The aroma of Old World baking fills the air. ... European heritage and American ingenuity combine to create wonderful cookies you can enjoy every day'.[154] In addition, there is an Old Fashioned collection ('Cookies that could have come right out of Grandma's cookie jar').

Conclusion

In this chapter, I have sought to make a case that more and more areas of modern life are becoming themed in a similar way to the sense in which Disney theme parks are themed. Walt Disney did not invent theming and the use of simulations on which theming thrives, but between them, his theme parks have provided rich exemplars of what theming entails and the kinds of use to which it can be put. There are undoubtedly numerous examples of theming prior to 1955 but Disneyland was a high-profile and hugely successful paradigm of its potential which has been widely drawn upon. The Disney theme parks are emblems of the process of theming, as they are with the other dimensions of Disneyization discussed in this book. Increasingly, theming has been used as a means of differentiating service providers as diverse as restaurants, malls, shops, zoos, and holiday destinations. The more standardized services and places become,[155] particularly as a result of the homogenizing tendencies of McDonaldization, the more important theming becomes as a mechanism of differentiation. Theming becomes a mechanism for distinguishing otherwise identical and unremarkable venues and products.

Critics of theming often disapprove of the use of symbols of nostalgia for thematic cues. Drawing on faux designs and histories, theming in terms of nostalgic references is often depicted as presenting a sanitized history, one that removes any reference to hardship and conflict in the cause of consumption. Their critique is therefore levelled at the commodification of these emblems of the past that resonate in our culture. Interestingly, many of the companies that guard their copyright images, logos and works most tirelessly, such as Disney and Nike, are precisely the companies that draw on the public domain emblems of heritage and popular culture with impunity. Their use of images is a one-way street so far as copyright permission is concerned, since impressions of the Wild West, seafaring, and ancient Egypt can be plundered more or less free of constraint.

In addition to theming being depicted as part of a strategy of differentiation, it is sometimes suggested, especially in connection with shopping, that it is deployed so that people lose themselves in the experience and are more likely to buy. This may happen to some people some of the time, but as several commentators have pointed out, this is to construe the consumer as a kind of cultural dope who mindlessly buys in response to the confusion that themed environments inflict on normally reasonably rational consumer behaviour. We should be wary of such a view. Most people are very familiar with themed environments and their attractions, and are not taken in by the seductive experiences they offer. The plight of themed restaurants since the late 1990s is a good illustration of this point. It was precisely because many of them offered an experience at the expense of good food that they were increasingly shunned. This rationality in consumer taste and behaviour is testament to the resilience of consumers to the allure of theming.

Theming may also be spreading, not just because service providers and others perceive it to be a weapon for getting money out of our pockets. It may also be spreading because it has a kind of multiplier or snowball effect in our consciousness: we increasingly expect the accoutrements of theming. Just like the shoppers at the mall studied by Sandicki and Holt who found it dull and boring,[156] there is a growing expectation of a level of theming. Shoval notes that in Israel, holy sights are increasingly themed.[157] It might have been expected that these sights could speak for themselves, that they would have a kind of intrinsic significance and message because of their religious and historical connotations and importance. He suggests that the reason is that around 80% of visitors come from Europe and North America where theming has become a key element in tourism and other consumption activities. In other words, theming may have (or be seen to have) its own momentum because of the expectations and requirements of consumers.

Notes

1 Wolf (1999).
2 Ritzer (1999).
3 Bitner (1992).
4 Solomon (1998).
5 Pine and Gilmore (1999).
6 Gottdiener (2001).
7 Schmitt and Simonson (1997).
8 Ritzer and Stillman (2001a).
9 Beardsworth and Bryman (1999: 243).
10 Schmitt and Simonson (1997: 124).
11 Euro Disneyland S.C.A. Offer for Sale of 10,691,000 shares by S.G. Warburg Securities. Quotation is on page 13.
12 Bryman (1995).
13 Quoted in Mosley (1986: 221).
14 Findlay (1992: 80).
15 Adams (1991); Weinstein (1992).
16 Kasson (1978: 69).
17 Quoted in Kasson (1978: 69).
18 Bright (1987).

19 Thomas (1976: 251).
20 Findlay (1992); Nelson (1986).
21 Kasson (1978: 23–4)
22 Harris (1997).
23 Marling (1997: 45).
24 Marling (1994: 105).
25 Weatherford (1998).
26 Hannigan (1998: 201).
27 Doss (1997: 189).
28 Beardsworth and Bryman (1999).
29 Beardsworth and Bryman (1999).
30 Shoval (2000: 261).
31 Kirshenblatt-Gimblett (1998: 171).
32 www.blackbeardscave.com/rest.htm consulted on 4 December, 2001.
33 www.poole-associates.com/house_of_ mao1.htm consulted on 20 August, 2003.
34 Bagli (1998); Mccalla (1999a).
35 'Crash-themed restaurant scrapped following attacks'. 25 September, 2001

www.news-journalonline.com/cgi-bin/printtext.pl. Consulted on 4 December, 2001.

36 Mccalla (1999a).
37 Quoted in Mccalla (1999a).
38 Quoted in Mccalla (1999a).
39 Quoted in Mccalla (1999a).
40 A term used by Pine and Gilmore (1999) to refer to an economy in which consumers expect memorable experiences from services and goods that they purchase.
41 Beardsworth and Bryman (1999).
42 Quoted in Barber (1995: 128–9).
43 Quoted in Fantasia (1995: 227).
44 Manning and Callum-Swan (1994: 473).
45 Twitchell (1999: 177).
46 Bagli (2001).
47 Schlosser (2001: 233–4).
48 Yan (1997).
49 Waples (2001).
50 Bone (2001: 9).
51 Gordon and Meunier (2001).
52 Pine and Gimore (1999).
53 Turner (2001).
54 themeparks.universalstudios.com/orlando/website/resort_hotels/ consulted on 21 February, 2003
55 Gottdiener (1997: 13).
56 Crawford (1992)
57 Kirshenblatt-Gimblett (1998: 171).
58 Shoval (2000).
59 www.taupo.caboose.co.nz (consulted on 4 December, 2001).
60 Dedman (1998).
61 www.madonnainn.com/tour/index.asp (consulted on 21 February, 2003).
62 www.seevue.com/rooms.html (consulted on 4 December, 2001).
63 Gottdiener (2001).
64 Cohn (1996: 4.1, ellipses in original).
65 Crawford (1992: 16).
66 Hamilton (2000: E1).
67 Chaney (1990).
68 Jenkins (1998).
69 Crawford (1992: 14–15).
70 Sandicki and Holt (1998: 327).
71 Quoted in Sandicki and Holt (1998: 327).
72 Ball (1991: 81).
73 www.faneuilhallmarketplace.com/info/design/PMPNew/exp_explore.cfm consulted on 24 February, 2003.
74 Goss (1996).
75 Waitt (2000).
76 Goss (1996).
77 Boyer (1992: 191).
78 Waitt (2000).
79 Bryman (1995).
80 Judd (1999).
81 Pine and Gilmore (1999: 39).
82 Ritzer (1999: 111).
83 Goldberger (1997a).
84 Wolf (1999: 63–4).
85 Pine and Gilmore (1999: 36).
86 Klein (2000).
87 Goldberger (1997a).
88 Wallendorf et al. (1998).
89 Wallendorf et al. (1998: 187).
90 Wallendorf et al. (1998: 190).
91 www.cnn.com/2000/FOOD/news/05/19/nra.restaurant (consulted on 4 December, 2001).
92 Peñaloza (1999); Sherry (1998).
93 Goldberger (1997a).
94 Hannigan (1998: 92).
95 Peñaloza (1999); Sherry (1998).
96 Quoted in Sherry (1998: 115).
97 Peñaloza (1999: 376).
98 Mullan and Marvin (1999).
99 Hamilton (1999).
100 Anderson (1995: 290).
101 Malamud (1998: 79).
102 Davis (1997: 71).
103 Tarpy (1993).
104 Anderson (1995: 290–1); Croke (1997: 76–84).
105 Anderson (1995).
106 Dibb (1995: 263).
107 Conway (1996: 27).
108 Malamud (1998: 79).
109 Davis (1997).
110 www.chesterzoo.org consulted on 6 June, 2003.
111 Quoted in Tomkins (1998: 9).
112 Quoted in Churchill (1998: 3).
113 For example, Jamieson (1995); Malamud (1998).
114 Mintz (1998: 52).
115 Fainstein and Judd (1999).
116 Urry (2002: 130).
117 Lanfant (1995: 32).
118 Edensor (2001: 68).
119 Squire (1993).
120 Pretes (1995: 8).
121 Mordue (2001).
122 Urry (2002).
123 Cohen (1997: 82).

124 Pretes (1995: 7).
125 Sherwin (2001).
126 Norton (1996).
127 Nuttall (1997: 226).
128 Goss (1993b).
129 Milne et al. (1998).
130 Urry (2002: 92).
131 Harley (2002).
132 Byrne (1997); Young (1998).
133 Robbins (2002).
134 Urry (2002: 137).
135 Raz (1999: 154).
136 Frantz and Collins (1999: 116).
137 Frantz and Collins (1999); Pollan (1997); Ross (1999).
138 Huxtable (1997). Kenny and Zimmerman (2004), for example, show how theming in terms of nostalgia was a core component of the New Urbanist redevelopment of Central Milwaukee. This included reference to the city's 'grounding in traditional Midwestern values' and 'the cultural capital represented by the late nineteenth-century era industrial landscape' (2004: 76). However, as the authors observe, the process of transformation 'by nostalgically celebrating a heritage of ethnicity and industrialization' (2004: 94) uncritically presupposed values that were in short supply in the old neighbourhoods. Similarly, Falconer Al-Hindi and Staddon (1997) depict the appeal of Seaside, Florida, as based on an idealized past in which a sense of community is taken to be a key ingredient. According to Falconer Al-Hindi and Till (2001), developments associated with New Urbanist principles could be found in at least 45 states.
139 Urry (2002: 123).
140 Gottdiener (2002).
141 Hendry (2000: 1)
142 Kirshenblatt-Gimblett (1998: 9).
143 Handler and Gable (1997).
144 Hendry (2000: 137).
145 Robinson (2003).
146 *Investor's Chronicle*, 24 March, 2000: 26.
147 Baldwin (2002).
148 Sherman (2001).
149 Ritzer and Liska (1997).
150 Wood (2000).
151 Wickers (1999).
152 Pine and Gilmore (1999: 41).
153 Ritzer (1999).
154 Quoted in Schmitt and Simonson (1997: 122).
155 Goldberger (1997b).
156 Sandicki and Holt (1998).
157 Shoval (2000).

Chapter Three
Hybrid consumption

By 'hybrid consumption' I mean the general trend whereby the forms of consumption associated with different institutional spheres become interlocked with each other and increasingly difficult to distinguish. What we end up with under hybrid consumption are de-differentiated forms of consumption in which conventional distinctions between these forms become increasingly blurred to the point that they almost collapse. By 'forms of consumption' I mean such things as: shopping; visiting a theme park; eating in a restaurant; staying at a hotel; visiting a museum; going to the cinema; playing and/or watching sports; and gambling in a casino. With hybrid consumption systems, forms of consumption are brought together in new and often imaginative ways.

Why Create Hybrid Consumption Environments?

If adjacent attraction and differentiation are the principles that underlie theming, as outlined in Chapter 2, with hybrid consumption the master principle is getting people to *stay longer*. Essentially, the more consumption items that are fused, the longer people will stay in the venue to which they have been attracted in the first place. In the extreme, the aim is to create a *destination*, somewhere that people go to as a significant venue that will keep them there for some time. As destinations, hybrid consumption locations become venues akin to holiday destinations. The merging of different orders of consumption, particularly when accompanied by theming, creates a spectacular consumption site, which frequently evinces a sense of awe, partly because of its size but also partly because of its innovativeness in bringing together unusual types of consumption.

The reality of the 'stay longer' principle can be detected in the comments of many designers and managers of late modern consumption destinations, several of which will be encountered again in this chapter. Goss quotes a senior vice-president of leasing and marketing with respect to shopping malls in the US as saying: 'Our surveys show [that] the amount of spending is related *directly* to the amount of time spent at centers. ...Anything that can prolong shoppers' visits are [sic] in our best interests overall'.[1] He goes on to quote a marketing executive in connection with Franklin Mills, one of the malls in the Mills Corporation stable which was referred to in Chapter 2: 'The entertainment at Franklin Mills keeps shoppers at the centre for 3–4 hours, or twice as long as a regular mall [and] the more you give shoppers to do, the longer they stay and the more they buy'.[2] Crawford quotes a mall developer along similar lines: 'The more needs you fulfill, the longer people stay'.[3]

Layers of theming help to add to the sense of a destination and provide further reasons for staying longer. According to the editor of *Visual Merchandizing and Store Design*: 'There is less leisure time today so people need to have fun. You have to use every trick in the book to keep those shoppers lingering longer'.[4] A similar point was made by the manager of Forum Shops which is attached to the Caesar's Palace Casino-Hotel in Las Vegas:

We like to compare ourselves with like Disneyland, where you feel good about where you are. And when people feel good they tend to want to stay longer. So that's what it's all about – making people feel good about where they are and making sure they have an enjoyable experience. If they're coming here to see the entertainment, that's a plus. And in their way to seeing some of these [audio-animatronic] shows they bypass Banana Republic or you know whatever other shops and they might think 'Gosh, you know what, I might love to get a new blouse for this evening' or 'I might pick up that dress I saw in the evening.' So it all ... sort of, one hand shakes the other.[5]

Similarly, Davis shows in connection with Sea World in San Diego how important it is for the park to make sure that visitors stay as long as possible: the longer they stay, the more they spend. Like all theme parks, they do this by trying to create as many reasons as possible to stay in the park. This includes having a large number of attractions and making sure that restaurants and other amenities are available. It also includes increasing the tactile emphasis of some attractions, since, according to the vice-president for entertainment 'people stay longer if entertainment is less passive, less dependent on just watching and more physically involving'.[6]

The message from these various comments is clear. The goal of hybrid consumption sites is to give people as many reasons as possible for staying at the sites. The more needs that can be met, the longer visitors will stay and the more money they will spend. Also, there are more reasons for visiting them in the first place so that they become destinations in their own right.

Hybrid Consumption at the Disney Theme Parks

Walt Disney realized at a very early stage that Disneyland had great potential as a vehicle for selling food and various goods. Main Street USA typified this in that its main purpose is not to house attractions but to act as a context for shopping. As Umberto Eco puts it: 'The Main Street façades are presented to us as toy houses and invite us to enter them, but their interior is always a disguised supermarket, where you buy obsessively, believing that you are still playing'.[7] Nowadays, the Disney theme parks are full of shops and restaurants to the extent that many writers argue that their main purpose increasingly is precisely the selling of a variety of goods and food. The shops and restaurants are designed to merge seamlessly, in terms of their theming and location, with the attractions. With many attractions, visitors are forced to go through a shop containing relevant merchandise in order to exit (for example, a shop containing Star Wars merchandise as one leaves the Star Tours ride in the two American Disney parks and Disneyland Paris). In Epcot's World Showcase, representations of different nations are the main focus, but one of the chief ways in which the nations and their nationhood is revealed is through eating and shopping. Indeed, some of the buildings, which iconically represent some of the countries, do not contain attractions at all (for example, Britain and Italy), or perhaps contain little more than a film about the country concerned (for example, Canada and France). However, each 'country' has at least one restaurant (some, like France, Mexico and China, have two) and at least one shop. It is not surprising, therefore, that many commentators portray Epcot and indeed the other Disney parks as vehicles for selling goods and food. Thus, the Euro Disneyland share prospectus presented as one of the main management techniques associated with 'the Disney theme park concept' the fact that 'Disney has learned to optimise the mix of merchandise in stores within its theme parks, which consequently are highly profitable and achieve some of the highest sales per square metre for retail stores in the United States'.[8] If we add hotels into this equation, the case for describing the parks as sites of hybrid consumption is even more compelling.

At Disney World the number of hotels has grown enormously since Michael Eisner took the helm at the Walt Disney Company in 1984. Eisner and his team felt very strongly that this was one of several areas that needed attention. It was felt that too many theme park visitors were staying off Disney property and that as a result the company was losing a huge revenue stream. Also, if people went off Disney property at the end of the day, they would be less likely to be spending their money in theme park restaurants and on merchandise. As a result, over the succeeding 20 years Eisner and his team have massively increased the number of Disney hotel rooms and in the process pursued an accelerating hybrid consumption strategy. This has been done by building less-expensive hotels, as well as the more traditional upmarket ones.

In addition to being themed (see previous chapter), there has been a clear attempt to increase the number of guests staying in its hotels by emphasizing their advantages over non-Disney ones. For example, Disney guests are able to enter the parks earlier and can therefore get to the main attractions before the arrival of hordes of off-site tourists. They are also able to secure tables for the sought-after restaurants (especially the Epcot ethnic ones) from their hotels rather than having to take a chance on their availability when they turn up at the parks. Also, for some time now Disney has been offering its hotel guests inclusive length-of-stay passes to the parks. It is striking that it was recognized during the days when the financial troubles at Disneyland Paris were common knowledge that one of the reasons for its problems was not the number of visitors to the parks but the fact that they were not spending as much on food, souvenirs and Disney hotels as had been predicted.[9] Thus, we see in the Disney parks a tendency for shopping, eating, hotel accommodation and theme park visiting to become inextricably interwoven. Any distinctions are further undermined by the fact that Disney have created what is essentially a mall in the centre in Disney World (Disney Village, formerly called Disney Marketplace), a strategy that has been followed through at Disneyland and Disneyland Paris.

An extension of this strategy at Disney World is that Disney have turned it into a resort. Disney World is not a theme park – it is a resort with four major theme parks, some water parks, a nightclub area, hotels, restaurants, an educational venue (Disney Institute), a sports area, and a shopping district. Essentially, the strategy is one of seeking to give guests as few reasons as possible for wanting or needing to leave Disney property. This strategy has also been followed at Universal Resort Orlando, which not long ago was just Universal Studios Orlando. Since then it has added a new theme park (Universal Islands of Adventure), a nightlife area (Universal CityWalk including clubs, restaurants, a cinema, and shops), and themed hotels. Disney has adopted its own strategy at Disneyland, which is now Disneyland Resort. By opening a new theme park – Californian Adventure – and a new hotel and shopping area, it has given guests more reasons for staying on Disney property and more opportunities to spend their money. The point is simply made by Kerry Hunnewell, a former Walt Disney Co. vice-president: 'The Orlando philosophy is to get you there, keep you there, and to make sure you spend all your money with them. ...In Anaheim, we needed a reason for folks to stick around'.[10]

Precursors of Hybrid Consumption

Hybrid consumption is not new: what *is* new is the systematic way in which different forms of consumption are being tied together with the goal of turning places into destinations where visitors will stay longer. Amusement parks have always had cafes and restaurants; museums have always sold a few souvenirs; and hotels have invariably had restaurants. What is also new is the sheer variety of forms of consumption that are being brought together to create new hybrid forms and formats.

Over the last century it is possible to detect a number of contexts for hybrid consumption. The department store is an obvious candidate. It brought together under one roof different types of goods and services (notably restaurants, tea rooms) that previously had been (and which often still are) located in different shops. Shopping arcades operated with the same underlying principles but were somewhat less integrated than the department store. As with the larger and more lavishly themed malls, department stores and arcades could often produce a sense of awe at the spectacular nature of the locations and the sheer plenitude of goods and services on offer.[11]

The supermarket and its various extensions into hypermarkets and beyond can also be seen as an early form of hybrid consumption. The supermarket has gradually incorporated more and more forms of retailing under its roof, as meat, vegetables and fruit, and alcohol – formerly the province of specialist shops – were gradually included. Since then, a vast array of goods have slowly been included and today form key areas of profitability: clothing, recorded music, do-it-yourself and gardening equipment, electrical products, pharmaceuticals, and so on, as well as coffee shops, restaurants and other services. Hybrid consumption is therefore an extension of a trend that has been underway for decades.

The Disney theme parks may even have influenced many of the developments to be discussed below by virtue of their successful policy of bringing together different forms of consumption. For example, one of the Ghermezian brothers who own and operate the company that was responsible for the design of West Edmonton Mall, one of the most noted sites of hybrid consumption, was apparently very influenced by the Disney theme parks.[12] It seems likely that hybrid consumption is in part a case of structural Disneyization but also of transferred Disneyization.

The Diffusion of Hybrid Consumption

In this section, a variety of ways and contexts in which hybrid consumption occurs nowadays will be outlined. Initially, some major combinations of consumption forms will be concentrated upon.

Hotels and casinos

Las Vegas is possibly a better illustration than the Disney theme parks of Disneyization in the form of hybrid consumption. The themed hotels mentioned in Chapter 2 could equally be described, and probably more accurately, as casinos. Each houses a massive casino, although they could equally be described as casinos with hotels attached. But in recent years, hybridization has proceeded apace in Las Vegas. You may enter the Forum Shops (also mentioned in Chapter 2) at Caesar's Palace on the moving walkway but the only exit is to walk through the casino. Many of the other large themed hotel-casinos in Las Vegas have attached upmarket shopping malls to their buildings. Blackpool's proposed Pharaoh's Palace will adopt a similar combination of consumption opportunities in order to become a Las Vegas-style resort. Atlantic City, New Jersey, also has some giant casino-hotels with added attractions.

In addition, in order to attract families and a wider range of clientele, the casino-hotels in Las Vegas have either built theme parks (for example, MGM Grand, Circus Circus) or have incorporated theme park attractions (for example, Luxor, Stratosphere, New York New York, Treasure Island, Excalibur). Figure 3.1 shows Hotel New York New York with its Manhattan skyline and one of the cars on its roller coaster just coming into view.

In 1994, one journalist felt compelled to write:

> The old Sin City ... has traded in its G-string for a G-rating. So much for the garish neon signs, topless showgirls and smoke-filled casinos. Las Vegas has become Disneyland in the Desert, a family resort instead of an adult playground. Or, at least, that's the impression left by a flood of recent newspaper and magazine articles.[13]

In the process, conventional distinctions between casinos, hotels, restaurants, shopping, and theme parks collapse. In addition, the Las Vegas hotel-casinos are also major venues for elaborate shows and sometimes indoor sporting events like boxing. Crawford has written that 'malls routinely entertain, while theme parks function as disguised marketplace',[14] but current trends imply that even this comment does not capture the extent of hybrid consumption in Las Vegas where several formerly distinct forms of consumption are merged under one roof.

In fact, the suggestion that Las Vegas hotel-casinos rushed headlong into the family market is an exaggeration.[15] While the number of families treating Las Vegas as a family destination undoubtedly increased, many of the hotel-casino operators were concerned that the expenditure on and the allocation of space for theme park entertainments would not be offset by the lower levels of spending on gambling (the city's prime mover). Also, there was a concern among some of the hotel-casino operators that an excessive emphasis upon families could detract from the sense of Las Vegas as an adult Disneyland. The common description of Las Vegas as a Disneyland for adults denotes that it is a playground for adults, *not* that it is a Disney-style theme park for families.

Figure 3.1   Hotel New York New York in Las Vegas including its roller coaster

Some casino operators included somewhat more limited family attractions in their portfolios of tourist activities. Thus, the Hilton built a Star Trek ride along with related elements, such as a shop selling Star Trek merchandise and a bar called Quark's. These themed elements were designed to link seamlessly with the gambling, especially since people did gamble in the 'real' Quark's in *Star Trek: Deep Space Nine*. This is an example of a limited and circumscribed design of attractions for the family. Others built water parks that would appeal to adults as well as to families, thus increasing the degree of hybrid consumption at the Las Vegas hotels.

The attachment of family theme park attractions to hotels has not been an unequivocal success. There has been a feeling that some adults may have been put

64

off coming to Las Vegas because of its family-friendly image, preferring more exclusively racy destinations. By the early 2000s, the emphasis was beginning to switch away from a family orientation. A *Times* journalist, for example, quotes a spokeswoman for the city's Convention and Visitors Authority as saying: 'We don't want to discourage families, but Vegas is an adult party town'.[16] Also, some theme park attractions simply have not been able to justify their cost. Probably the most significant failure is the theme park that was attached to the MGM Grand. This was probably the most ambitious of all the attractions built for families in that it was a full theme park in its own right but closed down a few years after opening because of insufficient numbers of visitors.

Theme parks, shopping and restaurants

Most theme parks follow the Disney example in seeking to maximize visitors' opportunities to shop and eat in restaurants or at kiosks *en route*. Sales of goods and food contribute greatly to the profitability of parks. Theme parks are nowadays replete with shops selling goods loosely linked to the park's themes and also in the form of what is referred to in Chapter 4 as licensed merchandise bearing the logo of the park or of its emblems. In addition, they offer a vast array of eating opportunities, including reflexively themed restaurants, like McDonald's and KFC.

Sea World in San Diego, California, provides a good illustration of the process. Davis has written of the park:

> Sea World's designers and engineers focus on the problem of intensifying spending. To keep people buying food and souvenirs, they know that they must be made comfortable, kept interested, and moved at the right pace through a landscape they find appealingly different…[17]

One way in which they do this is to create the impression that the park is not too packed with people, since people tend to spend less if they feel that an environment is too crowded. Davis quotes the vice-president for operations as saying that he aims to create a rhythm for the park that will make sales of goods and food more likely. The management experiment with the schedules of Sea World's shows to maximize possible sales. In addition, the layout of the park is such that the visitor is being led to gift shops that are themed in relation to the park's animals, such as its leading star Shamu, the performing killer whale, the penguins in Penguin Encounter, manatees and so on. Food stands help to make the restaurants slightly less busy at times of the day when people are most inclined to want to eat but also help to promote needs the consumer would not otherwise have realized he or she had. As a result of these strategies, Davis estimates that 50% of park revenues derive from food, drinks, merchandise and similar sources. While smaller theme parks may appear less well equipped than major ones like the Sea Worlds, they undoubtedly employ similar tactics to cultivate sales and keep visitors staying longer.

The shopping mall has become a major location for hybrid consumption. This occurs in numerous and fairly well-known ways, whereby malls seek to incorporate many types of consumption and functions so that there are as few reasons as possible for the shopper to leave the mall. Indeed, the mall frequently becomes a venue for activities other than shopping as such and in the process becomes a destination in its own right.

Malls now incorporate a wide variety of restaurants, snack bars, and coffee shops. In addition, they often have banking facilities in the form of actual bank branches or ATMs (automatic teller machines). Cinemas have become an increasingly common component of the standard mall combination of elements. At the large malls, designers have built theme parks and other leisure facilities. At Mall of America is a seven acre theme park called Knott's Camp Snoopy, which features 23 rides. There is no entrance fee and visitors pay for each ride. In the first six months of operation, the park had more than four million riders.[18] Early research showed that the average visitor spent 3.1 hours in the mall which includes a half-hour visit to Camp Snoopy, although since then the average visit to the mall has been calculated as 2.6 hours.[19] West Edmonton Mall has similarly incorporated a giant water park and theme park attractions in 'Fantasyland' and now also incorporates a mini-golf course and a chapel.

Most shopping malls do not have the extraordinary extent of combinations of hybrid consumption that are found in West Edmonton Mall and Mall of America, but they are able to follow some of their leads. The MetroCentre in Gateshead, England, contains 'an enormous fantasy kingdom of fairground rides'.[20] The Trafford Centre just outside Manchester, England, includes a tenpin bowling alley, a virtual reality games section, and dodgem cars. Figure 3.2 shows one of the restaurants in its food court area next to the centre's games section against a backdrop of Aztec and ancient Egyptian images. The developers of Bluewater Mall in Kent, England, have promised regular concerts and performances as part of the range of leisure options available.[21]

One journalist has written in connection with the Trafford Centre: 'The shopping centre as theme park, appealing to all sexes and ages, is the key to the Trafford Centre's marketing policy'.[22] It is likely that this process is only partly to do with the theming of areas of the centre in terms of parts of the world or the changing sky that it borrowed from the Forum Shops in Las Vegas. It is also to do with introducing a wide range of leisure facilities that can increase the range of family members wanting to visit the centre and the number of reasons for keeping them there. Like some other large malls, the centre also has its own hotel within the complex, a strategy that has been especially significant at West Edmonton Mall. Ontario Mills in California has over 200 stores, an indoor zoo, two ice rinks, and a motion simulator ride, as well as an entertainment setting in the form of a Dave and Buster's (see the following section for these venues).[23] Several new large malls have been built in Bangkok and several of them have

Figure 3.2   The restaurant and games area in the Trafford Centre

included small theme parks and areas for family entertainment; in Sydney, Australia, there is a large retail area that encompasses theme park attractions and rides, themed restaurants, a Sega World and street theatre.[24]

The trio of forms of consumption that are the focus of this section are also brought together in many of the far eastern theme parks that have emerged in the years after Tokyo Disneyland. In this connection, it is striking that the passage quoted on page 50 from the work of Hendry concerning the Japanese *gaikoku mura* (foreign country villages) mentions that there is at these venues 'an abundant stock of food, drink and ornaments from the area in question'.[25] As an example, at Glücks Königreich, a park themed on Germany, there are a variety of eating opportunities for appropriately ethnic food as well as shops, and a reproduction castle that functions as a luxury hotel. The park also includes a restaurant, conference facilities and a sports club. Similarly, Huis ten Bosch, which is themed on Holland and is the largest of the *gaikoku mura*, contains a wide range of shops and restaurants as well as a hotel (Hotel Europe).

In addition to shopping malls as locations where theme park attractions, shopping and restaurants merge, large complexes like the festival marketplaces and tourist enclaves (see Chapter 6 on the latter), provide examples of locations where different forms of consumption are brought together. Wolf mentions several complexes that combine a variety of consumption forms. He cites: Fox Studios, Australia megaplex – 16 theatres, soundstage with a backlot for public viewing, adventure playground, area with stores and restaurants; Crown Resort, Melbourne with a casino, hotel, restaurants, bars, nightclubs, and a theatre; and Genting, City of Entertainment, Malaysia, which comprises gambling, golf courses, convention facilities, restaurants, sports facilities.[26] Along Philadelphia's waterfront, a large number of themed bars and restaurants have opened, along with a Dave and Buster's (see next section), a seaport museum, ice skating rink and a Hyatt hotel.[27] New York's controversially rejuvenated Times Square is yet another example, with its striking combination of themed restaurant, bars, theatres, stores, all linked to a general tourist entertainment theme. Of course, cities have invariably contained combinations of leisure facilities, but what is significant about such developments is the coordinated way in which these hybrid consumption areas are assembled and the fact that this tends to occur in a clearly defined enclave.

Hybrid consumption within outlets

Related to hybrid consumption of the kind found in malls, as outlined in the last section, is that many outlets seek to incorporate more and more consumption opportunities under their roofs. Placing coffee shops within book store chains like Barnes and Noble and Borders in the US and Waterstone's in the UK is an example of the way in which some outlets seek out a symbiotic relationship between different forms of consumption in order to enhance the general ambience of their main offering. This kind of twinning is also very much to do with the stay longer principle outlined above. At the time of writing, many branches of Abbey National, a chain of banks in the UK, include a small Costa coffee shop within each branch (Costa is one of the main chains of coffee shops in the UK).

Another example of the process is Dave and Buster's where several different adult entertainment activities, such as video games, restaurant, billiards room, and a nightclub are brought together under one roof. The Dave and Buster's chain is often found in malls, especially those with a strong entertainment orientation. Since the chain's outlets include several consumption activities, they serve to increase the range of hybrid consumption in these malls. Disney's ESPN Zone chain also functions in a similar way as a resort for adult sports enthusiasts where they can eat in the restaurant, be spectators of sports, participate in interactive video games, and purchase sports souvenirs in the shop.[28] In the UK, at Girl Heaven, a chain of retail stores for girls aged three to 13 and themed on the concept of 'girl power', the aim is to provide a platform for a total makeover into a 'princess', so the outlets include hairdressing, manicure, and make-up along with clothing.[29]

Hotels

Hotels are often at the heart of hybrid consumption settings because the bigger they are, the more likely it is that people will be prepared to stay longer and therefore they are more likely to consider staying in a linked hotel. We have seen this principle in connection with the casino-hotels and the Disney theme parks have used this strategy. Many other theme parks are doing likewise and Universal Orlando, which was mentioned previously, has developed a great deal in this area. Other theme parks are following suit, in that there is a Legoland Hotel at Legoland in Holland, while Alton Towers theme park in England now has two themed hotels on the site.

Similarly, some large malls are including hotels in their complexes. Even the Hamburger University in Illinois, where McDonald's franchisees and managers are trained, has its own Hyatt.[30] The new football (soccer) stadium that is the home of Bolton Wanderers, known as the Reebok Stadium, has a hotel attached to it, reflecting a growing tendency for sports venues to be sites for hybrid consumption (see the section on sports stadiums below). The large Las Vegas hotel-casinos are not only platforms for shopping and restaurant opportunities, they are also frequently venues for shows of various kinds and sporting events, thereby further extending the ways in which hotels are implicated in hybrid consumption.

Sports stadiums

Many sports stadiums, and the modern baseball park in particular, are increasingly a home to a variety of forms of consumption.[31] They are no longer solely locations for watching a favourite team play. One writer on sports marketing writes that 'today's ballparks have ATM machines, virtual shopping malls, and ... restaurants and hotels' and observes that the Skydome in Toronto 'offers dinner views of the park, hotel rooms with views of the diamond, and even a swinging Hard Rock Cafe in right field'.[32] According to a journalist from the *Wall Street Journal*, at Tropicana Stadium, the home of the Tampa Devil Rays baseball team

> fans can get a trim at a barber shop, do their banking and then grab a cold one at the Budweiser brew pub, whose copper kettles rise to three stories. There is even a climbing wall for kids and showroom space for car dealerships.[33]

At the MCI Center in Washington, DC, Ritzer notes that there is a Discovery Channel store, a sports gallery that includes museum displays, and an electronic games arcade. Regarding baseball parks, there is now a growing number that include among the various consumption elements: shopping malls, food courts, beer gardens and bars, video games arcades, museums, some amusement park attractions, and banking facilities.[34]

McDonald's

There are two main ways in which hybrid consumption can be seen in relation to McDonald's. One is through the way its tie-ins with companies like Disney become the context for the distribution of toys or when it latches onto new toy crazes like the Beanie Babies.[35] These toys have attracted enthusiasts who collect them and maintain a website for sharing of information about them and there is an annual convention for collectors.[36] Most new Disney films are involved in cross-promotional tie-ins with McDonald's. As Pecora and Meehan report in the context of their US component of the Global Disney Audiences Project (see Box 3.1): 'Given Disney's promotional agreement with McDonald's, the McDonald's in the mall had been decorated with *Hunchback* streamers and promotional displays. It offered special *Hunchback* meals with *Hunchback* place mats, napkins, paper cups, etc'.[37] But it is the distribution of free toys that is the key feature for us in terms of hybrid consumption. The exclusive McDonald's/Disney alliance produced a 23% increase in Happy Meals in the United States.[38] In 1997, this made for a 7% increase in sales. In the process, McDonald's became the largest distributor of toys in the world. It is not surprising therefore that the participant researchers in the Global Disney Audiences Project noted that their interviewees in several countries frequently remarked upon the prominence of tie-ins with Disney films (see Box 3.1). However, it is not just Disney films that are tied in

---

Box 3.1 The Global Disney Audiences Project

The Global Disney Audiences Project comprises a series of linked investigations that were concerned to examine the reception of Disney products around the globe. Researchers from 18 countries (one of which was the United States, where five different locations were studied) were involved in the overall project. In each case, researchers in the countries concerned carried out interviews and administered questionnaires to audiences to gauge the reception of Disney products internationally. In addition, national profiles dealing with Disney's marketing of its products in different countries and unique aspects of the national context that impinged on reception were explored. The questionnaires and interviews dealt with such issues as possession of Disney goods and viewing Disney films, feelings about the company, perceived values associated with Disney products, and the perception of Disney as a culturally imperialist institution (or otherwise). In each country, the target respondents were university students.

Source: Wasko, Phillips and Meehan (2001)

---

to McDonald's, in that films like *Space Jam*, have also been involved in this way. Although writers like Wolf claim that such tie-ins can result in very significant improvements in food sales for McDonald's, the movie tie-in with food is by no means a recipe for success, as Taco Bell found with its cross-promotion with *Godzilla*. The significance of such tie-ins for the present discussion is simply that the distribution of free toys as a lure for children can be viewed as evidence of hybrid consumption since it involves elements of the sale of both food and toys. It should also be noted that this form of hybrid consumption is often a focus for criticism because it is seen as evidence of the manipulation of consumers and of children in particular. The Archbishop of Canterbury has criticized such tie-ins and singled out Disney for particular disapproval. He expressed dismay at the way in which companies cultivate consumerism among children, particularly through tie-ins and recognized the influence of Disney on this process. He was quoted as saying: 'The "tie-in", the association of comics, sweets, toys and so on with a new film: the Disney empire has developed this to an unprecedented pitch'.[39]

The second main sense in which we find hybrid consumption in relation to McDonald's is the way in which it is frequently implicated in settings that bring together a variety of forms of consumption. Examples are the obvious ones like the presence of McDonald's in malls, but there are others too, such as its location in theme parks. McDonald's is also often found in the modern ballpark.[40] This kind of diffusion of McDonald's into a variety of settings has been a clear strategy for the company. In the Afterword to the autobiography of Ray Kroc, the founder of McDonald's as we know it today, Kroc's co-author Robert Anderson mentions with satisfaction the appearance of McDonald's outlets in a hospital, tollway services plazas, military bases, shopping malls, and amusement parks. He quoted from the 1985 annual report: 'Maybe – someday – McDonald's will be found on aircraft carriers and commercial airliners. In sports stadiums and fine department stores'.[41] Some of these developments have indeed materialized. However, as a strategy, this is not always successful, as the company found when it was forced because of poor levels of patronage to close many of its outlets that were located in Wal-Mart stores.[42]

Zoos

Zoos too are implicated in hybrid consumption. Disney's Animal Kingdom is an extreme in this respect and it is hardly surprising that a Disney location should be a major site of this aspect of the Disneyization of zoos. In placing a zoo in the midst of Disney World, which comprises theme parks, water parks, nearly 20 hotels, six golf courses, and numerous restaurants, including one of the Rainforest Cafe chain in the Animal Kingdom and a hotel very close to it, hybrid consumption in relation to zoos is magnified. Like Busch Gardens, West Midlands Safari Park and several other zoos, it includes theme park attractions within its grounds. The Animal Kingdom has a thrill ride tellingly called Countdown to Extinction. Busch Gardens has numerous thrill rides which are organized in terms of African lands, and Sea World in Orlando has a flume ride entitled Voyage to Atlantis and a roller coaster. Some theme parks, like Drayton Manor in the UK, incorporate a zoo amid the various rides and attractions. Similarly, Marine World Africa in California has been described as: 'Part zoo, part theme park, part circus, even part carnival'.[43] Aqualeon, just outside Barcelona in Spain, combines a water park with the display of wild animals, as well as shows which actively involve some of these animals. Dibb, in the context of her examination of UK zoos and wildlife parks, notes:

> Throughout the 1980s the growing popularity of the theme park provided a significant challenge to the role of zoos. Increasingly, establishments are choosing to combine the lure of wild and domestic animals with other entertainments. For example, UK animal attraction Whipsnade has introduced a range of new activities to encourage visitors to spend more, visit more frequently and stay longer. West Midlands Safari Park and Chessington World of Adventures [which started life as a zoo] combine rides with wildlife.[44]

We see in these examples a tendency for the distinction between zoo and theme park to become blurred.

A further aspect of this issue is the fact that the large American zoos and aquaria (Animal Kingdom, Busch Gardens, Sea World) include extensive shopping and eating facilities. While most zoos cannot match this provision because of their much smaller scale, it is conceivable that these features will become more prominent and will gradually supplant the standard cafe or tea room and small gift shop at the exit. Merritt and Cain point to the growing commercialism of American zoos and aquariums and the significance of restaurants and gift shops selling soft toy animals and other merchandise as part of that strategy. The authors even suggest that zoo managers need to be more aware of the ways in which such institutions can be developed as businesses.[45]

At one point, Ontario Mills in California included a small themed zoo within its walls. Moreover, zoo-like attractions are sometimes included in settings where they might not be expected. At the Mirage hotel-casino in Las Vegas, in addition to a giant aquarium behind the check-in desk, there are tigers on view in fabricated settings that can be viewed much like a conventional zoo. The tigers are used in a long-standing magic act in the hotel (the Siegfried and Roy show, which at the time of writing was closed).

One further way in which hybrid consumption might be viewed as occurring in zoos is that as the theming of zoos, particularly in terms of animal habitats and conservation, has intensified, the emphasis on simply gazing at animals has shifted. Increasingly, the zoo is a place where education of a limited kind takes place. In order to counter public unease about simply gawking at animals, many zoos have placed a greater emphasis than in the past on educating the visitor. This is especially important for zoos at a time when many are repositioning themselves as agents of conservation with strong breeding programmes. Promoting an understanding of the processes involved requires educating visitors in the craft of rearing animals and preserving species.

Museums

Museums are involved in hybrid consumption in three contrasting and interesting ways. First and most obviously, they are increasingly tuned to providing shopping and restaurant opportunities for visitors. These are invariably a major source of income and have moved far beyond the small shop you pass through as you exit the museum or the tiny restaurant serving a limited range of drinks and food. Nowadays, especially in the larger museums, shopping and eating are major components of revenue and are catered for with often more than one shop and restaurant.[46] For major museums, retailing has become a major activity and can contribute as much as a quarter of its earned income. For the Museum of Modern Art store in New York has sales of $1,750 per square foot which compares with $250 for the average US mall and $600 for the Mall of America.[47]

Second, museums are sometimes part of general hybrid consumption settings. Large sports clubs often include a museum or at least some museum displays as part of the range of consumption forms that they offer. Previously, it was noted that MCI Center in Washington, DC, includes some museum displays and in many stadiums there are full-blown museums. Spanish football clubs Barcelona and Real Madrid both have large museums, as does Manchester United at its Theatre of Dreams, Old Trafford. Universal CityWalk in Universal City includes a Museum of Neon Art among its themed restaurants and shops.[48] Some companies, such as Hershey, Crayola, Goodyear, and Hormel Foods (Spamtown), in the US and Cadbury in England, have added museums to the attractions that have been created around their manufacturing plants.[49] For a short time, there was a Coca-Cola museum in the Showcase Mall in Las Vegas, but it closed down due to lack of interest.

Third, what is and is not a museum is becoming increasingly difficult to determine. As Macdonald observes, 'the boundaries between museums and other institutions have become elided'.[50] In part, this is because museums have taken on many aspects and characteristics of a theme park that is consequent on their theming (see Chapter 2). Another factor is the emergence of what Urry has termed 'a postmodern museum culture in which almost anything can become an object of curiosity'.[51] However, even more than this, museum-like exhibits sometimes permeate non-museum environments. In the Past Times chain of shops in Britain, simulated artefacts of the past are for sale in museum-like surroundings. Nowhere is this trend more apparent than at Niketown Chicago. As noted in Chapter 2, the store was designed to have the features of a museum, such as memorabilia in boxed glass cases, as well as those of a store. The museum mode of exhibiting memorabilia caused considerable confusion on the part of shoppers who were concerned about whether they could purchase anything and whether they should pay an entrance fee. However, the museum atmosphere was generally well received by visitors. Drawing on her ethnographic study of the Chicago store, Peñaloza quotes one visitor (a white male in his 30s) as saying, while gesturing to display cases of Air Jordans 'I didn't expect this. *It's like a museum*. This is great'.[52] The fact that store staff were located in each room like museum attendants further led to the misapprehension on visitors' part that they were in a museum.

Airport terminals

A further illustration of hybrid consumption is the way in which many airports and terminals are being turned into mini-malls. Not all that long ago, many terminals boasted little more than a duty free shop, a restaurant, and a shop selling newspapers and a small selection of books. Hamilton and Harlow noted a considerable growth in this area and suggested that in the early 1990s sales at airport shops were growing three times faster than on the high street.[53] Airports and terminals have attracted big name stores such as Selfridges, Harrods and House of Fraser, which use the outlets as a way of showcasing their local presence in cities, as well as selling souvenirs, gifts, and other merchandise. In addition, airports have been attracting chains of shops, such as bookshop chains. Restaurants and coffee shops have also proliferated and some of the big high street names now have a presence in terminals, such as McDonald's, Starbucks, Nathan's, Chilli's, TGI Friday's, and Planet Hollywood. Many terminals now have a video games room as well.

However, the principle underlying hybrid consumption at airports is different from most of the other instances covered thus far. It has been argued that a major principle behind hybrid consumption forms is that of staying longer. This principle does not translate entirely to the airport context because the main object of being in an airport terminal is that you are in transit. Some people may arrive slightly early to give themselves a little time for last minute shopping or to grab a meal before a flight but they are unlikely to be seduced by the stay longer principle because if they did they would miss their flights! Instead, the principle lying behind the proliferation of shopping and eating outlets and other elements in hybrid consumption is that these are captive shoppers, diners and game players. Shopping, dining and playing games offer diversions from the boredom of waiting for a flight. People may only go into a shop intending to browse but there is a fair chance that some will be seduced into buying. They achieve one of the highest levels of sales per square foot of any form of shopping; airport malls like that at Pittsburgh International can achieves sales per square foot that are as much as three times that of a traditional US mall.[54] Major railway stations, like New York's Grand Central, are similarly waking up to the shopping opportunities offered by such developments.[55]

Cruise ships

The large cruise ships have become contexts for hybrid consumption forms. At one level, they are about tourism and going to a variety of destinations. But many of them have gone well beyond this and are now resorts in their own right, in that they encompass so many forms of consumption that they are destinations independently of their ports of call. These huge cruise ships include a host of shops (some ships essentially have their own malls), many restaurants, shows and variety acts, casinos, banking facilities, and sporting facilities (including ice rinks and golf courses). Carnival Cruise Lines' *Destiny* includes: a massive casino; four swimming pools and sports facilities; a jazz club; a huge disco; a comedy and dance lounge; Las Vegas-style shows; and many restaurants in addition to the dining rooms.[56]

There are signs that this process of adding more and more forms of consumption is likely to accelerate. At a speech given to the Seatrade Asia Pacific Cruise Convention in Singapore in December 1996, the Italian architect who designed the *Crystal Harmony* cruise ship and Huis Ten Bosch, one of the most successful of the Japanese *gaikoku mura* (foreign country villages) referred to in Chapter 2, suggested that the large cruise ships will eventually become floating theme parks.[57]

Other domains of hybrid consumption

The foregoing discussion has emphasized some of the major spheres in which hybrid consumption has taken place in late modern society. However, it does not exhaust all of them by any means. The following is a catalogue of others along with a brief discussion of each.

- *Weddings* These are among the more surprising elements to be included in the range of consumption offerings. The Disney wedding has become a popular rite of passage at Disney's American theme parks, but it is not the only hybrid consumption venue where they take place, since they take place at Mall of America too.[58]

- *Family entertainment centres* Often located on the edges of cities, family entertainment centres are sites where a variety of leisure experiences are combined in one setting, with a multiplex cinema frequently forming the leisure hub.[59] Star City in Birmingham, England, combines a huge Warner Village cinema, amusement arcades, various restaurants, a night club, some shops, and a health club. A similar kind of development is Xscape just outside Milton Keynes, which has an indoor ski slope as its hub and includes climbing walls, bowling, a multiplex, interactive games area, cafes and restaurants, and some shops, and which attracts five million visitors per year.[60] At night, the tenor of the complex changes in that a nightclub and bars become the main focus for clientele.[61] In San Francisco, Sony's Metreon Center comprises a multiplex, IMAX cinema, video games, an adventure simulation, theme park attractions, shopping with an emphasis on games and entertainment, and restaurants.[62]

- *University campuses* Several commentators who have noticed the way in which many American university campuses increasingly look like malls in which a large array of shops and restaurants are available, many of which are national chains.[63] A similar process is happening to some UK campuses, which are increasingly becoming home to a wide variety of consumption forms, such as banks, shopping facilities (such as supermarkets, travel agents, opticians), and restaurant chains. Many include hotels and sports facilities for students and staff as part of a total consumption package that includes a university education.

- *Hospitals* Hospitals are increasingly sites for a considerable variety of consumption opportunities, most notably shops and restaurants, including fast food chains like McDonald's and Pizza Hut. In addition, fitness centres in hospitals have become a major development in medical real estate in Florida and are increasingly replacing independent gyms.[64]

- *More prosaic hybrid forms* Many of the forms and context of hybrid consumption referred to in this chapter have been high-profile elaborate forms. There are also more pedestrian forms which are worth a brief mention. Petrol or gas stations frequently function as small supermarkets selling a wide range of goods, including, in the UK, post offices and other facilities. Ritzer and Stillman mention laundromats with exercise equipment and internet cafes as further examples of a process in which the boundaries between different forms of consumption are broken down.[65]

Conclusion

In this chapter, my main aim has been to make a case that in much the same ways that the Disney theme parks are not just amusement parks that are themed in that they incorporate an array of consumption opportunities, so too have many areas of social and economic life come to fuse different forms of consumption. Increasingly, a visit to these new hybrid consumption contexts is presented to us as a way of taking in more than one consumption opportunity. Two principles have been presented as laying behind the emergence of many if not most forms of hybrid consumption. One is the destination principle. The idea here is that by including several different forms of consumption in one place or nearly one place, a destination is created that is more than the sum of its parts. Gottdiener quotes one commercial developer: 'Just as with food courts, restaurant-plexes and movie multiplexes, if there is enough choice, the project itself will become a destination, and the entertainment selection will be made on arrival'.[66] For the merchant, in addition to attracting customers who specifically want its fare – a film, a meal, its wares – others may be attracted who are visiting the venue for another reason. The quotation on page 58 from the manager of Forum Shops is also indicative of this kind of thinking. The second principle is the stay longer principle and is essentially saying that the more needs a venue can fulfil the longer people will stay. The two principles are, of course, connected because if people are attracted to hybrid consumption sites as destinations and stay in them longer, the more likely they are to have an unanticipated want created.

However, there is a further point that can be made that is very much in tune with the kinds of observations that were being made at the end of Chapter 2. Combinations of different forms of consumption can become mechanisms for differentiating identical or at least similar places. By introducing unique blends of forms of consumption, especially when combined with theming, the planner is able to differentiate sites that might otherwise appear unremarkable. The blending of different forms of consumption serves to create environments that are construed as being spectacular.[67] This feature is also significant as a means of combating home shopping and internet shopping. The internet merchants have been fighting back by creating their own forms of hybrid consumption. Wolf describes PepsiCo's website, Pepsi World, as a means of engaging in a variety of forms of consumption, such as watching a video clip or playing a game, which together are designed to keep the surfer at the site.[68] Similarly, Pine and Gilmore quote the president and CEO of AOL: 'We see online as a whole packaged experience that we want to bring to consumers. This package increasingly includes some new areas, and more of what we already have – multiplayer games, shopping and financial services'.[69] Thus, as the internet portals fight back, they create their own forms of hybrid consumption.

The observation being offered here that new forms of hybrid consumption frequently provide a means of differentiation can be usefully extended by suggesting that unusual combinations will become even more arresting and therefore help to draw attention to otherwise commonplace contexts. This kind of reasoning is especially significant in a world in which not only are many nations' consumption spheres dominated by ubiquitous chains but one where the chains are often put together in combinations that are unmemorable and lacking in a clear identity. The use of theming and unusual blends of forms of consumption helps to create extra-ordinariness where otherwise ordinariness reigns. Chains of identical shops and restaurants in unimaginatively reproduced locations have no identity – they could be anywhere. They are what both Augé and Zukin have termed 'nonplaces',[70] that is, places without a sense of identity or of being rooted in a recognizable space, and examples of what Ritzer terms 'nothingness', that is, spaces that have no distinctive substance.[71] In a world of such standardization, a state of affairs to which processes like McDonaldization have contributed considerably, theming and hybrid consumption offer commerce and planners ways of differentiating and of creating a sense of place.

Notes

1 Quoted in Goss (1993a: 22).
2 Quoted in Goss (1993a: 28).
3 Quoted in Crawford (1992: 15).
4 Quoted in Barber (1995: 325).
5 This quotation is from 'Shopology', the second of two television programmes shown on BBC2 on 9 September, 2001.
6 Quoted in Davis (1997: 103).
7 Eco (1986: 43).
8 Euro Disneyland S.C.A. Offer for Sale of 10,691,000 shares by S.G. Warburg Securities. Quotation is on page 13.
9 Bryman (1995: 77).
10 Quoted in Grover (2001).

11 Chaney (1983).
12 Hopkins (1990: 9–10).
13 Quoted in Gottdiener et al. (1999: 64).
14 Crawford (1992: 16).
15 Gottdiener et al. (1999).
16 Chesshyre (2002a).
17 Davis (1997: 82).
18 Spellmeyer (1993).
19 Cohn (1996).
20 Urry (1990: 149).
21 Rugoff (1999).
22 Jenkins (1998: 20).
23 Wolf (1999: 10).
24 Hannigan (1998).
25 Hendry (2000: 1).
26 Wolf (1999).
27 Hannigan (1998: 191).
28 Sherry et al. (2001).
29 Russell and Tyler (2002).
30 Schlosser (2001: 31).
31 Ritzer (1999); Ritzer and Stillman (2001b).
32 Schlossberg (1996: 176).
33 Quoted in Ritzer (1999: 140).
34 Ritzer and Stillman (2001a).
35 Barboza (1999).
36 Kincheloe (2002: 28–9).
37 Pecora and Meehan (2001: 315).
38 Wolf (1999: 55–6).
39 Quoted in Gledhill (2002).
40 Ritzer and Stillman (2001b).
41 Quoted in Kroc (1987 [1977]: 209).
42 Barboza (1999).
43 Desmond (1999: 193).
44 Dibb (1995: 261).
45 Cain and Merritt (1998).
46 See for example, Huxtable (1997: 84).
47 Leong (2001a: 147, 149)
48 Hannigan (1998: 112).
49 Pine and Gilmore (1999: 20); Ritzer (1999: 142–3).
50 Macdonald (1996: 1).
51 Urry (2002: 97).
52 Peñaloza (1999: 367, emphasis in original).
53 Hamilton and Harlow (1995).
54 Steinhauer (1998).
55 Leong (2001b).
56 Ritzer (1999: 167–8).
57 Wood (2000).
58 'Shopology'. Second of two television programmes shown on BBC2 on 9 September, 2001.
59 Hubbard (2002).
60 Waples (2003).
61 www.xscape.co.uk/xplained.
62 www.metreon.com.
63 For example, Klein (2000: 98).
64 Ross (1999: 259).
65 Ritzer and Stillman (2001a: 92).
66 Quoted in Gottdiener (2001: 101–2).
67 Ritzer (1999).
68 Wolf (1999: 196).
69 Pine and Gilmore (1999: 39).
70 Augé (1995); Zukin (1991).
71 Ritzer (2004).

Chapter Four

Merchandising

In this discussion, 'merchandising' refers to the promotion of goods in the form of or bearing copyright images and logos, including such products made under licence. As such, it includes such things as t-shirts and mugs bearing logos and models of proprietary characters. Merchandising is a form of franchising, in the sense that it is a mechanism for leveraging additional uses and value out of existing well-known images. Increasingly, a movie is not just a movie but a platform from which a variety of different extensions of the movie can be launched. To the extent that it can be used as a launch pad for a plethora of spin-offs, merchandising can be said to have taken place. Merchandising has its roots in the mass production of souvenirs but extends this phenomenon by associating the notion of a souvenir with copyright logos and images.

Merchandising has strong affinities with hybrid consumption. In fact, in his discussion of Disneyization in relation to the American criminal justice system, Robinson links the two so that they almost form a single dimension.[1] Hybrid consumption frequently entails the sale of goods that are based on the merchandising principle of extending images and concepts. As we will see, a theme park, as was discussed in the previous chapter, is the location for several different forms of consumption. One of the main ways in which this occurs is through the sale of theme park-related merchandise. Nonetheless, a distinction is still worth preserving between hybrid consumption and merchandising because there are several important aspects of the latter that are independent of the former. Not least of these is the fact that the development of merchandisable objects has become a goal in its own right and is not something that is necessarily part of a hybrid consumption context or framework.

Why Merchandise?

The key principle behind merchandising is a simple one of extracting further revenue from an image that has already attracted people. To the purveyors of merchandise, merchandising is a means of building on and extending an image and people's enjoyment of it. As Wolf observes: 'It is no longer sufficient merely to turn out a hit movie, television show, magazine or book, because in many cases these products cannot be profitable on their own. A hit must become a franchise and, in so doing, becomes the hub from which a wide-reaching variety of products emanates'.[2] Merchandising can be hugely profitable. It means that items that cost very little to make can be sold for substantial amounts simply by adding a logo or image to them or by manufacturing a doll or soft toy into a well-known and immediately recognisable form, such as Mickey Mouse or Darth Vader.

'Synergy' is a relevant term here. The point about merchandising is that it may actually help to promote other related activities, as well as being profitable in its own right. As a writer for the *Economist* puts it: 'when Viacom licenses *Rugrats* toothpaste and *Rugrats* macaroni cheese, it both makes money and promotes the direct-to-video movie launched last year and the full-blown animation feature due out later this year'.[3] Merchandising becomes part of a mutually referential system of cross-promotion which can take in theme park rides, clothing, computer games, toys, television programmes, books, videos, and so on. It keeps the images in people's minds and acts as a constant advertisement for existing and forthcoming spin-offs. There are two main reasons for the widespread use of movie tie-ins with fast food meals and cereals, whereby toys associated with a new film either come free with a meal or are sold at a very low price (a form of hybrid consumption as noted in the previous chapter). First, they act as a lure for the purchase of the fast food meals and cereals themselves. In addition, they also help to promote the movie and other merchandise. Davis suggests that theme parks have become major vehicles for merchandising and that this at least in part accounts for the growing tendency for media conglomerates to buy or build them. As she puts it: 'Licensed images and ... merchandise are at the heart of the matter, and the potential of the theme park industry to sell and support licensed products is central to synergy'.[4]

For those who buy merchandise in the sense in which the term is used here, the items serve as reminders of visiting a place, of having a particular kind of experience, or of their enjoyment of a character or prop. Increasingly, people anticipate the possibility of being able to buy merchandise and may even be disappointed if the opportunity to do so is not available. However, merchandising does not rest on principles that are automatically destined for success, since the images and logos must be nurtured in order to create the valuable and franchisable commodities that are revered. Creating merchandise with the appeal and recognizability of the Disney logos and characters or the first raft of *Star Wars* images is a kind of holy grail which few companies can attain but increasingly has become a goal that is potentially hugely profitable. As will be seen below, the success of merchandising is not always predictable and there are some well-known and fairly spectacular failures in this area.

In certain respects, merchandising and hybrid consumption merge into each other. Hybrid consumption contexts are frequently environments for selling merchandise of the kind discussed in this chapter. This is particularly the case with theme parks and with themed restaurants, where it is often the selling of licensed merchandise that is the main facet of the shopping component of the hybrid forms in which shopping is combined with another form of consumption. For example, in Chapter 3 Sea World's strategy for increasing the likelihood that people will purchase goods was referred to. Much of what is sold in the outlets that the parks' designers and management position so carefully is merchandise bearing Sea World's image or logo and representations of its creatures, especially Shamu. However, the shops do not exclusively sell such goods; they also sell goods that are thematically relevant to a certain attraction. Similarly, but looking at this issue the other way around, not all merchandise is sold in hybrid consumption contexts. A *Jurassic Park* t-shirt sold in an independent shop is not part of the hybrid consumption format that was described in Chapter 3.

Merchandising at the Disney Theme Parks

The Disney theme parks have two points of significance in relation to merchandising as a component of Disneyization. First, and most obviously, they are contexts for selling the vast array of Disney merchandise that has accumulated over the years: from pens to clothing, from books to sweets and from watches to plush toys. Sales from merchandise are a major contributor to profits from the parks. The parks are carefully designed to maximize the opportunity for and inclination of guests to purchase merchandise. Second, they provide their own merchandise. This occurs in a number of ways, including: t-shirts with the name of the park on them; Epcot clothing or souvenirs with a suitably attired cartoon character on them, such as a 'French' Mickey purchased in the France pavilion or a sporty

Goofy purchased in the Wonders of Life pavilion; merchandise deriving from characters specifically associated with the parks, such as Figment (a character in the Journey into Imagination ride in EPCOT); and a petrified Mickey looking out from the top of the Twilight Zone Tower of Terror (a Disney-MGM Studios attraction) emblazoned on clothing. It is sometimes suggested that the Disney theme parks sell merchandise that is available through any Disney Store in a mall or high street.[5] This is simply not true: there is a vast array of merchandise in the parks that is not for sale outside them. Most of this is merchandise specifically linked to the parks and their 'lands', such as the petrified Mickey previously referred to.

The parks are designed to maximize opportunities and rationales for purchasing merchandise. Main Street USA acts as a funnel. Visitors move from wide open spaces after the entrance, are then channelled along Main Street with its many shops selling merchandise, and then emerge again into open spaces. Not only do they have to walk down Main Street to get to the attractions, they are placed in a position where they are more likely to be lured into the shops.

Precursors of Merchandising

Merchandising is by no means a phenomenon that should be attributed only to the Disney theme parks. For example, there was a large amount of Pooh-related merchandise from 1929 onwards, including such artefacts as Christmas cards and calendars, books, and notepaper.[6] Walt Disney certainly did not create the idea of merchandising or even of merchandising animated cartoon characters. Felix the Cat was the focus of a large range of merchandise in the mid-1920s. An American writer in a trade journal in Britain, where Felix was especially popular, recorded:

> It is almost incredible, but the most popular outstanding figure in the film trade at this moment, throughout every nook and cranny of the Kingdom, is Felix the Cat. ...There are Felix songs, Felix tie pins, Felix brooches, Felix silver spoons, little and big Felix dolls, Felix pillow tops, Felix automobile radiator tops, Felix candy, Felix blankets, Felix street vendor novelties and more other publicity producing angles than a centipede has legs.[7]

However, Disney itself probably provides one of the best examples of pre-Disney theme park merchandising. This is a realm in which Disney have been preeminent. Walt Disney's first animated star was arguably not Mickey Mouse, but Oswald the Lucky Rabbit, around which he and his studio had created a popular series of animation shorts in 1927. When he tried to negotiate a better financial deal over these shorts, Walt found that it was not he but the distributor who owned the rights to them. As a result, the studio had no rights to Oswald's name and therefore to the small range of merchandise that had begun to appear bearing the character's name and image. Thereafter, he zealously guarded his rights in this regard. A major factor may well have been the revenue-producing capability of merchandise bearing Oswald's image, including a pop-up puppet, stencil set, celluloid figures and posters.[8] According to legend, to which Walt amply contributed, on his train journey back from his thwarted negotiations in which he attempted to increase the studio's share of receipts from the Oswald shorts, he dreamed up the idea of a cartoon series based on a mouse named Mortimer. His wife, Lillian, liked the idea but not the name, and out of that discussion Mickey Mouse was born.

Merchandise and licensing proliferated in the wake of Mickey's arrival in November 1928. A year later, Walt Disney Productions was transformed into four separate companies, one of which dealt with merchandising and licensing. By 1932, a journalist reported that between 50 and 60 firms were producing Mickey Mouse merchandising which was sold in 200,000 stores.[9] Deals were handled first of all by George Borgfeldt and from 1934 onwards by the flamboyant Kay Kamen. By 1948, the company's deals with Kamen had resulted in the sale of the five millionth Mickey Mouse watch (see Box 4.1) and in that year alone goods bearing the images of Disney characters brought in revenue of $100 million.[10]

Box 4.1 The Mickey Mouse watch

The Mickey Mouse watch is one of the great success stories in the realm of merchandising. The idea of a watch with Mickey on the dial was developed by Kay Kamen who sold the idea to the Ingersoll-Waterbury Company, which had been on the verge of bankruptcy at the time. The watch, whose first version appeared in 1933, saved the company. The first wristwatch retailed at $3.75 and a pocket watch at around the same time for $1.50. Macy's in New York sold 11,000 watches on just one day soon after they went on sale. At both Macy's and Marshall Fields in Chicago, the watches were the focus of spectacular window displays. At the 1933 World's Fair in Chicago, Ingersoll provided a small factory where the manufacture of the Mickey watches was demonstrated. The watch became seen as a stylish item and Ingersoll were able to add 2,800 new employees to its small workforce of 200 in the space of just two years. At the 1939 World's Fair in New York, a Mickey watch was placed in a time capsule. Mickey Mouse watches are still produced today and indeed watches bearing the images of a host of Disney animated characters are on sale. They come in a variety of shapes and sizes and are sometimes produced to celebrate Disney events or anniversaries. The style is often ironic nowadays, such as a Dick Tracy watch bearing an outline that has features of both Tracy and Mickey. A wide variety of manufacturers are involved in their production nowadays, such as Lorus and Fossil.

Source: Heide and Gilman (1997)

Walt realized the immense profitability of merchandising and the significance of the role it could play in the company. In the years after Mickey's arrival, the company did not make large sums from its cartoons, because Walt's incessant quest for improvements in the quality of animation cut deeply into the studio's profits. To a very large extent, he was able to finance expensive technical innovation and his unyielding insistence on quality by using profits from merchandise. About half of the studio's profits were attributable to merchandise.[11] Indeed, some writers have suggested that in later years, the design of cartoon characters, in particular their 'cuteness', was at least in part motivated by a consideration of their capacity to be turned into merchandise.[12] Certainly, it seems that cuteness increasingly became a yardstick against which the design of characters was measured. Fogacs points out that during the 1930s, cuteness was frequently mentioned. For example, notes from the story conference for *Snow White* include the following: 'Walt points out that the animators must always try to feel the cuteness of these characters. ... Dopey could become very grotesque, unless he is kept in a cute little manner'.[13] Above every animator's desk at the studio was the instruction 'keep it cute'.[14] This emphasis on cuteness may also account for the changes in Mickey's increasingly less rodent-like and child-like appearance over the years.[15] The stress on cuteness may at least in part have been motivated by the greater merchandising potential of cute characters. Similarly, Walt had to persevere for many years to secure the rights for *Jungle Book*. His story editor said around the time of the film's release that one of the reasons for Walt's persistence was that 'it has a little boy in it, Mowgli, and a lot of animals and both are great for merchandising'.[16]

The Diffusion of Merchandising

In this section, a variety of ways and contexts in which merchandising occurs nowadays will be outlined.

Merchandising at Disney

Since the early years, merchandising has been a major activity for Disney. At the time of the release of *Snow White and the Seven Dwarfs* in 1937, Disney had signed at least 70 licensing deals.[17] In 1958, an article in *The Wall Street Journal* noted the importance of merchandising for Disney and observed:

> Disney figures it's created approximately 2,000 imaginary personalities over the years and, at last count, over 140 US firms and more than 700 abroad were helping Disney to cash in on the popularity of some 50 of these characters. About $2 million in royalties came in from these merchandising activities last year.[18]

While these figures show a substantial increase in merchandising activity over those that prevailed at the time of *Snow White*, they pale into insignificance when compared to the situation nowadays, even allowing for inflation and other changes (see below).

However, between the time of the death in 1971 of Walt's brother, Roy O. Disney who took over the reins after the death of Walt in 1966, and the arrival of Michael Eisner as chairman and his team, there is evidence that merchandising was not being pursued as actively as it might have been. At the time of Eisner's arrival, Disney was languishing and had barely managed to fight off a takeover aimed at plundering its stock of films and intellectual property which was seen as a cash cow. Also, the theme park visitor numbers were down so that less money was being spent on merchandise and other on-site facilities. Consequently, the hugely profitable revenues and profits that could be derived from merchandise sales were not being realized. Disney adopted five major strategies that would increase its commitment to merchandising. In each case, merchandising was not the *sole* reason for the strategies – nothing ever seems to be done by Disney for a single reason because of its commitment to synergy.

First, Disney increased visitor numbers in two main ways. Advertising and promotion were greatly stepped up. Prior to the arrival of the Eisner team, there had been very little of either. Second, attractions that would appeal to teenagers were developed and introduced into the parks, such as a simulator ride based on *Star Wars* and a 3-D film with Michael Jackson as the captain of a space flight. The strategy was extremely successful in spite of the team pursuing an additional strategy that might have had an opposite effect on visitor numbers, namely, regularly increasing the cost of admission, which was seen by Eisner and his team as too low.

A third component of Disney's post-1984 strategy that was geared towards merchandise was to take a more active role in developing deals. Eisner has written that at the time of his arrival 'licensing was essentially a passive business. Disney played almost no role in the production, distribution or marketing of these products.'[19] By 1994, operating profits in consumer products had quadrupled. A fourth component is the Disney Store, the first of which opened in 1987 in Glendale Galleria in Southern California and which has since been rolled out worldwide. When the idea of a Disney Store was floated to Eisner, he has written that he liked the idea because they could promote Disney films and theme parks, as well as sell merchandise.

A fifth strategy was to increase the production of animated feature films. Prior to Eisner's arrival, the quality and quantity of Disney animation had fallen. Animation had come to be seen as costly and the full range of advantages of animation had not been fully appreciated. In 1979 one of the leading animators, Don Bluth, left the company with a number of others, citing the problems that they were having with the production of good quality animation as the reason for their departure. Producing uninspiring and often poor quality (by Disney standards) animation had had a deleterious effect on merchandise sales deriving from the films, quite irrespective of the previously mentioned passive approach to licensing. The animation department produced a series of feature films that were well received at both the box office and critically, culminating in *Beauty and the Beast* (1991) which was released to great acclaim.

But it was *The Lion King* in 1994 that was the turning point. A major reason for the revival of animation at Disney was the Disney team's conviction that animation was, or at least should be, at the centre of the company's activities. A successful Disney animated feature, they felt, led to success in other spheres of the company's portfolio of activities. Nowhere was this clearer than with merchandising, since animated characters are extremely adaptable and amenable to being transformed into merchandise. A successful feature heralded the prospect of greater profitability elsewhere, not just in the feature itself. Interestingly, the article in *The Wall Street Journal* that was quoted from above included a diagram with a Disney copyright indicator showing the links between the company's various activities (television, Disneyland, merchandising, comics, publications, and music), but at its centre was its films. Somehow in the years after Roy O. Disney's death, the significance of this point seemed to have been marginalized.

The Eisner team were right to restore animation to the centre of its activities and in a sense even more correct than they had anticipated. Masters has written of the release of *The Little Mermaid* in 1989: 'Disney had not really been prepared for the bonanza and didn't have nearly as much merchandise on hand as it could have sold. … Disney began to appreciate the staggering amounts that could be wrung from a medium that allowed the studio ultimate control and didn't include any live actors who were in a position to demand a percentage of the gross'.[20] However, this box office and merchandising success paled into insignificance when compared to *The Lion King*. Not only was the film a massive box office success, it represented a merchandising bonanza for Disney that vastly exceeded expectations. Giroux has suggested that it was so successful that it became a model for marketing and extracting value from subsequent animated feature films.[21] *Lion King* toys achieved retail sales in the US of $214 million by Christmas 1994, which made it a tough act to follow.[22] In its 1996 Annual Report, Disney reported that comparable sales at the Disney Stores were down 2% from the previous year 'primarily due to the strength of *The Lion King* merchandise in the prior year'.[23] It is generally reckoned that revenues from the film amount to just under $1billion, of which around one-third is from the box office. The rest will have been made up from revenues from videos, computer games and from licensed merchandise, as well as other sources. Since *The Lion King*, Disney has been even more enthusiastic about animated feature films and has been producing nearly one animated feature a year (which is much more frequent than in Walt's later years when animated feature films were being released every three years). This includes films using traditional 'flat' animation techniques (albeit enhanced by computer animation) and 3-D animated features produced through computer graphics: the two *Toy Story* films, *A Bug's Life*, *Dinosaur*, *Monsters Inc.* and *Finding Nemo*.

Interestingly and indeed surprisingly, Disney was caught out with insufficient merchandise again for the first *Toy Story*.[24] There were well-publicized shortages of Buzz Lightyears in particular. Nowadays, there tends to be a wide range of merchandise on offer. Pecora and Meehan sought out merchandise relating to *The Hunchback of Notre Dame* in Tucson Mall, Arizona. Even though the observations were being done after the merchandising for the film had reached its peak, 320 items were uncovered. They report:

> Our observations confirmed that *Hunchback* merchandise was everywhere. Up-market department stores, mid-market department stores, and many specialty stores offered *Hunchback* products as well other Disney merchandise. The same Esmeralda dress could be bought in both the anchors and at the Disney Store; the same *Hunchback* T-shirt was offered in the anchors as well as in gift shops. Small stores specializing in greetings cards, paper goods, candy, books, recorded music, pre-recorded videos, toys, etc. offered numerous *Hunchback* items as well as other Disney items. The Disney Store expanded on these offerings, stocking *Hunchback* merchandise that was only available through Disney's own retail operations. Given Disney's promotional agreement with McDonald's, the McDonald's in the mall had been decorated with *Hunchback* streamers and promotional displays. It offered special *Hunchback* meals with *Hunchback* place mats, napkins, paper cups, etc.[25]

The promotional tie-in has become one of the major merchandising vehicles for Disney's animated films. For the first *Toy Story*, $125 million was spent on such tie-ins by firms such as Burger King, Nestlé, Frito-Lay, Minute Maid, and Payless ShoeSource. Burger King alone spent $45 million in order to be able to boost sales of its food by giving away *Toy Story* figures and also selling *Toy Story* puppets for $1.99. Goodwin reports: 'Some Burger King stores have reported such a huge demand for the toys that they ran out of a 5½-week supply in just 10 days'.[26] Seven years later with its latest computer animated film (like *Toy Story* produced with Pixar), an even wider spread of deals was negotiated. The tie-ins are important for Disney in drawing attention to the film in as many quarters as possible. Indeed, tie-ins and other merchandise-related activities are brought out months before a film's release in order to acquaint children with the characters and the film's major themes. According to the vice-president of marketing at Buena Vista UK, Disney's distribution arm: 'These movies are very expensive to make and release and these tie-ins get us exposure we could not afford to buy'.[27] For the other side of the tie-in, the implications can be considerable in terms of profitability, as was noted in relation to McDonald's and hybrid consumption in Chapter 3. In the case of *Monsters Inc.* and one of Disney's product partners, Fairy Liquid, a washing up liquid, the appearance of characters on the bottles resulted in its having a record month.

Disney then, has turned merchandising into a major income stream. Even its town of Celebration, which was referred to in Chapter 2, has its own merchandise shop (Figure 4.1). It is a good example of Disneyization because the company excels in the range of merchandise it generates and the degree to which it makes such a significant contributor to revenue. The company assiduously protects its proprietary images against misuse and is often involved in litigation over copyright protection.[28] However, few can match the company in the way in

Figure 4.1   Merchandising Celebration

which merchandising is part of a synergistic system in which different components feed off and point to each other. Nowadays, an animated feature film is part of a network of activities, wherein it has the potential for: release on video and DVD, CD-roms, computer software, theme park rides, being shown on the Disney Channel, spin-off television series, spin-off videos in limited animation, books, magazines, and other merchandise which can be sold in its Disney Stores and theme park shops. No one can match Disney for such a synergistic complex of mutually reinforcing commercial activities. On the other hand, Disney has become a model of what is possible and as such has been much emulated.

Feature films

Over the years, it has become increasingly apparent that more money can be made from feature films through merchandising and licensing than from box office receipts as such. While hugely successful merchandise bonanzas like those associated with *Star Wars*, *Jurassic Park* and *The Lion King* are by no means typical, they represent the tip of a lucrative iceberg. As Wolf puts it, increasingly a film is being regarded as an 'anchor product that gives birth to other businesses'[29] and gives the example of *Jurassic Park*:

> *Jurassic Park* became a brand that meant dinosaurs. The two films have grossed more than £1.5 billion worldwide. … The theme-park ride is one of the most successful attractions in Universal Studios in Hollywood and Florida. The home videos flew off the shelves, selling $454 million. Merchandise sales, including toys and video games, reached an estimated $1.5 billion. Adding in other revenue streams, Universal built a $5 billion brand empire.[30]

Wolf's assessment is interesting and very relevant but possibly misleading in one respect in its comment about a film being an 'anchor product'. It clearly is this in the case of *Jurassic Park* and the same point could be made about the *Star Wars* films, the Harry Potter films, and the *Lord of the Rings* movies, *Spider-Man*, as well as Disney and other animated cartoon movies. But what binds all these films together is that they are either aimed at children or have a strong appeal to children. Critically acclaimed films like *Schindler's List* or *The Hours* do not generate large quantities of popular merchandise, though they undoubtedly fare well in terms of video and DVD sales. Films aimed more or less exclusively at adults, even those without an 18 rating, do not engender the kind of 'anchorage' that Wolf refers to and in this connection it is not irrelevant that he takes *Jurassic Park* as his illustration. While not a film exclusively for children, it certainly has a strong appeal to children who seem to find dinosaurs fascinating. Warner Brothers' new strategy in 2001 and 2002 entailed turning as many films as possible into brand names through franchising, in which merchandising plays an important part, but it is striking that the bulk of the films that they have in mind in a *New York Times* article reporting this approach seem to be for children.[31]

Walt once remarked that he made films for adults, not for children. In a sense, he was being disingenuous too, because his films typically appealed to both adults and children. It is the latter who would typically ask to be taken to the cinema to see his films and to be bought Disney merchandise. But what he was also saying, in much the same way that he wanted Disneyland to appeal to adults (see Chapter 2), was that unless adults also found the movie and its concept appealing, they would not take their children to see it or buy its merchandise, even when confronted with a torrent of pestering. It is specifically and almost exclusively films which draw children that are typically the focus of wide ranges of merchandise and Walt realized this point and sought to cater for, and indeed pander to, this disposition with the emphasis that he and his successors placed on cuteness. Nowadays, with even greater awareness of the potential of merchandising, there has been a considerable increase in the number of children's films (a term I am using to include films that appeal to children as well as adults like *Jurassic Park*, *Star Wars* and the *Star Trek* films). Moretti has observed that during the period 1986–95, 25% of box office top five releases in the United States were for children.[32] The percentage was even higher in several other countries: Slovakia, Poland, Puerto Rico, Egypt, Luxembourg, Sweden, the UK, Austria, France, Switzerland and Japan. Moretti compared the situation with the mid-1950s when he was a child and found there were extremely few children's films then. In the mid-1950s, not one film for children was in the *Variety* top 20 for the year, although as he points out, *20,000 Leagues Under the Sea* (a Disney film) and *Around the World in 80 Days* could be construed as for children. One factor behind the considerable growth in children's films could well be their potential for merchandising and other spin-offs including television series.

This is not to suggest that films made more or less exclusively for adults are devoid of merchandise potential. Estée Lauder, for example, marketed a makeup range called Face of Evita, capitalizing on the popularity of *Evita* in 1996. However, according to Pat Wyatt, at the time president of licensing for Fox, family films have the greatest merchandise potential, especially when there is a fantasy element to the film. In part, this is because children's films with a strong fantasy element include many non-human characters which, according to Wyatt 'do better than representations of people because kids can project a broader fantasy into their play'.[33] A further problem with much merchandise based on people in films is that actors are sometimes difficult about agreeing to their likenesses, as well as the problem of getting the image right initially.

The Harry Potter films serve as a reminder of the profitability of merchandising. The release of the first film was accompanied by a raft of merchandise, such as games, a Lego Hogwarts Castle (which performed particularly well[34]), t-shirts, and a Hornby Hogwarts Express train set, as well as the appearance of Potter-related images on a variety of goods, such as bubble bath.[35] Hamleys, the huge toy emporium in London, even opened a Harry Potter shop within the store. It was in a position to sell over 200 lines of Harry Potter merchandise.[36] A Nottingham company, which had exclusive rights for manufacturing official Potter socks, was turned into the fastest-growing sock-maker in England around the time of the first Potter film when 50,000 pairs were being sold per week.[37] As a result of her share of the vast array of merchandise for sale, it was projected that the author of the series of books, J.K. Rowling, would become the first billionaire author and that at the very least, her earnings from merchandising would exceed her royalties which had already made her one of the wealthiest women in Britain.[38] It was calculated in 2003 that Harry Potter merchandise was bringing in revenue of £1 billion per year and that J.K. Rowling would earn £10 million from quidditch turning into a computer game.[39]

However, by no means all children's films, let alone all films, generate successful lines of merchandising and there have been some interesting and even surprising failures. If a movie flops, like *Judge Dredd*, even though based on a popular comic book character and having apparent merchandise potential, or if a film does not appear to have good potential for merchandising, products will either not be licensed or will not be sold. Also, the merchandising of even fairly successful films like *Flintstones* and *Casper* can be disappointing.[40] Certainly, Disney seems to have been very disappointed with the merchandise sales associated with *Dick Tracy*, produced by Touchstone Pictures, one of its film-making divisions.[41] Interestingly, even though the Harry Potter movie-related merchandise was hugely successful, in Britain it did not fare as well as that relating to Bob the Builder, a children's television series that was very popular around the same time.[42]

There may even be some quite surprising failures in the area of movie merchandising. The classic example is *The Phantom Menace*, the first in the Star Wars trilogy of 'prequels'. In the months leading up to the release of the film, a range of merchandise was made available. In part, this was in anticipation of the level of massive demand for merchandise that had accompanied the first series and which had been a major influence on the perception of movie-related merchandise as a major income stream.[43] While there were some worries that there might be over-exposure,[44] toy makers and others did not want to get caught with insufficient stocks, which is what had happened first time around. In fact, the merchandise for the film flopped. Two British companies – Character Group and Dorling Kindersley, a publisher – ended up nursing huge losses in 2000, the year after the film's release. The losses in both cases were almost entirely attributable to the failure of the Star Wars merchandise.[45] In the case of Character Group, its share price had slumped to 62.5p from 440p a year earlier. In the case of Dorling Kindersley, the debacle resulted in the transformation of a £4.7 million profit into a £25 million loss and in the resignation of its chief executive and the loss of 140 jobs.[46] For the second prequel, *Attack of the Clones*, only half the number of licensed products were signed up and the general approach to who was given licenses was much more selective than for *The Phantom Menace*. However, although the sale of merchandise was disappointing at the time of *The Phantom Menace*, it nevertheless achieved sales of $2 billion in 1999.[47] The problem seems to have been that expectations were too high and that some injudicious decisions about goods and licensees had been made.

A further issue that relates to films is that to extend the franchise as much as possible, further episodes need to be made. However, this means that in order to wring as much as possible out of merchandise sales, the manufacturers of goods need to come up with new and exciting ideas. Simply recycling old toys is insufficient. To a certain extent, the films' storylines are likely to induce new characters and props with merchandise potential, but even though there is a need for continuity between episodes innovation is still required. One extreme way of doing this occurred with the second *Jurassic Park* film, *The Lost World*, where one of the licensees persuaded the film-makers to include in the plot a truck that could be turned into an attractive toy.[48]

Television series

Like many movies, television series also often form the basis for successful lines of merchandise and indeed it has sometimes been suggested that they are devised with merchandise and licensing potential very much in mind. Certainly, Kline argues that when children's television advertising was effectively deregulated in the USA in 1980, the merchandising tie-in became 'the preferred tactic of children's programming and consequently made the ability to move product the overriding consideration in the scripting of television'.[49] Television programmes were developed with the creation and promotion of characters at the forefront of writing and programming. Kline argues that this allowed two important childhood elements to be brought together: stories and play. By placing characters in a coherent narrative and emphasizing how they could be used by children in play through both advertising and the programmes themselves, the creators of television-related toy merchandise could capitalize upon these two powerful elements of childhood. Characters were increasingly developed with the creation of a strong character in mind. Especially useful in this regard were series like *My Little Pony* and *Care Bears* where the main figures were distinctively different (while simultaneously being part of a 'set') and therefore lent themselves to being collected. In the case of the *He-Man and the Masters of the Universe* series, the costs of setting up the production were split between a toy company (Mattel), the producers and a licensing agency, demonstrating the significance of the television series as an advertising and promotion medium.

The television series has been a prominent strategy for launching merchandise worldwide. *Thomas the Tank Engine*, which is based on a series of books, has over 2,500 product lines. Characters like Bob the Builder, Angelina Ballerina, The Powerpuff Girls and the Teletubbies have resulted in large revenues from merchandising. The potential deriving from franchising such characters is so great that it seems unlikely that they are not being developed with their capacity to be merchandised as a major consideration. For example, a new cartoon character, PC Pepper, was bought from its creator, Rob Lee, by Galleon Group, a media company. The character is a friendly policeman stationed on an island. The company was then reported as intending to invest money in the character for a television series. It was also reported that it will 'invest in licensing the character for merchandising – more than two-thirds of the profits from cartoon ventures come from this kind of activity'.[50] This is a common pattern whereby characters are developed for series with an eye on their merchandise potential at an early stage rather than as an afterthought. The arrival of new BBC television networks for children undoubtedly helps this development process, at the same time as boosting revenues for the BBC itself. PC Pepper may not become a Bob the Builder but the process by which these characters are developed into television series and more or less simultaneously into merchandise is one that is repeated.

One surprise merchandising bonanza was in 1998–1999 when the cartoon series *South Park* was used on a vast array of merchandise. In the UK alone, between August and December 1998, £50 million was spent on *South Park* merchandise.[51] What makes this success warrant being called a surprise is that unlike most of the major merchandising successes, it was not aimed at children. Indeed, because of its adult content, the products and the advertising for them were aimed at those aged over 18. In fact, the series and its merchandise are hugely popular with children and what made the products so successful was that it appealed both to them and 20-somethings – a rare occurrence. In a sense, the *South Park* phenomenon underwent a transformation for the latter group. Armstong argues that as we get older, we usually switch from 'entertainment merchandise' to 'brand merchandising', like CK, Ralph Lauren, The Gap, and so on.[52] He argues that the case of *South Park* merchandise defied this law, but in a sense perhaps this misses the point. For these 20-somethings, *South Park* became a brand. How else can we understand the fact that the numbers viewing the series in the UK was relatively small, but the merchandise was a massive success? This is an interesting case of a situation in which merchandising associated with entertainment elided with brand merchandising. However, the main point to register is that television series can become the catalyst for extremely successful merchandising lines.

Theme parks

Unsurprisingly, in view of the likely influence of the Disney theme parks, theme parks are major sites for the sale of all kinds of merchandising bearing copyright logos and images relating to the parks or to their themes. Thus, at Universal Studios, not only are items sold with the park's name and logo emblazoned on them, but also images from the studio's vault of films, often accompanied by the park's name, are also sold. For theme parks without such ready-made images, they have to be created. Thus, at Sea World, Shamu, the orca whale that acts as an icon of the parks and whose show is one of their park's major attractions, filled a void in this regard. Giving Shamu a name and an identity through its interactions with its trainers in the show acts as a merchandise lure. Shamu is by no means the only source of merchandise, since the park can draw on its other animals and on its claim that it provides a foundation for conserving endangered animals, which is a means of linking images from nature with commercial concerns. Similarly, at other theme parks characters have been invented to provide a focus for merchandising. At Parque España in Japan, Don Quixote and Sancho Panza have been turned into cartoon characters (as dog and racoon respectively) and the greater potential of such emblems for merchandise may well have contributed to such a development.[53]

Themed restaurants and themed hotels

It would be a mistake, of course, to view merchandising purely in terms of movies and cartoon characters, though these areas have certainly been ones in which merchandising has been particularly developed. The themed restaurant chains all follow the lead of Hard Rock Cafe of developing extensive lines of merchandise, including the ubiquitous t-shirt which simultaneously informs where wearers have been on their holidays and literally acts as a walking advertisement for the chain. You do not necessarily have to eat in the establishment in order to purchase the items. Very often, if not invariably, you can enter the shop area without needing to eat the food. In the case of the Rainforest Cafe chain, the shopping area is frequently as big as many restaurants. The ESPN Zone in Chicago has some of the features of a museum presentation but sells its branded merchandise and some other items (see Figure 4.2). Previously, many of the themed restaurant chains just had small merchandise booths attached to the restaurants, but nowadays the areas are much larger. This combination of themed restaurants selling items with their licensed logos on them has become a prominent strategy.

Some themed hotels have adopted a similar approach. In particular, the large themed hotel-casinos in Las Vegas have large shopping areas in which they sell a wide range of goods relating to the overall theme, including licensed merchandise. Hotel Luxor, for example, has a shop selling lots of fake ancient Egyptian artefacts along with t-shirts, mugs and many other objects with the hotel's logo and signs on it.

Zoos

All of the large American zoos sell extensive ranges of merchandise – t-shirts, baseball caps, wallets, pens and pencils, and so on. However, there is evidence that this feature is becoming much more widespread. The Director of Zoo Atlanta, Terry Maple, has argued that such merchandise is important because it produces revenue and also provides publicity and enhances the zoo experience. He has written that 'we must be prepared to provide our supporters, partners, and guests with specialized bumper stickers, pins, T-shirts, ties, and coffee mugs'.[54] In addition, he proclaims that in his own zoo, 'we adopted some of the techniques and methods commonly used by entertainment and amusement enterprises, like Disney World and Six Flags'.[55] Merchandising is reinforced through the creation of representations of 'iconic' animals (e.g. tigers, manatees, giant pandas) and other species seen as threatened with extinction or as having a particular magnetism. Such representations can then be directly incorporated into merchandise items. Thus, the presentation of animals and animal performances by zoos can feed directly into the generation of commodified images, which can have considerable commercial potential. As Desmond observes, the commodification of wild animals is ironic because they are invariably depicted as symbols of pristine

Figure 4.2   The Merchandise Shop at ESPN Zone in Chicago

nature and therefore as beyond the clutches of a commodified world.[56] However, surrounding the zoo with an aura of research, conservation and education helps to legitimate this commodification and helps to resolve the irony.

Maple's reference to the influence of the Disney theme parks suggests that in many instances of Disneyization the process may be a direct one (i.e. transferred Disneyization) involving imitation in a manner that has occurred in relation to museums.[57] Nor is Maple the only writer to draw attention to the potential and actual influence of the Disney and other theme parks on zoos. The Director of the National Zoological Park in the USA has written:

Theme parks are attracting people to subjects that many museums find difficult to exhibit in a way that is engaging. We need to borrow from the best exhibit techniques and quality management practices, without emulating the lack of social concerns, intellectual challenges, and real controversy that marks much of media output.[58]

Similarly, Coe notes that the San Diego Zoo and Wild Animal Park 'borrow heavily from theme park marketing, visitor services, and management concepts'.[59]

McDonald's

There is evidence of merchandising in McDonald's as well as theming. It can be seen in the availability of a wide range of merchandise bearing its logos or main character, Ronald McDonald. The McDonald's website has a very large amount of merchandise for sale, including clothing items like baseball caps and t-shirts to nostalgia items like cookie jars. The McDonald's in the Disney Village in Orlando had a particularly wide range of merchandise when I visited the area in 2000. Schlosser notes that at the Ray A. Kroc Museum you are forced to walk through McStore where 'You can buy bean-bag McBurglar dolls...telephones shaped like french fries, ties, clocks, key chains, golf bags and duffel bags, jewelry, baby clothes, lunch boxes, mouse pads, leather jackets, postcards, toy trucks, and much more, all of it bearing the stamp of McDonald's.'[60]

Merchandising has been extended by the McKids range of children's clothing. Referring to this range, in his *Foreign Policy* interview, Jack Greenberg (then CEO of McDonald's) said: 'It happens to be licensed to Wal-Mart, but it's our brand and we get a royalty for it.'[61] While merchandising in McDonald's is by no means as extensive as in Disney theme parks, there is evidence that the restaurant chain has incorporated this element of Disneyization.

Sport

Professional sport has succumbed to the attractions of merchandising in that major clubs and events can be the focus for successful merchandising. Major clubs in the most popular sports sell wide ranges of merchandise which are sold in their own shops, sometimes ones that are not attached or close to their stadiums, as well as through sports shops more generally. Clubs like Manchester United FC, New York Yankees, Real Madrid, Chicago Bulls, and Dallas Cowboys have their names and logos on a massive range of merchandise. The same applies to events. At the time of the Euro '96 football (soccer) tournament in the UK, it was reckoned that £120 million of merchandise would be sold with the tournament's logo on it, though the proposal for it to be on condoms was rejected.[62] To give an idea of the scale of the growth of merchandising in football and of its significance for clubs, Kuper has written that Manchester United Football Club 'tripled its turnover to £60m over the last five years, largely thanks to merchandising'.[63] In the early 1980s, merchandising was only a fraction of top clubs' income but by 2001 merchandise sales were just under 40% of income.[64] In English football, merchandising in the form of items bearing a clubs' crests (especially clothing) has been one of the main ways that clubs have increased profits.[65] In addition to the vast array of club and event merchandise, sporting bodies like the World Wrestling Federation have also entered the world of merchandising. Wolf estimates that in 1997, total National Basketball Association league revenues were 'dwarfed' by the revenue from merchandise sales, which amounted to over $3 billion worldwide.[66] College sports in the USA had merchandise sales in 1997 of $2.75 billion.[67] Around the mid-1990s, US sports fans were estimated to be spending $12 billion annually.[68] Moreover, lack of consistent on-field success does not necessarily imply poor merchandise sales. The Dallas Cowboys, who have an extensive and hugely popular merchandise range, ranked third in 2002–3 among NFL teams in terms of merchandise sales, in spite of three less than successful seasons.[69]

Other domains of merchandising

The foregoing discussion has emphasized some of the major spheres in which hybrid consumption has taken place in late modern society. However, it does not exhaust all of them by any means. The following is a catalogue of others, along with a brief discussion of each.

- *Universities* For many years, universities in North America, especially the major ones, have sold a wide array of merchandise. For large universities like UCLA and Harvard, merchandising is a very significant income stream and many other US universities have off-campus shops. UCLA even has a shop in Universal CityWalk adjacent to Universal Studios in California. While British universities have lagged behind their North American counterparts, it appears that they too have realized the potential of what one news reporter appropriately refers to as 'Disney-style merchandising'.[70] For example, Oxford Ltd was reported in 1997 as projecting sales of official Oxford merchandise in excess of £4 million, which represented a doubling of revenue within three years from this source. Most of its sales are in South East Asia and Japan, a feature that parallels Manchester United's merchandising success in these regions.

- *Princess Diana* An American firm has produced a Diana doll and other Diana merchandise has also been produced.[71] On the face of it, this would not seem to be a case of merchandising as defined in this chapter, since it has been defined in terms of copyright logos and images. On the other hand, the Diana, Princess of Wales Memorial Fund sued the makers because it was argued that the firm had failed to obtain consent to use her intellectual property rights and identity.[72] Thus, what is and is not a copyright image or logo may be controversial, and in fact the Fund was unsuccessful in its action. It has since linked up with one of the American company's main competitors to produce Diana merchandise.[73]

- *Police forces* Robinson observes that there has been a big increase in demand for merchandise featuring the logos of police officers and firefighters following the September 11 tragedy.[74] Some of the merchandise that has become available is unofficial and therefore illegal. London's police force has also begun moves to enforce copyright of its various insignia, such as the famous helmet. As a result, not only will it be able to license items bearing its logo, it will be able to reap the benefits of the use of props in television series featuring the police force.[75] The Royal Canadian Mounted Police (the Mounties) signed an agreement in 1995 with Disney to license Mounty merchandise throughout the world. The deal was criticised in Canada for its association with a company strongly linked to cultural imperialism but was defended on the grounds that it would allow greater control over the brand from a company with so much experience of such activities.[76]

- *Art* The licensing of art has become a growth business in recent years. Art galleries have for many years sold reproductions of works of art, but the range being sold now extends to an array of items like fridge magnets, ties, coasters and mouse mats adorned with galleries' artistic images.

- *Dance clubs* Dance clubs like Ministry of Sound and Cream increasingly use their logos as the basis for merchandise. On a telelvision programme, a representative of the latter group claimed that his club 'doesn't make us that much money – it's all of the other products we do'.[77] He was referring to such items as records and t-shirts.

- *The Vatican* It has been reported that the Vatican is planning a chain of shops selling licensed items and gifts based on exhibits in its museum.[78] Vatican merchandise has been for sale for some time, but the plans imply increasing the scope of items on offer considerably.

Reflections of Merchandising

The potential that is often seen in characters from films, television series and books is particularly apparent in a trend that has been noticeable in recent years. This is the way in which older cartoon and other characters are resuscitated and bought and sold like commodities. Sometimes, this trade in such characters is done with a view to update what are regarded as franchises with potential that have fallen out of favour. In recent years, British characters like Sooty, Pingu the Penguin, Captain Pugwash, and Noddy have been traded between companies keen on developing their merchandise potential.[79] Many of Enid Blyton's characters are similarly being reinvented, their copyright having been bought by a British company keen to enhance their merchandise potential.[80] In the United States, the revival of the Marvel comic heroes can be seen as part of the same process of raising the profile of previously popular characters with potential.[81] This trade in copyright logos and images gives a sense of their importance if the potential value of their franchise is fully realized.

Merchandising strategies have to be careful not to engage in over-exploitation. Movie companies and toy firms are often accused of exploiting children and by implication their parents by creating too much merchandise or of using strategies that are aimed at manipulating children. It was reported, for example, that J.K. Rowling was being very careful about the amount and type of merchandise that would be made available at the time of the first Harry Potter film.[82] It was claimed that she was concerned that children and their parents should not be exploited by the merchandising deals. Nonetheless, a promotional tie-in with Coca-Cola became the focus of controversy when she was accused of associating herself and her literary works with a product that may harm children's teeth.[83] Although she claimed that the tie-in was being used to promote children's literacy, the case of the Harry Potter and Coca-Cola tie-in demonstrates that merchandising can easily become a focus of controversy. Similarly, some football clubs have been accused of over-merchandising and of exploiting fans. Parents of football-crazy children have long felt they were being exploited by clubs which changed their strips (jerseys, shorts, and socks) regularly in order to reap merchandise profits and this has led to a fall in sales.[84] The sheer range of products associated with the Manchester United brand (the most powerful football brand in the world after Real Madrid) has also led to accusations of them taking advantage of fans.[85]

Excessive merchandising can lead to accusations or feelings of commercialism which can taint and harm a venture. It has been suggested that one reason why *Hercules* was a less successful film for Disney than its predecessors was that its tie-ins and merchandise made it seem according to a *Los Angeles Times* writer 'less as a movie than as a giant marketing venture'.[86] Even the self-parody in the film of a Hercules Store stuffed full of animated Hercules merchandise could not quell the sense of marketing overkill.[87] Indeed, many of the respondents in the Global Disney Audience Project (see Box 3.1) found the growing commercialism of the company, as revealed in merchandising, something that respondents found distasteful and felt was dangerous for children. While the Disney merchandise items that interviewees themselves had received as children were remembered fondly, they tended to feel that the current Disney marketing policy went too far. Also, the synergistic links between films, theme parks, merchandise and advertising were often seen as manipulative. However, it should be appreciated that the interviewees in each country were university students, who might be expected to have a more critical stance. Similarly, the rock concert Woodstock '94, which was meant to reprise the famous event of the 1960s, was criticised for being too commercial because of the volume of concert merchandise on sale.[88]

Owners of the rights to license copyright images and logos, like the protectors of brands more generally, have to be sensitive to the possibility of extending them to products that could be deemed inappropriate to the brand. The extension of the Harley-Davidson images and logos to toiletries was regarded by many as a failure. As the managing partner of one marketing consultancy argued: 'How could they take an icon of liberation, something that was all about feeling the wind in your hair, and put it on a cheap product, in pseudo-macho packaging?'[89]

A major problem for those involved in merchandising and licensing is that fashions change. Themed restaurant t-shirts and replica football shirts no longer represent the fashion statements that they did in the mid-1990s.[90] Princess Diana memorabilia, which had been the subject of a court case, were faring poorly by the middle of 2002.[91] The BBC's Teletubbies, which had been a massive merchandising success in 1998 and 1999, saw a large fall in profits in 2001, just three years later.[92] Even Elvis merchandise has shown signs of falling away, largely due to changing demographics, although fashion may also have a role in the process.[93]

Conclusion

As the reflections in the previous section suggest, merchandising is not a licence to print money. There are numerous pitfalls and risks in the whole process. For one thing, it is difficult for the owners of copyright to know how far the franchise should be extended. Second, it is difficult for licensees to know which images and logos to pursue and on which products. While they can be cautious and opt for established images, like Harry Potter which was already well established through the series of books, or television series that have done well, fashions change and they may find they end up with stock they cannot sell but still have to pay the licensing fees for the images and logos. Third, the outlets that carry the merchandise are likely to be uncertain about how much stock to carry because, for the same reason as the licensees, there are few certainties.

On the other hand, merchandising is a hugely profitable area if the participants get their calculations right. What is striking about merchandising is that it has in a sense ceased being icing on the cake and has become a major ingredient of the cake in its own right. Increasingly, films, television series and themed restaurant chains are developed with an eye firmly on their merchandising potential. Merchandising is no longer just an added benefit. Disney has shown the way in this regard but few can match its synergy. When others have tried they have rarely fared as well. The closure of many Warner Bros. Studio Stores and of two Hanna-Barbera stores in the Los Angeles area soon after opening in 1990,[94] are illustrations of Disney's unique position, as well as an indication of the fragile nature of a merchandising strategy. So too are the Viacom stores that were planned as outlets for merchandising relating to the company's holdings. However, by early 2003 there were clear indications that the Disney Stores were under-performing as well.

Merchandising is closely bound up with hybrid consumption, because in many hybrid consumption environments, such as theme parks and themed restaurants, licensed merchandise is one of the major items for sale. However, the two should not be fused, because there is a distinctive cluster of merchandising activities that we have seen in this chapter, most notably in connection with films and television series. For their part, the merchandisers have to tread a very careful line between appealing to children, probably the most influential target group, and disillusioning the parents through creating children's 'must-haves' that are likely to have as limited a shelf life in their bedrooms as in the stores.

Notes

1 Robinson (2003).
2 Wolf (1999: 227).
3 Quoted in Wasko (2001: 8).
4 Davis (1996: 407).
5 Fainstein and Judd (1999: 15).
6 Sparks (1998).
7 Quoted in Canemaker (1991: 88–9).
8 Tumbusch (1989: 28).
9 Anon. (1932).
10 Anon. (1948).
11 Klein (1993); Merritt and Kaufman (1992: 144).
12 For example, Bryman (1995); Forgacs (1992).
13 From a story conference 3 November, 1936, quoted in Forgacs (1992: 364).
14 Bailey (1982: 75).
15 Gould (1979).
16 Quoted in Fessier (1977: 19).
17 Schlosser (2000).
18 Gordon (1958: 12).
19 Eisner (1998: 241).
20 Masters (2000: 229).
21 Giroux (1999).
22 Pereira (1999).
23 The Walt Disney Company, 1996 Annual Report: 57.
24 Masters (2000).
25 Pecora and Meehan (2001: 314–15).
26 Goodwin (1995: 10.7).
27 Quoted in Sherwin (2002: 11).
28 Litman (1994).
29 Wolf (1999: 228).
30 Wolf (1999: 229).
31 Holson and Lyman (2002).
32 Moretti (2001).
33 Quoted in Handy (1996: 56).
34 Voyle (2001).
35 Cunningham (2001).
36 Reid and Peak (2001).
37 Akwagyiram (2001).
38 Chittenden and Winnett (2001).
39 *Sunday Times Rich List 2003*; Boztas (2003).
40 Pereira (1996).
41 Grover (1991: 261).
42 Studd (2002).
43 Simensky (1998).
44 Whittell (1999).
45 Armstrong (2000).
46 Ashworth (2002).
47 Goodman (2002).
48 Handy (1996).
49 Kline (1993: 218).
50 O'Donnell (2002). Similarly, Larson (2003: 64) notes that the merchandising of *The Simpsons* was a critical event for companies making animated television series because it brought home a full realization of its potential. It is believed that as much as $1 billion in revenue was generated from ancillary sales, particularly merchandise, for FOX.
51 Armstrong (1999).
52 Armstrong (1999).
53 Hendry (2000).
54 Maple and Archibald (1993: 79–80).
55 Maple and Archibald (1993: 89).
56 Desmond (1999: 148).
57 King (1991).
58 Robinson (1996: 50).
59 Coe (1996: 114).
60 Schlosser (2001: 31).
61 Anon. (2001: 36).
62 Longmore (1996).
63 Kuper (1996: 2).
64 Television programme 'The Men Who Changed Football', shown March 13 2001, BBC2.
65 King (2002: 136).
66 Wolf (1999).
67 Klein (2000: 96).
68 Schlossberg (1996: 172).
69 Durrett (2003).
70 Swanton (1996: vi).
71 Elliott (1998).
72 Bale (1998).
73 Ashworth (2000).
74 Robinson (2003).
75 Ludlow (2002).
76 Wasko (2001).
77 Episode in the television series 'Logo' shown on BBC Choice 27 November, 2001.
78 Jones (1999).
79 Fox (1996); Hopkins (2002); Waples (1997).
80 Koenig (1996).
81 Alexander (1993); Brodie (1996). Interestingly, Nel (2003) has observed

that in spite of his reservations about commercialization, Theodore Seuss Geisel (Dr Seuss) did permit some licensing of the characters in his books. The conversion of some of his books into films and television specials increased the pressure for such merchandise among prospective licensees, production companies, and others. Since his death in 1991, there has been a huge increase in licensed merchandise based on his characters.

82 Chittenden and Winnett (2001).
83 Koster (2001).
84 Fresco (2001).
85 Nicolas (2002).
86 Quoted in Wasko (2001: 80).
87 See Giroux, (1999: 161) for a summary of merchandise generated by and for the film.
88 Klein (2000).
89 Quoted in Nicolas (2002: 34).
90 Fresco (2002).
91 Hamilton (2002).
92 Midgley (1999); Steiner (2002).
93 Gwynne (1997); Goodwin (2002).
94 Simensky (1998).

Chapter Five
Performative labour

Mini Contents

There is a growing trend for work, particularly in service industries, to be construed as a performance, much like in the theatre. The employee becomes like an actor on a stage. By 'performative labour', then, I simply mean the rendering of work by managements and employees alike as akin to a theatrical performance in which the workplace is construed as similar to a stage. In the Disney theme parks, the metaphor of the theatrical performance is explicit with the references to 'cast members', 'auditioning', 'onstage', and 'backstage'. For the two management consultants who coined the term 'the experience economy', the metaphor of the theatre is central when they suggest that at 'every level in any company, workers need to understand that ... every business is a stage, and therefore work is theatre'.[1] The work of the person who stages the experience is crucial for the experience to remain in the customer's memory. They urge worker-performers to engage customers 'as if your work depended on it!'[2] One of the main elements in generating the sense of a performance that is particularly notable at the Disney theme parks is through *emotional labour*, which is the main focus of this chapter.

Emotional Labour

Emotional labour refers to employment situations in which workers as part of their work roles need to convey emotions and preferably to appear as though those emotions are deeply held. The writer most closely associated with the term has defined it as 'the management of feeling to create a publicly observable facial and bodily display'.[3] The emotions that the emotional labourer might convey can be positive or negative ones. In the latter case, an example of which is the bill collector, the emotions that are supposed to be conveyed are ones that are largely dispassionate, uncaring, and even mildly threatening. However, this is not the kind of emotional labour that is being considered in this chapter. Instead, the emphasis will be upon the display of *positive* emotions, namely, ones that are supposed to make the recipient of the emotional labour feel good about the worker and the organization for which he or she works.

Emotional labour is always about acting, but Hochschild draws an interesting distinction between surface and deep acting. The former essentially entails going through the motions of displaying the correct emotional form. The bodily gestures are appropriate but lack real feeling or conviction. There is likely to be considerable variance between the outward display of emotions and the way in which the emotional labourer actually feels. With deep acting, the emotional labourer really feels the emotions that are being exhibited. Deep acting is much more difficult than surface acting to cultivate among emotional labourers. Nonetheless, it is a kind of holy grail to which many service organizations are committed as a means of improving service delivery.

Emotional labour does not exhaust the ways in which emotions relate to and are influenced in organizations.[4] There are several ways in which emotions take on significance in organizations, but in drawing attention to emotional labour the focus is being placed on a feature of the Disney theme parks that is spreading throughout the service sector. Relatedly, one of the most notable developments since the 1970s has been the gradual shift from an emphasis on control to the production of commitment in organizations.[5] Increasingly, organizations seek to motivate employees by raising their commitment to a firm or to a team, so that they become emotionally tied to it. As a result, they are expected to commit themselves, not just to their jobs, but to the organization and all that it represents. Developing mission statements and designing organizational culture values are among the ways that employees' emotions are enlisted for organizational ends. Tying employees emotionally to the organization and manipulating organizational culture to create a sense of meaning and attachment for them are among the main mechanisms for creating that bond. Management gurus like Tom Peters and his colleagues advocate the creation of strong cultures that will instil a sense of passion and meaning for employees.[6] Similarly, Hamel and Prahalad write about 'strategic intent' which conveys a sense of direction, much like Peters's strong cultures. Strategic intent provides 'the emotional and intellectual energy' for getting to a certain point in the future and 'aims to create employee excitement'.[7] While there is scepticism about the degree to which organizational cultures can be changed and manipulated in the way implied by such writers,[8] there is little doubt that many consultants and organizations have sought to create high-commitment cultures that draw on employees' emotional resources. This aspect of emotionality in organizations will be addressed briefly at least in part because it is one of the ways in which emotional labour is cultivated.

Why Promote Emotional Labour?

Emotional labour is closely associated with the delivery of services, most notably perhaps those in which the service entails a commercial transaction. The link is so close that the quality of the service delivery, of which the display of positive emotions is an important component, is increasingly being associated with the quality of the service itself or of the goods that are supplied in the course of a service transaction. This means that diners in a fast-food restaurant are more likely to respond positively to a meal that is supplied in a pleasing way rather than in a surly or morose manner. This is especially likely to be the case as services assume greater prominence in the economy and as customer expectations of service quality and delivery are ratcheted upwards.[9]

Probably nothing epitomizes or exemplifies emotional labour more than *the smile*. The smile, along with other elements of a positive emotional display such as eye contact, transfers to the service transaction a generally upbeat set of impressions that are meant to improve the aura surrounding the service. When Hochschild conducted research on flight attendants, she noted that during a training session at which she was present one of the trainees had written 'Important to smile. Don't forget smile'. The directive had come from a pilot who had said: 'Now girls, I want you to out there and really *smile*. Your smile is your biggest *asset*. I want you to go out there and use it. Smile. *Really* smile. Really *lay it on'*.[10] Moreover, the fact that one of the airlines she researched emphasized in one of its jingles that its 'smiles are not just painted on', suggested that the smile was supposed to come from within and therefore should not be mere surface acting.

The reason for inculcating emotional labour on the part of service staff is that there has been a growing recognition that the style and quality of the delivery of a service are crucial to how it is perceived.[11] In many instances, and the work of flight attendants is an example of this, the display of positive emotions becomes a component of the service. In other words, emotional labour is a source of *differentiation*. It is a means of differentiating services that are otherwise more or less identical or whose products are served up through service transactions that are more or less identical (as may be the case with fast food restaurants or retail outlets). How else, the reasoning goes, might we distinguish flights between New York and Chicago, other than through the quality of the flights, assuming seat pitches or styles and safety are more less indistinguishable? The interface between the attendant and the passenger, of which the emotional element – how the passenger is treated – is crucial, becomes a major factor in terms of how the service is perceived and received. Similarly, it is not the case that the quality of a hamburger in a fast food restaurant is irrelevant, but given that there is frequently little to distinguish one restaurant's hamburgers from another, the quality of the transaction, as evidenced in the way in which the service is delivered, is likely to assume greater importance and significance than otherwise. In these cases, if the service is a memorable one (or at least not memorably disappointing) the customer is more likely to return.

One of the main ways in which emotional labour in service delivery has diffused in relatively recent years is through customer care programmes. The greater salience attached to emotional labour in work roles is related to a growing under-standing of the importance of positive service encounters for the customer and of the influence of the frontline service employee on customers' impressions.[12] It can also be seen as being very much associated with the related issue of the way in which customer satisfaction is increasingly depicted by service firms as of para-mount importance, because it is crucial to repeat business. For example, there is evidence that as many as two-thirds of customers stop purchasing a service or product because they are dissatisfied with the employee.[13] These considerations have been important factors behind the growth of customer care programmes.

The customer nowadays is frequently described as 'king' (a principle also often referred to as 'consumer sovereignty') and satisfying the king's needs has become of central importance to many organizations in the service sector. Of major significance has been the growing impact of customer care programmes that have been influenced by Total Quality Management (TQM) and the particular form that it has assumed when applied to the service sector, namely, one of making the satisfaction of the customer's needs a central tenet of operations.[14] TQM in the service sector has meant that the emphasis in the quality movement on 'fitness for use' or 'fitness for purpose' was translated into a focus on 'fitness for the customer'. Satisfying the customer's needs became a paramount concern. The major impact of this orientation has been to make the frontline employee and the service that he or she delivers the focal point of the quality revolution.

We can therefore see two related processes behind the diffusion of emotional labour. First, customer care programmes, especially those influenced by TQM, are predicated upon the principle of consumer or customer sovereignty, which ascribes paramount importance to satisfying customers' needs so that they will be more likely to return. The quality of service delivery, of which emotional labour is an important ingredient, therefore becomes crucial and is the main rationale for customer care programmes. Second, in a world in which there is little to distinguish many products and services the quality of service delivery, including emotional labour, may be the major distinguishing factor. In such circumstances, ensuring the satisfaction of the customer's needs becomes especially crucial and again is frequently a spur to the introduction of customer care initiatives, like TQM. These customer care initiatives are often inextricably linked to programmes (of the kind briefly mentioned above) that seek to enhance employees' organizational commitment, since they are more likely to accept the demands of emotional labour when ties to the organization are close. With all of these developments, generating an organizational framework that is designed to satisfy the needs of sovereign consumers is the prime mover, and fostering emotional labour is a crucial component of the framework that is meant to satisfy those needs.

Emotional Labour in the Disney Theme Parks

Emotional labour is in many ways exemplified by the Disney theme parks. The friendliness and helpfulness of Disney theme park employees are renowned and is one of the things that visitors often comment on as something that they liked.[15] Moreover, anyone with even a passing knowledge of the parks *expects* this kind of behaviour. The ever-smiling Disney theme park employee has become a stereotype of modern culture. Their demeanour coupled with the distinctive Disney language is designed, among other things, to convey the impression that the employees are having fun too and therefore not engaging in real work. Disney are fully aware of the significance of the Disney touch. As Michael Eisner observes: 'Nothing so visibly defines Disney's parks as the warmth and commitment of our cast members over the years, and the appreciation guests feel for the way they're treated.'[16] An article on Disney theme park employees in the *Disney Magazine*, presents the following anecdote:

> It's a typical summer day at Disney's Blizzard Beach Water Park. The lines are long, the guests are hot, the noise is pounding, and the action is frenzied. At the top of the Teamboat Springs Raft Ride, a young woman in a bright red bathing suit loads families into the round rubber rafts, tugs them through the pool of water in the holding area, and then uses all her strength to push the heavy rafts onto the start of the slide. Approximately every 40 seconds a new group begins its descent, meaning that she loads about 90 rafts an hour … But this young woman keeps smiling, greeting each new family with enthusiasm. 'How ya doing? Having fun? Do you have on plenty of sunscreen? Now hang on, because this gets pretty wild.'[17]

For Disney, inculcating forms of behaviour, gestures and impressions of this kind, and of emotional labour more generally, are very much part of what Disney nowadays refers to as its 'service theme': 'to create happiness for people of all ages everywhere'.[18] As part of their training (see Box 5.1), cast members are 'taught to take a wide responsibility for guest happiness, by being friendly, knowing the answers to common questions, and, when possible, guiding guests to their destinations'.[19] Performance tips are taught, which include exploring 'the effects of posture, gestures, and facial expressions on the guest experience'.[20] In an implicit recognition of the distinction between deep and surface acting, it is noted that: 'Practices such as smiling, greeting, and thanking guests are all well and good, but if these actions are restricted to rote, mechanistic behaviors, their effectiveness is severely limited'.[21] Unsurprisingly, the first guideline for guest service is:

Make Eye Contact and Smile!

Start and end every Guest contact and communication with direct eye contact and a sincere smile.[22]

Box 5.1 Introducing Disney theme park cast members to the Disney corporate culture

Central to the training of new cast members is the introduction to Disney traditions. This includes providing an induction into the company's history, its underlying philosophy (especially that of the theme parks), its quality standards, and its achievements. The training materials include motivational videos that include Walt himself. Trainees are instructed in the importance of creating a sense of happiness for guests and in the distinctive Disney language and the rationale for it. They are told about their roles in the 'show'. Cast members are then introduced to Disney policies and procedures, such as the regulations concerning appearance and dress, and to some of the benefits available to them. The overall goal is to secure cast members' commitment to the distinctive Disney culture.

Sources: Blocklyn (1988); Taylor and Wheatley-Lovoy (1998); Van Maanen (1991).

Little would seem to have changed from the late 1960s when John Van Maanen, a sociologist who worked briefly as a Disneyland ride operator, observed that the demeanour of cast members was governed by three rules that were implanted during training:

First, we practice the friendly smile.

Second, we use only friendly and courteous phrases.

Third, we are not stuffy – the only Misters in Disneyland are Mr. Toad and Mr. Smee.[23]

Similarly, Raz quotes from a Disneyland training manual:

At Disneyland we get tired, but never bored, and even if it's a rough day, we appear happy. You've got to have an honest smile. It's got to come from within. And to accomplish this you've got to develop a sense of humor and a genuine interest in people. If nothing else helps, remember that you get paid for smiling.[24]

Cast members must display emotional labour even in the face of difficult guests. One cast member of eight years told a reporter: 'We get daily abuse from customers but you have to keep on smiling. We're supposed to make eye contact, greet each and every guest and smile for eight hours. If you don't you get reprimanded.'[25]

It was not quite like this at the beginning however. In Disneyland's very early days, Walt was appalled by the behaviour of some of the park's staff toward visitors. The staff, many of whom had been hired by lessees, lacked training and were gruff and unhelpful towards visitors. Such behaviour was unacceptable to Walt who wanted to create an environment where people could forget the outside world and their troubles and be immersed in a magical experience. Unhelpful and discourteous behaviour are found abundantly in the outside world and therefore undermined the kinds of impressions he wanted to create. The only employees who exhibited the kind of behaviour Walt wanted were the attraction operators who had been trained by the company itself. According to Randy Bright, a Disney Imagineer: 'What Walt really wanted were employees with a ready smile and a knack for dealing pleasantly with large numbers of people'.[26] Walt told cast members that they should 'always smile' and that they should 'turn the other cheek to everybody, even the nasty ones'.[27] The Disney University was created precisely in order to inculcate the demeanour that Walt wanted to engender. According to the founder of the Disneyland University, one of the central elements of the early training approach was to introduce the principle that '[i]n addition to a "friendly smile", we sold the importance of "friendly phrases"'.[28] Since then, Disney has developed seminars which introduce executives from a variety of organizations to its distinctive approach to human resource management[29] and has publicized this approach more generally.[30] These seminars may have been instrumental in the further diffusion of this aspect of Disneyization. Moreover, a number of management texts have emphasized this ingredient of the success of the Disney theme parks.[31] Disney itself uses its training programme, which employs videos and talks on Disney's past and traditions, to secure commitment to the company and its values. Such a commitment is likely to facilitate emotional labour. As the then director of Disney's three-day training seminars for business executives from other companies points out: 'You can't force people to smile. Each guest to Disney World sees an average of 73 employees per visit, and we would have to supervise them continually. Of course, we can't do that, so instead we try to get employees to buy into the corporate culture.'[32] Similar approaches to training are common at large companies like McDonald's and Nike.[33]

Needless to say, the manifestations of emotional labour are sometimes repudiated in that behaviour inconsistent with Disney principles of how cast members should act is exhibited, as a number of commentators have observed.[34] However, to concentrate on these features is to miss the point: as Van Maanen observes, there is a significant acceptance among Disney staff of the emotional requirements of the job.[35] Similarly, adherence to the Disney Way of service delivery among Tokyo Disneyland cast members has been described as 'remarkable'.[36] Even among some former cast members who have had adverse employment experiences, there seems to be a certain ambivalence that combines a certain degree of admiration with a recognition that the job was not for them.[37]

Precursors of Emotional Labour

As with the other dimensions of Disneyization, emotional labour is not a new phenomenon. Nurses, doctors, midwives and others involved in medical services have frequently felt the need to engage in emotional labour: expressing joy at the birth of a healthy baby or a sombre demeanour when having to deliver bad news. Also, many jobs have a degree of emotional labour attached to them. We try not to fall out with colleagues, to be helpful to visitors to our organizations, to be solicitous when we need special consideration from a supplier, and to provide encouragement towards new recruits to an organization. In all such instances, it could be argued with some validity that emotional labour is being enacted.

What could be described as new in relation to the Disney theme parks and to the other modern examples of the diffusion of emotional labour is the prominence it is given, particularly in relation to commercial service delivery. Therefore, it is the formally prescriptive nature of the expression of emotions as part of the work role that is novel, even though emotional labour itself is not new. However, it would be wrong to associate emotional labour solely with formal prescription, since service workers are frequently fully aware of the significance of cultivating good relationships with customers in the interests of the performance of the organizations on which their jobs depend. Indeed, in some cases they may chafe under the yoke of an overly prescriptive approach to the display of emotional labour. For example, Rosenthal et al. show that workers in one of the main supermarket chains in Britain were able, following the introduction of an initiative that emphasized service quality for customers and removed many previous restrictions on employees, to engage in emotional labour in a way that suited them.[38] The more scripted approach that they had previously had to follow had been disliked because they felt they possessed the skills required to perform emotional labour. Emotional labour is not necessarily performed as a result of direct enticement, although this undoubtedly happens and is particularly prominent in Disney Parks, but also because employees frequently recognize the need for it. Such a recognition can arise as a result of contact with customer care programmes but also because there is a growing recognition of emotional labour as a component of good service.

Interestingly, the emphasis on emotionality at Disney predates the Disney theme parks at least in terms of the representation of the Disney employee. Walt was keen to give the impression that his animators were like children at play who loved their work. They were frequently described in articles on him or his studio as happy, carefree, smiling workers. A 1933 article in a popular magazine of the time said of the studio: 'Everybody wears a smile, and even the humblest employee addresses his chief as "Walt"'.[39] A 1940 article described the studio as 'the only factory on earth where practical jokes are a part of the production line'.[40] A movie released in 1941, *The Reluctant Dragon*, not only constituted the company's first live-action film but essentially provided a tour of the studio which served to give the impression of a fun factory. The reality was often at variance with the image that Walt was keen to convey of the studio. Walt himself was a hard task master who disliked being contradicted and who was ruthless with anyone who failed to agree with him. In fact at the time of *The Reluctant Dragon*, the studio was on the verge of a paralysing strike as a result of attempts to unionize the plant. Walt became increasingly intransigent and even after the conclusion of the strike was spiteful to those who had supported the dispute. Despite this, there is little doubt that many Disney studio employees felt that they were involved in a very special kind of activity and that the workplace itself had a magical quality. What is significant for our present purposes, however, is the fact that the company was keen to create an impression of a group of employees whistling while they worked in harmony. This management of the image of work at the studio was conducted so that it seemed like fun rather than real work. At the Disney theme parks, where providing a service was the goal rather than a product like an animated cartoon film, enticing employees to exhibit positive emotions became of key significance and not simply a matter of creating an impression for popular consumption. Emotional labour had to be delivered as a component of the frontline service interface.

The Diffusion of Emotional Labour

In this section, a variety of ways and contexts in which emotional labour occurs nowadays will be outlined. Hochschild calculated that for the early 1980s, around one-third of American workers were in jobs that included a substantial element of emotional labour and among working women, one-half of them had jobs of this kind.[41] These estimates have to be treated with some caution, not least because the level of the demand to exhibit emotional labour is likely to vary quite considerably among the occupations to which she refers. However, it is striking that such a large proportion of the workforce is affected by the requirements of emotional labour. Also striking is the fact that her calculations imply a greater likelihood of women being in jobs requiring emotional labour than men. The association of women with caring and nurturing may be a factor but so too is the fact that in many cases, emotional labour is sexualized and that women are more likely than men to be placed in positions where the allure of their sexuality is part of the service interaction. Moreover, in certain occupations women are often more likely than men to exhibit emotional labour.[42]

In one instance, at least, the diffusion of emotional labour from the Disney theme parks was very direct: the city of Anaheim's stadium and convention centre, built in the mid-1960s, consciously adopted a Disney-style approach to handling customers. Findlay quotes a local newspaper article as saying that at both organizations could be found 'an attractive and smiling staff' who had been tutored in a 'Disneyland vocabulary'.[43]

In this rest of this section, a variety of ways and contexts in which emotional labour occurs nowadays will be outlined.

Airline cabin crews

Hochschild's concept of emotional labour was originally developed in relation to airline cabin crew staff, primarily at Delta Airlines in the USA. Other researchers have confirmed the significance of emotional labour in this sphere of work. Taylor and Tyler found emotional labour to be a significant component of the work of flight attendants at two airlines, one of which was British. For example, they quote a training instructor:

> always walk softly through the cabin, always make eye contact with each and every passenger, and always smile at them. This makes for a much more personal service, and is what first class travel and (we) as a company are all about.[44]

Cathay Pacific stewardesses are similarly enjoined to smile and one of them is quoted in a newspaper article as saying:

> They are always telling us that we are pretty and intelligent and that we are a very important part of the company and they treat us as if we clean the toilets AND no matter what happens we must always SMILE.[45]

There is an unmistakable link here between sexuality and the display of emotional labour that was previously referred to and this connection is very much a feature of the advertisements for Asian airlines like Cathay Pacific that show images of alluring female stewardesses.

Some airlines feel a need to enhance the emotional labour component of their service delivery. It was announced in 1998 that British Airways cabin crews were to be trained so that they were less reserved, less inclined to exhibit the British stiff upper lip. They were to become more tactile and less aloof. According to a *Times* reporter: 'Cabin staff will be encouraged to crouch alongside passengers, offer the occasional consoling pat on the arm and maintain plenty of eye contact'.[46]

The article also hints that the pressure to exhibit such behaviour was in large part motivated by the fact that the cabin crews on one of its main competitors on trans-Atlantic routes – Virgin – are much more inclined to employ the kinds of behaviour that BA is described as being keen to encourage.

Shop workers

Shop staff are increasingly being encouraged to exhibit emotional labour. Perhaps one of the best known examples of this is Body Shop International. The company has long been known for its strong corporate culture and its use of training programmes as a means of getting that culture across and to secure commitment to it. Body Shop staff have been described as frequently engaging in emotional labour throughout the organization, not just in its shops.[47] One new recruit says that during her training

> We ... watch a sales video called Smile Dammit Smile, in which a very straight-faced blonde from head office comes on the screen to tell us that we should try saying the word 'yippee' to ourselves before we go on to the shop floor. 'It's a silly word and it will put a nice bright smile on your face.'[48]

Supermarket staff also have to cultivate such outward (and preferably inward) displays of emotion. Wal-Mart's friendly people greeters who are situated at the entrance to its stores (an idea adopted by Disney for its Disney Stores) are an illustration of the penetration of emotional labour into this area of retailing. ESPN Zone in Chicago also uses smiling people greeters.[49] The Wal-Mart greeters often wear a smiley face on the back of their uniforms, so that the shopper is met with a smile no matter which way the greeter is facing. Tolich studied the work of clerks in a supermarket (referred to as 'Raley's') in a rural area of California. He notes that the clerks were instructed to be friendly to customers and the training manual was explicit:

> It takes only a few kind words for customers to remember Raley's. In the checkstand it takes a smile, a friendly attitude, courteous service, accuracy, speed, and good appearance to make a customer want to come back to Raley's. You may be the last contact with customers as they leave the store. Make it pleasant and memorable.[50]

Similarly, at a national chain of convenience stores in place of a general request for clerks to be friendly to its customers, they were given training which 'instructed them to greet, smile at, establish eye contact with, and say "thank you" to every customer'.[51]

British supermarket chains have also sought to inject emotional labour into the service transaction, as the reference on p. 110 to the research by Rosenthal et al. suggests.[52] A study of four British supermarket chains by Ogbonna and Wilkinson found that three of the four groups had developed customer care programmes in which emotional labour was a central ingredient; the fourth chain competed on price rather than differentiation. In one of the three chains, a store manager indicated that checkout clerks 'are told to smile all the time' and to contact a supervisor or manager if a customer has a problem. A checkout clerk at the same store informed the researchers: 'We are given customer care training when we join the company and as an ongoing thing. We are told to smile all the time and that the customer is always right.'[53] Moreover, management at this store were keen that the smile should appear genuine and not superficial, so that in Hochschild's terms they should be displaying emotions through deep rather than surface acting.

McDonald's

Emotional labour is a key feature of McDonald's restaurants. It is a component of the Quality Service and Value ethos from Ray Kroc's days that remains a central tenet of the faith. Its importance is drilled into franchisees and managers at the Hamburger Universities. Crew members at the customer interface are widely expected to engage with diners in a friendly way in order to enhance the pleasurable nature of the dining experience and to increase the likelihood of more items being purchased. Drawing on her research in a McDonald's restaurant, Leidner found that window workers were expected to smile, be cheerful, and polite.[54] In addition, they were supposed to be themselves, meaning that they were not to repeat a script robotically but to go beyond the standard phrases and to inject some of their own personalities into the interaction. This arises out of a belief that a monotonous repeating of standard phrases and forms of behaviour frequently appears contrived and therefore not indicative of deep acting.

On the basis of his European research on McDonald's, Royle has suggested that the company's till employees 'are expected to control themselves *internally* by being pleasant, cheerful, smiling and courteous to customers, even when customers are rude and offensive'.[55] It is very much part of the show business atmosphere that Ray Kroc, the founder of McDonald's as we know it today, felt was such an important component of the success of the restaurants. It can be seen in the previously quoted remark by Jim Cantalupo (see p. 28), then president of international operations, when he refers to the significance of 'the smile at the front counter'. As Fantasia points out in connection with the reception of McDonald's in France, the American ambience is a very important aspect of its success there among youth, and it is the deployment of emotional labour that plays an important role in creating that ambience.[56] It is striking that when Kincheloe interviewed a woman originally from Hong Kong, she explained how as a girl her enthusiasm for McDonald's was such that she used to play role playing games in which she would 'churn up a big smile, and say, "How can I help you today? May I please have your order?"'.[57] However, there has been some speculation that McDonald's has allowed progressively less attention to be paid to service quality and that this was one of the main reasons for a downturn in its financial fortunes soon after the start of the new millennium and for its decline as a brand.[58]

It is not just crew workers who are involved in exhibiting emotional labour. Managers are also involved in a form of emotional labour in that they are trained and encouraged to become subservient to the McDonald's corporate ethos and culture. Leidner writes that the company seeks to produce managers with 'ketchup in their veins'.[59] The Hamburger University plays a significant role in inculcating this corporate spirit. In part, the training is conducted in order to instruct managers in the correct operational procedures in order to maximize the kind of uniformity of process and product for which the company is famous. But also, as Leidner observes, managers' zeal is worked on in order to ensure that they understand as fully as possible the reasons for adherence to protocol so that they are more likely to ensure that there is no transgression among their staff. The training is concerned therefore with 'building commitment and motivation' as much as instruction in McDonald's ways of doing things. The kind of company loyalty that is required and engendered involves an element of emotional labour on the part of those who are required to exhibit it. Much like Disney's University, the managers are also introduced to the company's history and to the words of its founder in order to enhance the emotional appeal of the corporate culture.

Other restaurants

McDonald's is by no means the only fast food chain that seeks to elicit emotional labour from its workers. It is evident in Reiter's research on Burger King which 'urges employees to be pleasant, cheerful, smiling, and courteous at all times' and to 'show obvious pride in their work'.[60] A flier given to cashiers as part of their training informed them: 'without the personal attention to good service that only you can give, our customers may not return ... Be fast and friendly, with a "smile". Make the customer's visit a happy one'.[61] Research into fast-food restaurants in New York (which included a McDonald's outlet) confirms the importance of emotional labour in the work of cashiers and other frontline service workers. As one worker put it: 'The first time I did the work, they said "smile, be polite." If some customers are impolite or not kind, we have to smile to everyone.'[62] Similarly, Leidner noted a sign outside a Kentucky Fried Chicken outlet that read 'Now hiring smiling faces.'[63]

Fast-food restaurants like McDonald's and Burger King are by no means the only types of restaurant in which emotional labour is likely to be found. In Chicago, at the Johnny Rockets restaurant (a chain of 1950s-themed diners) an instruction was written on a white board in the servers' food collection area

Figure 5.1

reading 'Always smile' (see Figure 5.1). Hall researched five restaurants in Hartford, Connecticut, which were quite different in character and clientele.[64] One was a franchise restaurant serving fairly standard fast-food fare; three were outlets of middle levels of prestige (an Italian restaurant, a trendy restaurant, and a formal restaurant whose waiters were in tuxedoes); and a prestigious and expensive three-star restaurant. At all of them a friendly manner was encouraged among serving staff. Hall explains that for all of the restaurants, the essence of the friendly service to do with being able to smile irrespective of how the server feels or how he or she is treated. At the upscale restaurant, the general manager encouraged servers to smile when they were failing to display the correct emotional state because it helps to create the impression that staff are enjoying themselves.

Of course, conforming to the smiling service worker is not exclusively a matter of managerial prescription. Servers in restaurants know that they are more likely to receive gratuities if they are friendly and pleasant towards diners.[65] However, this fact does not undermine the significance of this aspect of Disneyization. It is precisely because servers know that friendly, smiling service has become an expectation they recognize that they have to exhibit such behaviour in order to receive additional financial recognition. Moreover, they have a vested interest in patrons' returning to their establishments since they are more likely to keep their jobs and to receive a constant flow of tips.

Hotels

Reception staff in hotels are particularly likely to be required (or feel the need) to exhibit emotional labour. Evidence for this can be derived from a study of an American-owned multinational company with a string of hotels and other travel- and leisure-related activities. The company had introduced a TQM initiative which profoundly influenced the delivery of services. The initiative was designed to empower frontline staff to do whatever it takes to satisfy the customer. The company's mission is to ensure 'that every guest leaves satisfied' and staff are urged to ensure that they 'display genuine and enthusiastic interest in the guest'.[66]

Further evidence of emotional labour among frontline hotel staff derives from a study of the harassment of hotel workers. Employees were required to conduct themselves in a friendly manner even when faced with obnoxious behaviour. One of the researchers' informants described an instance whereby a man was sexually propositioning a female employee at the reception desk and said that the receptionist 'was sort of smiling and sort of playing along with it' while making excuses.[67] Another hotel worker described how 'you need to be friendly and you need to smile and even when you are shouted at ... it's a good thing if you can stay calm ... and just try to remember it's not you they are after, they are shouting at you but they are talking at the hotel ... it's not a personal attack'.[68]

Telephone call centres

Staff in call centres may not seem like obvious candidates for the display of emotional labour. They are unable to parade a smile because of the non-visual nature of their contact with customers. Also, they are particularly likely to encounter hostile customers, either because they are cold-calling on people who do not want to be disturbed or because they are the first port of call for customers who have a problem that needs to be resolved. Nonetheless, emotional labour has permeated this area of frontline service work too.

A case in point can be gleaned from a study of telephone sales agents working within a regional centre for a major British airline, referred to as Flightpath.[69] The work of the agents had been influenced by a customer service care programme in the form of TQM. Their work entailed dealing with members of the public who wanted to purchase or reserve tickets, or wanted any of the other travel services the company offered. Agents were encouraged to be themselves on the telephone, so that they did not sound robotic in dealing with customers. As noted above, there is a growing recognition that scripted forms of emotional labour sound very insincere and if anything undermine the very impression they are trying to engender. In effect, this means that agents are required to draw on their own emotional resources in order to deliver the kind of customer service the firm requires and to facilitate meeting financial targets. Each agent devised his or her own way of injecting emotionality into the interaction, though they were given training in how to deal with angry or difficult customers.

On the face of things, the framework within which these agents were working would seem to give them considerable autonomy in their emotional labour. However, as Taylor observes, the fact that they are required to work within a customer care programme and to be themselves, in addition to the fact that their calls monitored (an issue that will be returned to in the next chapter), meant that in order to deliver emotional labour they had to engage in the kind of deep acting to which Hochschild referred. Precisely because of company instructions about the need to cultivate customers and because of the preference for not using scripted emotional labour, in order to fulfil company demands concerning meeting customers' needs and to meet financial targets, deep acting was required. Similarly, emotional labour skills were found to be crucial for staff in call centres in several different countries (including Australia, the USA, and Japan) studied by Frenkel et al. These included 'the ability to remain calm amid the pressure of responding to a continuous stream of customer calls and the ability to maintain a friendly, positive, and tactful attitude while simultaneously remaining disengaged psychologically as protection from abusive customers'.[70] Further evidence comes from a study of a British company that is part of a US-based multinational which provides consultancy for handling calls and managing call centres. It was involved in a 'mystery shopper' examination of levels of customer care in the handling of calls. Three of the eight criteria of care – agent helpfulness, agent tone, and enthusiasm – are very much the kinds of features expected in emotional labour.[71]

Further evidence of the significance of emotional labour for call centre work comes from a study of customer service representatives at a call centre referred to as Telebank. The research shows that technical skills were far less important to recruiters than social and communication skills. As one manager put it: 'But we recruit attitude. You can tell by talking to someone during the interview whether they smile, whether their eyes smile. If you smile during your interview and you are enthusiastic, you'll be okay.'[72] Another manager suggested 'the only substantive differentiator between the banks [is] the personality of the individuals on the telephone. ... The differentiator is how they communicate with the customer. It is the overriding skill they've got to have.'[73]

Thus, in spite of call centre work not being an obvious candidate for the promotion of emotional labour, because of the non-visual nature of the interaction, it would seem to have infiltrated this type of service encounter as well, although the cultivation of deep acting can be especially difficult in this environment.[74]

Zoos

There is a growing expectation in zoos of good customer service and since the interface with the public is a component of this, it would not be too unwise to predict a growing tendency towards the use of emotional labour as zoos become more commercialized. Indeed, Dibb reports that encouraging staff to demonstrate 'a positive attitude toward customer service' is a preoccupation for managers of zoos and wildlife parks in the UK.[75]

When such service is *not* forthcoming the effects can create a highly negative response. A landscape architect described the enthusiasm of a group of his students for a zoo's exhibits concerning conservation

> until we reached the snack stand. The young woman who waited on us was so uninterested and the food ... was so poor that my students talked of nothing else the whole afternoon. The magical opportunity created by the $15 million exhibit investment was quenched by the most junior employee in the whole park![76]

Certainly, visitors will notice that emotional labour is definitely a feature of the Sea Worlds and Busch Gardens, and will also typically find it to be a feature of Disney's new Animal Kingdom.

In fact, Davis's study of Sea World in San Diego makes explicit reference to emotional labour as a feature of the park. She writes: 'Sea World employees must be friendly, cheerful, helpful, and always smiling to a vast throng of stroller-pushing pedestrians.'[77] According to the park's director of operations, supervisors check on the behaviour of staff:

> But they also check to see they're outwardly greeting people, and they're not just standing there. Even just smiling isn't enough of what we want. We want them to say things to people, and, as people are exiting stadiums, say 'Thanks for coming,' 'Have a nice day,' 'Anything I can do to help?' 'Can I help you find something?'[78]

In the zoo setting, the possibility exists that emotional labour can take a distinctive form, particularly in relation to environmentalist ethics and conservationist appeals. On the one hand, emotional labour may be used to induce a sense of guilt (in relation to environmental degradation, species extinction, etc.). On the other hand, it may be used to induce a 'feel good' factor in the minds of visitors, predicated on the proposition that by visiting the zoo and buying its merchandise, they are participating, however indirectly, in the lofty ideals of species and habitat protection.

Zoos frequently enlarge the field of emotional labour by conscripting their animal inmates, particularly the large mammals, into the performative realm that such labour inhabits. In effect, human emotional labour can be simulated when the animals are enticed to display behaviour that can be interpreted by the audience as indicative of an emotion, such as friendliness, humour, or mischievousness (as when Shamu soaks the first ten rows in Sea World's Shamu show). Such displays are not only spectacular performances in themselves, but also serve to increase the attractiveness of cuddly merchandise and souvenirs based on the animals concerned. Desmond also argues that the emphasis placed in such performances on the animals' 'love' of their trainers further serves to enhance the plausibility for the audience of these displays of apparent emotional expression that is an ingredient of emotional labour.[79] It also brings out the performative element that is a feature of most emotional labour.

Other domains of emotional labour

The foregoing discussion has emphasized some of the major spheres in which emotional labour has taken place in late modern society. However, it does not exhaust all of them by any means. The following is a catalogue of others along with a brief discussion of each.

- *American criminal justice system* The police and other agents of the American criminal justice system have long had to engage in emotional labour but Robinson has argued that the emergence of community policing is a particularly striking indicator of the growth of emotional labour.[80] Community policing entails an orientation to dealing with the problems that engender crimes rather than with crimes once they have occurred, which is traditional law enforcement. Robinson argues that the move towards community policing typically entails dealing with social services and with the public in a more friendly and accommodating way than is normally the case. In this way, the image of the police changes in the direction of a friendlier, more approachable group.

- *Fitness trainers* Fitness clubs are well-known for having a high 'churn rate', whereby it is difficult to retain members. There is often little to distinguish clubs in terms of equipment and facilities, so the role of frontline staff become paramount in keeping members. In a study of fitness trainers in the United States, Maguire found that there was a recognition of the need to demonstrate emotional labour.[81] The need for emotional labour was particularly evident when trainers had to act as motivators to clients who were often tired or not keen on training at a certain time. Trainers needed to use emotional labour to increase clients' motivation to work out, in large part because if clients become disenchanted with a fitness regime they will either leave the club or give up altogether.

- *Beauty therapists* In a study of beauty therapists in Britain, Sharma and Black note that the work of the women they studied is similar in certain respects to Hochschild's flight attendants.[82] Fliers are often anxious and insecure about flying, so that an important aspect of the attendant's emotional labour is one of putting them at ease. Similarly, the clients of beauty therapists are often anxious and insecure about their bodies, which they may believe conform poorly to the feminine ideal. Part of the work of therapists is to assuage such concerns and to help clients make the best of themselves. In addition, the therapists recognized the need to adopt a friendly, smiling demeanour since creating the right kind of interaction was crucial to the success of the business.

- *Insurance sales agents* Agents selling insurance in the field on a door-to-door basis at a company studied by Leidner – Combined Insurance – were also expected to exhibit emotional labour as part of their role, cultivating friendliness, eye contact and other signs of such work.[83] Particularly indicative of this aspect of their work is the Positive Mental Attitude, a philosophy developed by the firm's founder and to which trainees are introduced. The aim of the programme is in part to motivate future agents but also to enhance their optimism, enthusiasm and perseverance, which are part of an individual's emotional makeup. In addition, the agents were expected to exhibit the traits of friendliness and good humour that have been encountered frequently in this chapter.

Is emotional labour bad for you?

One of the distinctive features of Hochschild's explication of emotional labour is that she sees it as having a negative impact on those who enact it. This issue is not integral to the issue of Disneyization, but is worth a brief digression in view of its significance in terms of the broader implications of Disneyization and because it has been a focus for debate among writers and researchers concerned with this topic.

Hochschild argued that emotional labour creates a disjuncture between how workers act and how they feel and as such damages them psychologically.[84] The worker must exhibit emotions he or she does not really feel *and* must suppress emotions he or she does feel. Workers' sense of an authentic self is undermined, since emotions after all belong to a person's inner realm of self-expression and feeling, and they become alienated from their inner selves and true feelings. Even though the emotional display may be little more than surface acting, it is nonetheless a form of work that damages the individual's sense of self. Such a view would seem to imply that emotional labourers are deeply disturbed. There is no doubt that some research has supported such a negative view of emotional labour but it is by no means universal.

Like Hochschild, Wouters also studied the work of flight attendants.[85] He found that they often found it very gratifying when they used their skills to calm the fears of anxious passengers or when they built up a good relationship with some of them. Similarly, the beauty therapists studied by Sharma and Black were very often delighted by their ability to help their clients feel better about themselves.[86] Leidner's research on insurance agents at Combined Insurance also found that the requirement to engage in emotional labour did not seem to be interpreted in a negative way.[87] Three factors seem to be relevant. First, agents selling insurance door to door were on commission, so they had more to gain directly from the appropriate display of emotions. Second, they had much more autonomy than counter staff in a McDonald's, where Leidner had also conducted research, because they were out in the field more or less on their own. When engaging in emotional labour they were therefore able to inject more of their own personalities into the interaction. Third, the potential customer has to be persuaded to engage in any interaction at all with the agent. As a result, agents often got a thrill out of being able to engage in conversations with people when cold-calling them and even more so when they sold them a product.

This suggests that the supposed negative consequences of emotional labour may be contingent on the nature of the jobs concerned, such as the amount of autonomy. It has also been suggested that sometimes frontline service workers provide what has been called 'philanthropic emotional labour'.[88] This occurs when service workers essentially display emotional labour because they want to (for example, because they like the person they are serving or because he or she is a regular) rather than because it is part of their job or because they will get some kind of financial advantage, such as tips, for doing so. This form of emotional labour has also been discerned in relation to a study of British airline cabin crews, such as when a female crew member went beyond the call of duty to help and restore the dignity of a very sick passenger.[89] Such displays of emotional labour are unlikely to occasion the kinds of adverse consequences for the self that so concerned Hochschild and indeed point to a further way in which emotional labour can be something that sometimes is enjoyed in its own right.

Research by Wharton on emotional labour in a bank and large hospital in the USA confirms that emotional labour does not necessarily result in adverse psychological consequences for the individual.[90] Around a half of workers in these organizations had jobs that required at least some emotional labour. Wharton's research shows that emotional labour is problematic for some people depending on their personalities and on the kind of work they are engaged in. For example, as regards the second of these two factors that influence the response to emotional labour, Wharton confirmed the suggestion that autonomy in a job can help to shield workers who perform emotional labour from the negative psychological consequences that Hochschild emphasized. In itself, emotional labour does not necessarily result in such negative effects as emotional exhaustion and job dissatisfaction.

One further reason why emotional labour does not necessarily result in damaging psychological effects is that many workers who are enjoined to display emotions are able to distance themselves from the effects of emotional labour and to engage in other tactics of resistance to the requirement of displaying emotions. This is an issue that will further be touched upon in the next chapter.

Aesthetic Labour at the Disney Theme Parks and Beyond

In some discussions of and research into emotional labour the worker's appearance forms part of the analysis. For example, in research into airline cabin crews, it is difficult to escape the tendency for many members of the occupational group to be female (and therefore deemed to be more likely to possess caring skills) and attractive. This suggests that appearance is often an important component of managerial constructions of the right kind of frontline service employee, along with a capacity to exhibit emotional labour, and that hiring for jobs may in such circumstances take notions of presentability into account. Witz et al. have sought to conceptually disentangle this aspect of the service employee from the display of emotional labour. They employ the term *aesthetic labour* to describe 'a supply of embodied capacities and attributes possessed by workers at the point of entry into employment' that are then built upon by employers to mould the worker into someone who has the right kind of 'look' or 'sound' to represent the image of the company and of the kind of service it seeks to project.[91] In the process, the employees' bodies are commodified in that they come to embody the company and what it stands for in return for wages. Like emotional labour and indeed the other aspects of Disneyization described in this book, aesthetic labour forms part of a differentiation strategy.

Witz et al. demonstrate the emergence of aesthetic labour in areas like the retail, hospitality and banking sectors where a service-led orientation has become a major emphasis. They show that at the point of recruitment, applicants frequently failed to get jobs not because they did not have the right skills or experience (which were in fact low on recruiters' lists of priorities) but because they did not have the right look. Having the right look includes such features as dress, body shape, and personal style. Job advertisements frequently made reference to appearance as a qualification.

Frequently, it would seem that it is both aesthetic labour and emotional labour that companies seek, suggesting that the two many often go hand in hand. For example, the researchers were told that at one of the hotels in their investigation (Hotel Elba), the sort of person the company wanted to recruit 'had to be pretty attractive looking people ... with a nice smile, nice teeth, neat hair and in decent proportion'. A manager told them: 'There is probably a Hotel Elba look, not an overly done up person but very, quite plain but neat and stylish ... young, very friendly ... people that look the part ... fit in with the whole concept of the hotel.'[92] The quest for a particular look is transparent in these remarks, but the references to 'a nice smile' and 'very friendly' suggest that emotional labour or a capacity for it are being sought in conjunction with aesthetic labour. Nor is it just external features that are the focus of attention in that the authors found that for jobs in telephone banking a particular kind of voice and accent was required.

As style and image becomes increasingly significant components of both everyday life and commercial activity, it is quite likely that the requirement for aesthetic labour will grow. It is very much part of the performative aspect of labour that is the focus of this chapter. After all, acting requires that the actor possesses the right appearance, which is often embellished with make-up, props, and clothing. Indeed, as one of the researchers' informants from an upscale fashion retail company remarked of her job: it 'is a bit like acting. I mean it's like being in drama school'.[93] Moreover, aesthetic labour is an important feature of the Disney theme parks, where a strict appearance and grooming policy has long existed. Disneyland's ride operators have been described as follows:

> Single, white males and females in their early twenties, without facial blemish, of above average height and below average weight, with straight teeth, conservative grooming standards, and a chin-up, shoulder-back posture radiating the sort of good health suggestive of a recent history of sports...[94]

At Disneyland Paris, a similar aesthetic labour policy could be found. The vice president of personnel, who had been involved with staff at Tokyo Disneyland, specified in an interview the following criteria, which include a brief allusion to criteria that relate to emotional labour:

> We have appearance standards that are a condition of being hired. For men, it means no facial hair, a conservative haircut with no hair over the ears or the collar, no earrings, no exposed tattoos, and no jeans. For women, no extremes in dying hair or in makeup, and no long fingernails. We want a conservative, professional look; we want our employees to be warm, outgoing, and sincere. We don't want guests to be distracted by oddities or mannerisms of the cast members.[95]

Venues like Sea World, which has features of both a theme park and a zoo, also specify requirements for both the display of emotional labour and for a certain appearance. At Sea World in San Diego, California, there are

> dress and grooming codes. Interviewers in the personnel department are asked by management to be 'prejudiced' toward a 'clean-cut look.' As at Disneyland, posted regulations define standards for haircuts, makeup, jewelry, and fingernail length and care, and service employees, like all employees are encouraged to think of themselves as performers.[96]

Similarly, staff at Niketown in Chicago have been described as follows: 'Those I saw in the retail area were almost all young adults, beautiful and healthy in appearance. Their casual wear and friendly demeanor put customers at ease'.[97] At Smoky Joe's, a Southern American style barbecue themed restaurant in the south-east of England, staff were required to possess a mix of aesthetic qualities and emotional labour skills. Thus, kitchen staff were not allowed to walk through the restaurant because they did not possess the right visual qualities.[98] At Girl Heaven, a UK chain of retail stores for girls aged three to 13 and themed on the concept of 'girl power', a sales assistant told an interviewer that they needed 'to look right because we are there for the girls ... to copy'.[99] Once again, we see in these examples a merging of emotional with aesthetic labour in the interests of commercial activity.

The Spread of Performativity

As noted in the opening paragraph of this chapter, emotional labour has been the primary focus in the discussion because it is emblematic of the growth of the performative in many service encounters. Much the same point has been made in connection with aesthetic labour as well. Pine and Gilmore were noted at the outset for their recommendation that the performative aspects of work should be boosted.[100] Similarly, according to Eric Kuhne, an American retail architect: 'Everybody is discovering now in contemporary retailing that if you don't excite the senses, if you don't create a bit of an experience of a theatrical performance, you've lost it.'[101]

In addition to such general views about the importance of conveying a sense of service work as a theatrical performance, specific examples of the circulation of the performance metaphor are growing:

- At Sea World in California in 1992, large posters pinned up in the backstage areas were entitled 'Showtime!' and, according to the vice president for food services were there to remind the worker that he or she is 'a player on stage'.[102]

- At the American fast-food chain, Au Bon Pain, applicants are required to audition for their service roles and are observed for their acting ability.[103]

- Following a visit to the Disney Company, the Harrods personnel manager became convinced that 'like Disney, Harrods is theatre' and that staff should realize that they are part of an 'amazing' and 'spectacular' show for their 'guests' in order to push through the store's commitment to customer care.[104]

- At Girl Heaven, one of the co-founders informed an interviewer that 'staff don't see themselves as sales assistants but as performers, or as co-ordinators of a leisure experience.'[105]

- When Deborah Keily was appointed to a temporary Christmas job at a Body Shop outlet, she was told that the shop floor is 'onstage', the cash room was the 'box office', and the stockroom was 'props and backstage'.[106]

- Similarly, in the upscale fashion retail company that formed part of the investigation of aesthetic labour by Witz et al., a distinction was drawn between onstage and backstage regions.[107]

- At the themed restaurant, Smoky Joe's, new staff were given a handbook entitled 'It's showtime!' which instructed them to contact their 'show director' if they encountered problems. In addition, the shift roster was called 'cast performances'. The application form specifically asked for information about acting experience and in fact several staff had such experience and used these skills in connection with their work.[108]

- In her account of Niketown in Chicago, Peñaloza describes the work of the staff in terms of providing a performance where there is a clear distinction between 'frontstage activities' (greeting visitors, answering their questions, etc.) and 'backstage activities' (such as discussions about schedules and sales figures).[109]

- In Las Vegas's themed hotel-casinos, some staff are costumed according to the overall theme and are encouraged to interact with visitors as though performing a role in line with their attire.[110]

A further prominent form of theatricality in service provision is the tourist performance, where the tourist worker enacts and in the process embodies some aspect of the site in question. For example, as living museums have become more popular, museum staff become actors who don appropriate garb and demonstrate long-forgotten skills to show off exhibits and interact with visitors in a manner appropriate to the theme. For example, in his account of Quarry Bank Mill at Styal in Cheshire in the north-west of England, Urry describes the following scenario:

> Demonstrators, some dressed in appropriate clothing, show visitors how to spin cotton on a spin-ning jenny, how to hand-weave, how a carding machine operated, the workings of a weaving mule, and the domestic routines involved in cooking, cleaning and washing for the child workforce. ... The mill has made energetic efforts to attract the 'non-museum visiting public' by specifically increasing the entertainment elements of display. This is partly achieved by the use of people to demonstrate many of the processes and to interact in a role-playing way with the visitors.[111]

When Handler and Gable conducted fieldwork at Colonial Williamsburg in Virginia, they found different groups of staff involved in such work, including 'character interpreters' who were '"living history" performers who spoke to the public in the "first person"... that is, as eighteenth-century people'.[112] In addition, 'craftspersons' practiced various trades of the time. Similarly, at Plimouth Plantation, a living historical museum made up of buildings representing seventeenth-century pilgrim life, a brochure encourages visitors to 'talk with them, ask them about their lives, and listen as they tell you, in the seventeen regional dialects heard throughout the Village, what it was like to come to this foreign place and build their future'.[113] At a reconstruction of a Viking village in a Viking theme park in Norway, people attired in appropriate costumes conduct themselves as characters in a play, while at another reconstructed Viking village, Fotviken near Malmö in Sweden, costumed performers demonstrate handicrafts.[114] In all of these instances, performances for tourists are meant to convey a sense of what it was like to live during the period and at the location being represented, and as such to create a sense of authenticity.

In many spheres, then, the notion of work as a performance is not simply implicit, as it sometimes is with emotional and aesthetic labour, but explicit. In the latter case, there is a growing tendency for frontline service work to be con-ceived of as a performance much like in the theatre. This notion is particularly apparent in the Disney theme parks which employ the theatrical metaphor with its notion of employment as 'being cast for a role in the show.'[115] In other words: 'Jobs are performances; uniforms are costumes'.[116]

In fact, Disney is itself an important wellspring for the diffusion of the theatri-cal metaphor, the inculcation of emotional labour, and many other aspects of the company's distinctive approach to human resource management and customer care. At one level, the numerous visitors to the Disney theme parks and the frequent attention the parks receive in the mass media contribute to a basic aware-ness of many aspects of the Disney approach to people management. In addition, as we saw in connection with the Harrods personnel manager referred to on p. 125, many executives visit the company and attend its training courses for non-Disney executives. A book produced by the Disney Institute is full of references to organizations whose representatives attended such courses and that have since introduced Disney ways of managing people.[117] Examples include: Volkswagen Group dealerships, Start Holding (a temporary employment agency in Gouda in the Netherlands), and University of Chicago Hospitals and Health System, which is itself the focus of a case study of the application of Disney principles.[118] Regina Eisman attended one of the courses ('The Disney Approach to People Management'), which lasted three days and covered hiring, training and motivation approaches, supervisory skills, programmes designed to enhances job satisfaction, and strategies for listening to employees and customers.[119] Among the 52 course participants there was a hospital administrator, a personnel director at a tobacco and confectionary wholesaler, and a sales manager at a radio station. At the course McGill attended, there were executives from the Flamingo Hilton in Las Vegas, utilities, hospitals, education, airlines, and banks.[120] While Disney itself is by no means the only source of the aspect of Disneyization covered in this chapter, it would seem to have an important impact.

Conclusion

The main thesis of this chapter is that increasingly, frontline services are being influenced by the notion that work is a performance. Emotional labour and aesthetic labour are the primary forms in which this notion manifests itself. In much the same way that work at the Disney theme parks is construed in terms of a theatrical performance metaphor, in which the actor seeks to make an impression at least in part through the display of emotions and through the presentation of an embodied style, so too we find in many other areas of service delivery a similar set of impressions being created. One of the main moving forces behind this diffusion of performative labour is the growing recognition of the need to deliver a quality service and that frontline service staff are key to this requirement. In the case of many services, it is the main or at least a significant component of the service. According to the advocates of customer care programmes that adopt the consumer sovereignty principle, many of which have been influenced by TQM, it is crucial to leave customers with a set of memorable and positive impressions so that they are more likely to return. In restaurants, for example, the quality of the service provided can be almost as important as (if not more important than) the quality of the product. Moreover, the principles associated with emotional labour are spreading. Sturdy has shown that the growth of consumerism and the emergence of TQM and human resource management practices in Europe and the Asia Pacific region have been associated with more and more use of customer service initiatives, which invariably encourage emotional labour.[121]

As with other aspects of Disneyization, emotional and aesthetic labour form an important weapon in the battle for differentiation. Good, memorable service thus becomes a means of distinguishing one service from another. This feature is especially important when there is otherwise little to distinguish the services being delivered, as in fast food restaurants and airline services. In a sense, emotional and aesthetic labour become important for service organizations that have become McDonaldized and therefore highly standardized and homogenous. Critics of emotional labour have sometimes argued that it has a deleterious effect on those who are enticed to, or who feel otherwise compelled to, exhibit it in order to fulfil their work roles because it creates a sense of personal inauthenticity. However, the evidence for such a view is not entirely compelling; instead, it is apparent that many people derive considerable enjoyment from acting a role. Perhaps, as increasing numbers of workers are engaged in this kind of work, they become more used to it and it becomes less exceptional and therefore less problematic for them. However if this were to be the case, it would mean that a differentiation strategy based on performative labour is also becoming less exceptional, implying that that many organizations will begin to look for ever more distinctive ways of delivering services building on emotional and aesthetic labour within a customer care framework. Ultimately, then, differentiation strategies like emotional labour can become self-defeating if the strategy itself becomes commonplace.

Notes

1   Pine and Gilmore (1999: x).
2   Pine and Gilmore (1999: 112).
3   Hochschild (1983: 7).
4   Rafaeli and Sutton (1989).
5   Walton (1985).
6   Peters and Waterman (1982); Peters and Austin (1985).
7   Hamel and Prahalad (1994: 129, 134).
8   For example, Legge (1995).
9   Korczynski (2002: 62).
10   Hochschild (1983: 4, emphases in original).
11   Henkoff (1994).
12   Bitner et al. (1990).
13   Solomon (1998).
14   du Gay and Salaman (1992); Legge (1995); Sturdy (2001).
15   Sorkin (1992: 228).
16   Eisner (1999: 228).
17   Wiley (1999–2000: 54).
18   Disney Institute (2001: 30).
19   Disney Institute (2001: 61).
20   Disney Institute (2001: 85).
21   Disney Institute (2001: 87).
22   Disney Institute (2001: 86).
23   Van Maanen (1991: 65).
24   Raz (1999: 114–15).
25   Quoted in Ellwood (1998: 17).
26   Bright (1987: 111).
27   Quoted in Lipsitz (1993: 187).
28   France (1991: 22).
29   Blocklyn (1988); Eisman (1993).
30   For example, see Johnson (1991).
31   For example, Connellan (1996); Peters and Waterman (1982); Zemke (1989).
32   McGill (1989: 4).
33   Leidner (1993); Peñaloza (1999).
34   Koenig (1994, 1999); Van Maanen (1991).
35   Van Maanen (1991).
36   Raz (1999: 103).
37   Zibart (1997).
38   Rosenthal et al. (1997).
39   Quoted in Watts (1997: 172).
40   Hollister (1940: 697).
41   Hochschild (1983).
42   Bellas (1999).
43   Findlay (1992: 101).
44   Quoted in Taylor and Tyler (2000: 87).
45   Quoted in Linstead (1995: 197).

46 Crowley (1998: 17).
47 Martin et al. (1998).
48 Keily (1991: 4.3).
49 Sherry et al. (2002).
50 Quoted in Tolich (1993: 365).
51 Sutton and Rafaeli (1988: 464).
52 Rosenthal et al. (1997).
53 Ogbonna and Wilkinson (1990: 10).
54 Leidner (1993: 73).
55 Royle (2000: 63–4).
56 Fantasia (1995).
57 Kincheloe (2002: 32).
58 Rushe (2003).
59 Leidner (1993: 54).
60 Reiter (1996: 136).
61 Quoted in Reiter (1996: 136).
62 Quoted in Talwar (2002: 97–8).
63 Quoted in Leidner (1999: 82).
64 Hall (1993).
65 Butler and Snizek (1976).
66 Jones et al. (1997: 544).
67 Guerrier and Adib (2000: 697).
68 Guerrier and Adib (2000: 701).
69 Taylor (1998).
70 Frenkel et al. (1999: 70).
71 Bain and Taylor (2000: 10–11).
72 Quoted in Callaghan and Thompson (2002: 240).
73 Quoted in Callaghan and Thompson (2002: 241).
74 Callaghan and Thompson (2002).
75 Dibb (1995: 270).
76 Coe (1996: 112).
77 Davis (1997: 90).
78 Davis (1997: 91).
79 Desmond (1999).
80 Robinson (2003).
81 Maguire (2001).
82 Sharma and Black (2001).
83 Leidner (1993).
84 Hochschild (1983).
85 Wouters (1989).
86 Sharma and Black (2001).
87 Leidner (1993).
88 Bolton (2000).
89 Bolton and Boyd (2003).
90 Wharton (1993, 1999).
91 Witz et al. (2003: 37). See also, Nickson et al. (2001).
92 Quoted in Witz et al. (2003: 48).
93 Quoted in Witz et al. (2003: 39).
94 Van Maanen (1991: 59–60).
95 Quoted in Lainsbury (2000: 96)
96 Davis (1997: 89–90).
97 Peñaloza (1999: 371).
98 Crang (1994).
99 Russell and Tyler (2002: 628).
100 Pine and Gilmore (1999).
101 'Shopology'. Second of two television programmes shown on BBC2 on September 9 2001.
102 Davis (1997: 91).
103 Pine and Gilmore (1999: 157).
104 Quoted in du Gay (1996: 120).
105 Russell and Tyler (2002: 627).
106 Keily (1991: 4.3).
107 Witz et al. (2003: 39).
108 Crang (1994).
109 Peñaloza (1999: 377–8).
110 Ritzer and Stillman (2001).
111 Urry (2002: 122).
112 Handler and Gable (1997: 18).
113 Kirshenblatt-Gimblett (1998: 192).
114 Halewood and Hannan (2001).
115 Heise (1994: 18).
116 Disney Institute (2001: 62).
117 Disney Institute (2001).
118 Shueller (2000).
119 Eisman (1993).
120 McGill (1989).
121 Sturdy (2001).

Chapter Six
Control and surveillance

Mini Contents

In this chapter, the focus will turn to the ways in which Disneyization entails control and with it, surveillance. It is tempting to view control as a dimension of Disneyization much like the four aspects covered in the previous chapters. In a sense, it is a feature of Disneyization but it is more of an *enabling* one rather than an aspect of it *per se*. Control and surveillance permit Disneyization in the form of the four dimensions outlined to operate to its full capacity. In other words, without control, theming, hybrid consumption, merchandising, and performative labour are less likely to be effective.

Control is, of course, a dimension of McDonaldization. Ritzer[1] shows that in the McDonald's restaurant, the worker is controlled in various ways, such as through the division of labour; rule books concerned with the production of food and the nature in which it should be delivered; supervision; and the use of technology to regulate the workflow and the 'building' of burgers. He argues that along with the three other aspects of McDonaldization, control in these senses is spreading throughout society. Much of what Ritzer writes about control under McDonaldization is relevant to Disneyization as well, and in this chapter I will outline the ways in which it is an enabling feature of Disneyization too. Clearly, this is an area where Disneyization and McDonaldization overlap and indeed, the Disney theme parks exhibit aspects of control in the sense in which Ritzer employs the term, as do theme parks more generally.[2]

While control and surveillance are analytically distinguishable, in the contexts in which they occur in Disneyization they shade into each other. Surveillance can be a means of checking that control procedures are working as well as being a control device in its own right. It will, therefore, be covered in tandem with the discussion of control.

However, it is crucial that we do not end up with an overly pessimistic and deterministic picture of control under Disneyization. In fact, resistance frequently occurs and in this chapter such strategies of independence will be addressed, particularly in the context of the world of work where the evidence is especially striking. Such a discussion will be an important corrective to any implication that simply because control systems are in place they are necessarily effective and total in their impacts.

Control at the Disney Theme Parks

In this section, I will address the ways in which control can be seen to be an important feature, albeit an enabling one, at the Disney theme parks. Both Bryman and Wasko have found it useful to distinguish between six different levels of control and the discussion that follows will draw on the distinctions that these authors employ.[3] A seventh level of control has been added – control over visitors' behaviour – to provide a more complete account, particularly in the context of the wider ramifications of Disneyization. These seven levels of control differ in their relevance to the broader issues to do with Disneyization that will be tackled later in the chapter, but are presented for completeness and to give an impression of what the Disney theme parks are like.

Control over visitors' behaviour

In the Disney theme parks a high level of control is achieved over the movement and behaviour of guests. Control is achieved prior to entry to a park in a similar fashion to the way in which Disney theme park employees have to bear certain characteristics before being hired. For one thing, visitors must not be barefoot or be otherwise inappropriately attired, for example by not wearing a top. Once in the park, these norms of visitor appearance are similarly policed, as the vignette later in this section testifies. However, Disney has a further method of control in the form of the relatively high cost of admission which ensures that only visitors with appropriate characteristics – ones that are unlikely to be a source of problems – gain entry. Several writers have noted that white, middle-class families are the typical visitors to the American parks. In part, this is a refection of the underlying Disney philosophy of celebrating technological progress, commercial success, and the traditional family: a philosophy that is most likely to be attractive to this group. It is also likely to be the case that it is mainly people from this social group who can afford to visit and revisit the parks. As a result, the cost of admission acts as a device that ensures that visitors will be largely drawn from a group that the company understands and feels is least likely to cause problems in terms of behaviour.

From the moment visitors drive onto Disney property, they are being controlled. There are signs everywhere that direct visitors where to go both before and after leaving their cars. Once parked, they are told where to wait for a bus and what to do and what not to do once on the bus. Once in the park, there are instructions about directions and what is and what is not appropriate behaviour (for example, whether camcorders or flash photography are permissible). If all else fails, there is surveillance in the form of security guards to admonish any departures from Disney decorum. These reprimands are likely to be prompted by transgressions of norms of behaviour, such as unruly behaviour or eating and drinking while in lines, or of norms of appearance. As an example of the latter, a vignette from a criminologist, Clifford Shearing, is fairly instructive. During the course of a visit to Disney World, his daughter developed a blister on her heel and consequently removed her shoes to alleviate the discomfort and began to walk barefoot. He writes:

> They had not progressed ten yards before they were approached by a very personable security guard dressed as a Bahamian police officer, with white pith helmet and white gloves that perfectly suited the theme of the area … (so that he, at first, appeared more like a scenic prop than a security person), who informed them that walking barefoot was, 'for the safety of visitors', not permitted.[4]

Quite aside from the possibility that the guard also committed a transgression (referring to 'visitors' and not 'guests'), the incident is interesting for the speed with which the admonition was administered and because it therefore serves as an indicator of the Disney insistence on control. When Shearing explained the situation regarding his daughter's sore foot to the guard they were threatened with expulsion. As one critic of Disney World, the novelist Carl Hiaasen, has put it:

> Every now and then reality intrudes – a shoplifter, a flasher, a fistfight between tourists, an accidental fall, a fatal heart attack on the Space Mountain roller coaster. Such incidents are handled with astounding swiftness and discretion, the scene usually cleared and back to normal within minutes.[5]

Disney-style surveillance can therefore restore order very swiftly indeed.

In fact, most of the time, very little untoward happens because the high level of attraction throughput of visitors means that visitors become accustomed to conforming to Disney requirements. In the words of a Disney cast member: 'After a couple of rides, guests almost seem as if they are in a cattle round up or something.'[6]

In other words, the high level of control that Disney exerts from the moment visitors enter Disney property generates a kind of passivity or pliability that makes them more manageable and less disruptive to the company's routines. The fact that most visitors are in family groups or in tourist groups with a leader probably helps to minimize disorderly behaviour.

Control of the theme park experience

The layouts of the Disney theme parks are designed to channel the movement of visitors in certain directions, as the discussion of control of visitors' behaviour demonstrates. The number of routes that can be taken is restricted and various lures, which Walt called 'wienies', are used to entice the visitor in certain directions.[7] The different lands in the Magic Kingdom are sealed off from one another both visually and experientially, so that the visitor's appreciation of the narrative will not be undermined. Consequently, cast members in Frontierland garb must not be seen walking through Fantasyland when in costume. Visitors are even encouraged to take photographs at certain points (sponsored by Kodak) because they are deemed to provide especially good vantage points. In addition, food and drinks carts, restaurants, and shops are strategically sited to maximize consumption opportunities. Even the queues are tightly controlled in that they are designed to give the impression that they are not as long as they actually are. This impression is achieved by: the lines constantly weaving back on themselves; part of the lines not being visible usually because they stretch into a building; and by having pre-entertainment areas in which the prospective audience is entertained while waiting, usually through overhead monitors that are meant to add to the experience.

The attractions themselves are also highly controlled aspects of the theme park experience. Each person sees the same as everyone else so that the experience of many theme park attractions is controlled and thereby standardized. This control and standardization is achieved in a number of ways. One is though technology, so that visitors are loaded onto forms of conveyance (usually a kind of car) which takes each person through exactly the same vista and for exactly the same length of time as everyone else. In the case of some attractions, the forms of conveyance are programmed to swivel so that the visitor's gaze is directed towards exactly the 'right' spot (for example, in the Haunted Mansion). A second source of control and standardization is through scripted interaction, whereby the cast members closely follow a script, which varies very little from one occasion to the next, when announcing a show or when providing the patter for a ride. Third, the use of audio-animatronic animals and actors helps to control the theme park experience. Even when attending audience participation shows, the degree of control is very high. The so-called audience participation is invariably restricted to a very small number of people and is tightly circumscribed by the overall show template.

Control over the imagination

In Chapter 1, Sayers's critique of the Disney treatment of children's literature was noted for the accusation that it tended to leave little to the child's imagination.[8] This accusation of providing children with simplified and pre-digested versions of classic literature has often been repeated, but a similar claim is often made in connection with the company's theme parks. It is often suggested that the parks do not encourage visitors to use their imagination but instead consign them to a state of passivity, whereby they become onlookers – revelling in the imagination of others (Walt and his Imagineers) – rather than being active participants in the use of the imagination.

One of the ways in which the imagination is controlled is through an emphasis constantly being placed on certain key themes and a tendency to eliminate from view undesirable features. Examples are:

- An extolling of the virtues and accomplishments of industry and the corporation while simultaneously ignoring the damage they do to the environment (or if this issue is addressed, it is in terms of how industry has, can or will overcome the problems).

- An emphasis on the virtues of the traditional family, but ignoring non-traditional family forms, such as single-parent families, divorced families, and other kinds which are in fact becoming increasingly common.

- An accent on the nostalgia associated with the supposed purity of the small town, without any recognition of the reality of the lives that went on there in terms of hardships or racism.

- A very partial account of gender and racial discrimination as in the past and not rooted in real lives in the present day.

Opportunities for children to use their imagination are circumscribed though they have arguably become more numerous in recent times. Opportunities occur at such junctures as the Future World pavilions in Epcot which often given them the opportunity to rush around trying out different machines and electronic gadgets or at the end of the animation tour in Disneyland Paris, where children can try out animation skills on machines. In general, however, as several commentators have noted, the imagination of children is stifled by the routine of queuing, climbing onto ride cars, watching, getting off, and moving on to the next attraction.

Control as a motif

In some attractions, control is a topic in its own right. Nowhere is this aspect of control clearer than in the attraction in Epcot called Living with the Land, which is sponsored by Nestlé (formerly Listen to the Land and sponsored by Kraft Foods). The ride takes the form of a boat ride in which visitors are transported through various farming methods, inhospitable environments that are overcome by farmers (though in fact the farmers are often corporations), and given a glimpse of farming in the future where corporations and technology rescue agriculture from the vagaries of nature. Nature is presented as something 'that needs to be cajoled to behave itself'.[9] Thus, rather than listening to the land (the ride's original name) or living with the land (its current name), the land must be controlled by corporations or at least by the technologies they devise in order to extract its maximum potential and productivity. Control is therefore an overriding theme in which nature is viewed as untamed and problematic without some harnessing of its energies.

This attraction is by no means the only one in which control emerges as part of a narrative of progress. It can also be found in Frontierland in the Magic Kingdom, which is essentially a celebration of the conquest of the Wild West and of the American Indian. Adventureland is similarly imbued with a narrative of imperialism and of white triumphalism over natives. In the Animal Kingdom theme park in Disney World, the company rejoices in its manipulation of the land by creating environments for the animals that are replications of their normal landscapes. Trees, foliage, and other environmental features had to be introduced in order to create for the visitor the impression of being on a safari rather than in a zoo.[10] In various ways, then, control emerges as a motif that celebrates a sense of conquest over nature or of peoples.

Control over the behaviour of employees

The behaviour of Disney theme parks employees is tightly controlled and there are several dimensions to this control.

1. *Recruitment* The behaviour of Disney theme parks employees is in a sense controlled through recruitment (or 'casting' as the company prefers to call it) in that only individuals with the right kind of basic appearance and apparent capacity to behave in a Disney way are hired. This means that in terms of the issues explored in the previous chapter, they are hired for their prospective capacity for emotional and aesthetic labour.

2. *Training and socialization* Disney recruits are trained in Disney traditions and are encouraged to appreciate the company's unique culture and to become committed to its distinctive ways of doing things (see Box 5.1, p. 108). Such control amounts to cultural control.[11]

3. *Rules and regulations* Disney employees are also given instruction in Disney rules and regulations. There is a substantial set of rules and regulations governing rides, the distribution of food, relating to guests, and so on.

4. *Scripts* Employees are given scripts from which to work when interacting with visitors. They may be able to depart from the scripts but only within certain limits, so that the amusing patter of the Jungle Cruise guides is rarely ad libbed or spontaneous, but has invariably had to be cleared before being used in practice. In addition, cast

members have to employ the distinctive Disney language when interacting with visitors (see Box 1.2, p. 11).

5. *Technology* Disney employees are frequently controlled by the technologies that Disney has introduced. This is particularly apparent with the rides that are programmed to run on a regular basis for a set period of time. This McDonaldized aspect of the work of the ride operator's job means that to a large extent the work is pre-programmed and controlled by the pace and frequency of the ride, much like an assembly line. Similar principles underlie the work in the many fast-food outlets that populate the parks.

In addition, the behaviour of Disney theme parks employees is controlled through *surveillance*, about which more will be said below. There is clearly a considerable range of types of control that affect theme park employees and the ride operators in particular. In spite of this array of mechanisms, control is not total in the Disney theme parks any more than it is anywhere else, as will be seen in the context of the discussion of resistance below.

Control over the immediate environment

The Disney theme parks are themselves tributes to the company's capacity to control land having created fantasy worlds out of orange groves (in Disneyland) and swamp land (in Disney World). Indeed, the company revels in its mastery over the natural order and celebrates such things as importing flora from all over the world to create the right kind of vista for its attractions, such as the Jungle Cruise in the Magic Kingdom's Adventureland and Disney World's Animal Kingdom. There is therefore an affinity between its treatment of control as a motif in such attractions as Living with the Land and its own approach to controlling nature for the massive construction projects that it initiates. A further aspect of such control is the way in which utilities such as water, electricity, and waste disposal are banished below ground into huge corridors.

Even more significant is that Disney seeks to control the immediate environment surrounding the parks. One of the most frequently quoted maxims that Walt came up with was 'I don't want the public to see the world they live in while they're in the park'. Most likely, he meant that he wanted Disneyland to be a fantasy land in which visitors were not reminded of the outside world and its many negative features (work, traffic, ugly buildings, and so on). Disneyland was built in a way that minimized the visual intrusion of the outside world while the visitor was in the park. When in 1963 Sheraton sought to build a 22-storey hotel that would have been visible from within Disneyland, the company successfully lobbied to get it reduced to 16 storeys and also for a new ordnance that prohibited tall buildings in the park's vicinity.

Walt was also deeply distressed by the fact that the approach to Disneyland became populated by a strip of tacky hotels and restaurants. He felt that these establishments undermined the kind of magical environment he was seeking to create in Anaheim. In addition, of course, the nearby presence of these establishments meant that they siphoned off business that could have gone to the park's restaurants and to the Disneyland Hotel. In order to buy the land for and to build Disneyland, Walt had had to go deeply into debt and had not been able to buy sufficient land that would allow the kind of sealing off of the park from its environment and therefore from the parasitic hotels and restaurants that began to surround it. For Disney World, he ensured that he could buy sufficient land so that the same kind of experience would not be repeated. As a result, when visitors enter Disney World, they have to drive for a long time before arriving at their destination (park or hotel) on winding and somewhat disorientating highways. This land has allowed the company to build four major theme parks, water parks, numerous hotels, a shopping and eating area, and so on. But also, it allowed the company to seal Disney World off from the visual intrusion of other establishments and to have access roads unsullied by freeloading hotels and restaurants (though there are, of course, plenty of both of these in Orlando, but much further removed from the parks than at Disneyland). Ironically, it was not until after 1984, when Michael Eisner and his team took over the running of Disney, that the number of hotels at Disney World began to grow substantially. However, the basic point is that in this and other ways, the Disney theme parks seek control over their immediate environment. One facet of this relates strongly to the next section, since the control over the Disney theme parks' own destiny has been crucial to their ability to have control over their immediate environment.

Control over its destiny

Following some of the difficulties that he experienced at Disneyland, when Walt and his company began negotiations with the Florida authorities over the location and financing of Disney World they sought to create a situation in which they had more or less total control over such things as building and the provision of security in their Magic Kingdom. They were in an outstanding bargaining position for extracting benefits from the relevant authorities, because of the huge influx of new jobs, commerce, tourists, and ultimately dollars that Disney World would bring. As a result, the Disney negotiators were able to secure huge tax concessions and to receive financial support for construction of roads leading to the resort.

However, the benefits that Disney managed to secure pale into insignificance compared to the innocently named Reedy Creek Improvement District (RCID), which effectively turned Disney World into a kind of self-governing principality within Florida (see Box 6.1), leading one writer to call it 'a sort of Vatican with Mouse ears'.[12] RCID gave Disney World control over its destiny in that the company was able to arrogate to itself total control over its dominion, and therefore freedom more or less in perpetuity from the restrictions that other companies face when seeking to build on their land. Disney uses the legislation surrounding RCID whenever it needs to in order to justify actions, particularly with regard to construction projects, which might otherwise have been prohibited under state or county laws.

Box 6.1 The Reedy Creek Improvement District

The Reedy Creek Improvement District (RCID) may sound innocuous but it is in fact a fundamental facet of Disney's control of its destiny, in terms of such things as building regulations and autonomy from local control in Disney World. RCID is based on legislation passed in May 1967 which essentially gave Disney more or less exclusive control over what it did within the District, which in spatial terms is more or less coterminous with Disney World. Shortly before his death in December 1966, Walt filmed a presentation in which he made a plea that his company 'must have the flexibility in Disney World to keep pace with tomorrow's world. We must have the freedom to work in co-operation with American industry, and to make decisions based on standards of performance' (quoted in Zehnder, 1975: 95). This film was shown to a meeting of local officials in February 1967. A news release based on the meeting reported that:

> one of the principal purposes of the District will be to permit the landowners to control the environment, planning and operations of the services and construction essential to the contemplated improvement and development of the property. (quoted in Zehnder, 1975: 89)

One of the chief justifications for the freedom that was being sought was that it would be essential for the construction of the community that Walt had planned would be built at Disney World. He called it the Experimental Prototype Community of Tomorrow which, in the years after his death, became transformed into Epcot, which was in fact a theme park rather than a community in which people lived. It was not until the 1990s that his original vision began to take shape – in the form of Celebration – but in a rather different form from that which he had originally contemplated.

The RCID conferred sovereignty upon Disney that allowed it to build and develop its land in a way that was not hampered by regulations and restrictions that normally impede developers. As Foglesong puts it, Disney:

> was authorized ... to regulate land use, provide police and fire services, build roads, lay sewer lines, license the manufacture and sale of alcoholic beverages, even to build an airport and nuclear power plant. ... To the envy of other developers, Disney also won immunity from building, zoning, and land-use regulations. Orange County officials cannot even send a building inspector to Disney property... (Foglesong, 2001: 5)

> As Foglesong observes, while Disney's ability to extract tax concessions and help with road building from the local authorities was remarkable, it is the private government that it was able to create that is truly astonishing. What is more, the agreements that formed the basis for the RCID are in perpetuity, giving the company exceptional freedom over its destiny in the area.
>
> Sources: Foglesong (2001); Zehnder (1975)

Moreover, RCID seems to have engendered a mindset at Disney that leads to a belief in its right to get around the restrictions that other developers face. An illustration of this relates to Celebration. In order to make way for a new phase of construction, Disney needed to fell 172 trees, most of which pre-date the birth of Chief Osceola after whom the county in which the trees were located was named. Environmental officials objected citing an ordnance that required approval for such an action and also required the developer to replace the felled trees. Disney officials claimed they had exemption because of clauses in the planning documents that the county had previously approved. According to a local planning officer, RCID is an important factor in Disney's thinking on such issues because it has become accustomed to the kind of control over its dominion that RCID bestows.[13]

Disney has not been able to secure the same level of control over its destiny at its other parks that it was able to obtain in Disney World. However, it has nonetheless been able to secure significant concessions. At Disneyland Paris, it has been able to secure first refusal on 10,000 acres of land surrounding the park. This concession prevents other hotels and developments, such as restaurants, from springing up in the park's environs, as they did in Disneyland in Anaheim.[14]

Control and Surveillance Beyond the Disney Theme Parks

In much the same way that the Disney theme parks are built upon a foundation of control and surveillance, Disneyization more generally is frequently accompanied by similar approaches, though rarely with the totalizing impact that Disney and its parks are able to establish. The impact is rarely as great because few companies have as much control over all aspects of the building and running of Disneyized sites. In this section, I will examine some of the ways in which control and surveillance occur in Disneyized settings.

Control is a widespread phenomenon that occurs in ways that may have nothing or little to do with Disneyization, as the brief discussion of McDonaldization at the beginning of this chapter implies. I will concentrate on aspects of control that relate to Disneyization and on surveillance as a mechanism underpinning these aspects. Giddens has observed that surveillance 'is fundamental to all types of organisation associated with the rise of modernity',[15] but what marks the discussion of surveillance in this chapter is its intensification in the furtherance of consumption. Consumption is at the heart of Disneyization and as such issues to do with control and surveillance are intimately connected to maximizing the visitor/consumer's ability and inclination to consume goods and services. This storyline underpins and provides the focus for the discussion that follows.

Control of the consumer

Disneyization entails control over our movement in that we have to be placed in the right contexts to enjoy our destiny – consuming. A great deal of planning goes into the mixes of hybrid consumption sites like malls, in order to provide the right blend of elements, so that they become destinations in their own right and therefore worth visiting, and to maximize our propensity to consume once there. The optimum elements are given a great deal of consideration so that as wide a range as possible of consumption forms will be chosen. As a Trafford Centre Information Pack, that was available on the internet at the time of the mall's opening, put it: 'Throughout the development, the emphasis will be on equalising footfall by careful considerations of layout, geometry, architecture and retail-mix.'[16] Hybrid consumption environments are designed to capitalize upon consumers' availing themselves of consumption opportunities they had not envisaged until after their arrival, as much of the discussion in Chapter 3 sought to show. In addition to controlling movement through layout in the way alluded to by the Trafford Centre pack, music is frequently employed to affect movement. For example, the background music in the hallways in the Mall of America is designed to convey a sense of movement to discourage lingering or loitering and to encourage movement towards the Mall's consumption opportunities.[17]

Theming adds a further level of control by manipulating our gaze. It does so through the mechanism of adjacent attraction outlined in Chapter 2, but it also does so through the change in the way in which we may perceive themed environments. Such environments are meant to create a form of playfulness. In a study of visitors to the Disney theme parks, it was striking that most of those interviewed adopted a predominantly ludic response to their experience of the parks.[18] They were rarely critical, even of the blatant attempts to entice them to purchase merchandise and other items of consumption. It was almost as though people suspended their critical abilities and standards of decision-making when they became absorbed in Disney's themed settings. People felt pulled along and wrapped up in the fun of the place and seemed surprised if not perplexed when probed about possible negative reactions to the partial nature of the messages in many attractions or to the commercialism of the parks. Even among sceptical visitors to Disney theme parks, a similarly uncritical response is not uncommon. Buckingham quotes a British visitor:

> I enjoyed Disneyland in Paris. Against all my better judgement, I really enjoyed it. I went with a party of school kids – 10 kids – and I really expected to hate it. ... I went with all those assumptions of 'Disney, bloody Disney' – Americanization of culture, modulization of culture, all that. But it was really fun. I had a lovely time. I had a really, really good time.[19]

Predominantly ludic responses among visitors to the Disney theme parks, such as those emphasizing fun, have been described as uninteresting[20] but they are in fact indicative of the kind of uncritical reception that themed environments are capable of creating. These findings are consistent with those relating to the reception of Disney products more generally. Wasko summarizes findings from the Global Disney Audiences Project (see Box 3.1, p. 69) as follows: 'People's similar understandings of Disney suggest that there is relatively little room for active or alternative readings of texts, like Disney's, which are carefully coded and controlled, and not polysemic and open.'[21]

Consequently, theming in malls, restaurants, shops, and so on is often likely to be introduced in order to create a more playful reaction on the part of the consumer and in tandem a greater willingness to spend more than might otherwise have been the case. Shields, for example, has argued that malls like the West Edmonton Mall in Canada differ from what he calls 'conventional convenience-oriented malls' because the emphasis on theming and play 'places it outside the realm of the mundane and the quotidian. It promises a fulfilling fantasy and consumption experience as a break from the humdrum of everyday life'.[22] This sense of a different kind of environment, which mixes consumption with play, is the kind of context where the ludic response uncovered in the research on visitors to Disney theme parks is likely to be found. Hybrid consumption sites, like West Edmonton Mall, underscore the process by fusing shopping with activities that are more or less exclusively associated with leisure (cinemas, bowling alleys, theme park attractions, ice skating, and so on). Even the normally more cynical journalists can take this view, as the following remark in connection with MetroCentre in Gateshead and its Metroland amusement park shows:

> Campaigners weep for dying high-street shops. ... The malls are more fun. They remind me of the old Fun Palace at Blackpool pleasure beach. Coming in from the bus station at MetroCentre, you reach Metroland. A friendly dragon floats above the entrance. You can buy a day ticket for your children. A roller coaster whooshes overhead. A ferris wheel turns. The toy train ride clangs its bell without ceasing. The din is all very satisfactory.[23]

At the Girl Heaven chain of shops for young girls, there is an explicit organizational ethos of 'having fun' that staff are expected to personify.[24] The designer of the Girl Heaven concept has written:

customers are no longer willing to accept that the shops they visit are just places to buy goods. They demand drama and deserve to be delighted by the experience. Shops have become destinations in themselves – not only a place to purchase, but a place to be entertained, inspired and, in the case of Girl Heaven, to have loads of fun.[25]

Of course, consumers are not necessarily (and indeed are unlikely to be) duped by the machinations of theming and are frequently possessed of an ample store of *virtual capital*, that is, a stock of knowledge and images assembled by the individual from sources like television, film and advertising, plus a capacity for playful responses to mediated and simulated images.[26] On the other hand, the playful responses that themed environments entail may sometimes result in consumers dropping their normally judicious guards.

There are other common ways in which control is exercised in and through Disneyization. The growth of merchandising has resulted in a growing tendency for the souvenir to be thought of as something that bears a logo, whereas in non-Disneyized environments of the past and today, it was something that served as a memento of a visit. All souvenirs, especially those which are mass-produced, commodify memories, but the merchandise form takes the process even further in associating what constitutes a souvenir with corporations and their logos. Disneyization also controls our perceptions of places by plundering popular culture for images of what a place is like. For example, when the previously-mentioned Trafford Centre Information Pack refers to the mall's 'unique restaurant and leisure environment with themed areas from around the world including China, New Orleans, Egypt, Venice, New York and Morocco'[27] what it actually means is that it uses iconic representations of these places that are part of popular culture and recycles them back to us. Similarly, as was noted in the discussion in Chapter 2 of the theming of places, the publicity surrounding tourist destinations increasingly themes places in terms that will be recognizable and attractive to prospective visitors and as a result controls our perceptions of those places. Often, because of the inability of the tourist to enter the back regions of such destinations,[28] the visitor's perception of the place in terms of the themed features is unaffected by contact with it. Consequently, in a variety of ways, Disneyization controls (or at least has the potential to control) our perceptions of places and souvenirs. In addition, of course, control relates to merchandising in that consumers have to be placed in the right context for purchasing it, so movement is controlled in theme parks, museums, art galleries, themed restaurants, and so on to maximize the propensity to purchase such items.

New Urbanism towns emphasize control in at least two senses. One is that they derive from a master plan of social engineering, which is based on principles to do with restoring a sense of community and separating Americans from their automobiles. Second, in order to ensure that the town has a distinctive style, there are usually strict building codes that restrict the range of options within which housing designs can vary. This feature is taken to the extreme in Celebration where housing styles, colours, curtain styles, height of front hedges and fences, and the types of shrubs that could be planted are regulated.[29]

Control is similarly a requirement of tourist enclaves of the kind discussed in Chapters 2 and 3, such as festival marketplaces. In New York's Times Square, we see control in the form of a gradual cleaning up of the area, whereby the drugs pushers and fleshpots that previously had made it an unsafe area (or at least made it appear to be so), and of the creation of a safer environment with a mixture of shopping and shows which would not get in the way of consumption. Not all New Yorkers see this as a positive development and many rail against its sanitization but the links between control, safety and consumption are unmistakable.

The case of Celebration brings out an important consideration in connection with issues of control, namely, that those subject to it do not necessarily perceive it to be a bad thing. Indeed, they may even derive reassurance from being controlled. Frantz and Collins show that many Celebration residents bought into the ideals that the town offered and that there was a feeling that if anyone could deliver and implement them it was Disney.[30] Precisely because of Disney's legendary preoccupation with control, prospective residents know what kind of regime they would be confronted with in order for New Urbanist values to be realized and viewed it as an acceptable cost (if indeed it was seen as such) if those values were to be realized. A similar point is sometimes made about visitors to the Disney theme parks who often relish the control exercised by Disney because it enhances the predictability of the theme park experience and because it obviates the need for parents to worry about issues that confront them in the outside world, such as whether the children will enjoy the holiday, whether they will be in danger from vehicles or other hazards. While risks are dangled in front of visitors as lures (simulated dangers on rides or other attractions), they are 'safe risks'[31] or 'riskless risks'.[32] It is the very aura of control and safety that makes Disney theme park holidays attractive to parents.

Surveillance of the consumer

Surveillance in order to facilitate and to ensure that nothing gets in the way of consumption is widespread. It is particularly prevalent in shopping malls where it takes the form of both surveillance of and for consumers, though in practice the two are not easy to distinguish. As one writer puts it:

> Outside of Disney World, there is no better example than the mall of the wholesale use of architecture and decor as a means of promoting consumption – in an environment where there is probably more surveillance per square inch (both technological and human) than in any of today's underfunded public prisons.[33]

Surveillance of consumers obviously occurs to identify crimes such as shoplifting but it is also carried out to ensure that undesirable elements are kept out or if they gain entry, are not allowed to proceed further. The homeless and others who may be a source of concern to shoppers, such as groups of rowdy teenagers, are likely to be evicted, if indeed they have succeeded in gaining entry. At the same time, surveillance is also often regarded as *for* consumers, since its prevalence in the obtrusive form of security guards and CCTV (closed-circuit television) cameras is widely regarded as creating a sense of security and safety. Creating such a feeling of security is typically viewed as desirable since it allays consumers' anxieties so that they can proceed unhindered with their consumption projects. The CCTV system at the MetroCentre, for example, was designed 'to protect the landlord's investment and the safety of shoppers'.[34]

Certain groups are particularly likely to be watched by security guards in shopping malls. Security personnel are believed often to harass teenagers.[35] Ethnic minority teenagers are believed to be particularly likely to be trailed by guards.[36] This tendency was found in a study of two London shopping centres, even though one of the shopping centres (Wood Green) has a high proportion of black and working-class consumers.[37] Hybrid consumption sites like malls, amusement arcades and similar leisure outlets of interest to teenagers tend to be placed on the periphery so that they minimize the potential for overspill into the main shopping areas, pointing to a further way in which control of movement underpins such settings.[38] Some managers of malls have even attempted to control the hours that teenagers are allowed to shop without adult supervision.

A *Times* journalist has described Canary Wharf – a hybrid consumption site in London with offices, apartments, health clubs, restaurants, and shops – as like a gated community where the private security guards check all arriving vehicles. He goes on to write: 'Naturally, it is covered by a rash of CCTV cameras, making sure people are doing what they're supposed to be doing, going to work, leaving work, spending money'.[39] The various security precautions malls introduce are meant to create a sense of personal safety so that people can visit and consume in a place that is free of the worries that many see as present in city centre shopping areas. On the anniversary of the 10th birthday of the MetroCentre in Gateshead, one journalist reflecting on this and other British malls at the time (such as Meadowhall near Sheffield, Merry Hill near Dudley, and Lakeside in Essex) wrote:

> Enclosed and video-scrutinised, the new centres make people, especially women, feel safe. Shoppers and browsers walk down the arcades of Lakeside or MetroCentre with happy smiles on their faces. They have dressed up to come. There are no panhandlers, no alkies, no sad folk peeing on the street. Women don't need to carry their shoulder bags across their chest. American malls started the fashion for glass-sided crawler lifts, not because of the view out, but because of the view in. Rape is unlikely in a glass elevator.[40]

The mall's surveillance practices are thus widely viewed as offering the consumer a security that contrasts with the perception of the city centre as a risky shopping venue. Whether these perceptions, which malls are to a large extent complicit in promoting, are based in fact is a moot point. For example, in spite of its exclusion policies and surveillance systems, West Edmonton Mall is the setting for a surprising variety and number of criminal activities and various other disturbances.[41] Wooden has shown that crimes of various kinds are quite rife in North American malls: one upscale Florida mall reported in a two-year period in the late 1980s, 10 sex offences, 176 assaults, 64 hold-ups, 597 burglaries, 445 stolen cars, and round 2,000 larcenies, including shoplifting.[42] However, it is the *perception* that malls are safe venues that has led to the declining patronage of many city centres for shopping and other leisure activities. Moreover, it may be that the more Disneyized a mall or leisure complex is in terms of having theming, hybrid consumption, and similar dimensions of Disneyization, the safer the consumer feels because of the more ludic ambience that is created, especially when surveillance systems are clearly in evidence.

Shopping in large Disneyized malls is by no means the only way in which Disneyization is underpinned by surveillance. Tourist enclaves are frequently the focus of such systems, with the concomitant tendency for undesirables to be evicted. For example, homeless young people are tracked and evicted from the sidewalks of Victoria, British Columbia. The rationale for this activity is that the city is 'a tourist town with "Olde English" charm, a Scottish castle and a replica of Anne Hathaway's cottage'.[43] Not only do such undesirables undermine the charm, they might also prevent tourists from lingering and therefore spending money. Tourist enclaves like this tend to be subject to surveillance for these kinds of reasons. Indeed, one of the main ways that large cities have been able to entice tourists and often locals is to create such enclaves through redevelopment, as in New York's Times Square, or festival marketplace areas (see Chapter 3), like Faneuil Hall Marketplace in Boston[44] or Baltimore's Harborplace.[45] Surveillance is a marked feature of such tourist enclaves so that the perceived threats of the wider city can be kept at bay and affluent tourists and locals can be enticed back into cities for shopping, restaurants and other leisure activities.

Surveillance of the worker

In Chapter 5, a major element in the narrative was the importance of the frontline worker to the success of service companies, and in particular of the worker conforming to behavioural norms of emotional labour and to the appearance and style norms of aesthetic labour. While companies were described as going to great lengths to control the worker, most notably through training, rules and regulations and inculcating organizational commitment, surveillance forms a further element in their arsenal of methods to secure conformity with required modes of behaviour and style.

Surveillance of Disney theme parks employees

Just like the security guard dealing with a transgression by Clifford Shearing and his daughter (see above), security personnel also prowl the parks to check on the behaviour of cast members. This means that theme park employees are being watched to ensure that they follow rules and procedures properly and that they exhibit emotional labour in the expected way and to the correct degree. Any departures from appearance norms are also checked. Supervisors may be in uniform or dressed as tourists.[46] In addition, Disney uses 'shoppers', that is, employees who are dressed as tourists and interact with cast members in order to provoke them into a non-Disney response and then report (i.e. 'shop') them. One Disney cast member is quoted by Kuenz as follows:

> I was shopped one day. She gave me a good report because I'm always friendly to people. I had no idea who she was and still don't know. They come in. They buy two or three things, Disney gives them the money.[47]

The effect of such a form of surveillance, which is clearly known about among Disney staff, is that all visitors become potential 'shoppers'. Cast members must be on their toes, since the irritating guest who is being difficult in a restaurant at its busiest time could be trying to provoke them into an inappropriate response. The implications for failing to live up to Disney standards of service delivery are clear. According to the Disney Institute: 'Fulfilling the performance guidelines is a condition of employment at Walt Disney World. Cast members who do not use them are subject to progressive disciplinary actions.'[48]

Surveillance of frontline service workers

Frontline service workers generally are frequently subject to surveillance to ensure that service norms are followed. There are four major forms of surveillance. First, and most obviously, managers and supervisors check on the behaviour of service workers. For example, the behaviour of supermarket checkout staff is often monitored. Ogbonna and Wilkinson found that the staff were regularly monitored by checkout supervisors. A supervisor at one British supermarket company told the researchers: 'We are able to detect when a checkout operator is not smiling or even when she is putting on a false smile ... we call her into a room and have a chat with her.'[49]

A second form of surveillance is by mystery shoppers, that is, 'customers' who are hired by the company to check on the behaviour of its staff. They are like the Disney 'shoppers' referred to in the previous section. At the Californian supermarket chain studied by Tolich, 'company spotters' were employed to check on how far the checkout staff conformed to a list of required features of the transaction, including appearance and 'a pleasant greeting' and 'a pleasant and sincere thank you'.[50] Similarly, in the British context, according to Ogbonna and Wilkinson: 'Random visits by bogus shoppers and head office managements reinforce the threat of sanctions for undesirable behaviour or expressing one's true feelings to difficult customers'.[51] In April and May 2003, the British supermarket chain, Sainsbury's, printed the following message on one side of its plastic bags:

'our mystery shoppers regularly check the quality of our products and service of our staff' and on the other side 'are you standing next to one? our mystery shoppers ensure you're getting the best...' (ellipsis in original). The use of bogus shoppers would appear to be quite widespread. When Fuller and Smith conducted their research into 15 organizations in three metropolitan areas in the USA, only two did not use this surveillance strategy and both of them were hospitals.[52] Two companies actually wired the bogus shoppers so that the transactions could be heard via a microphone.

A third approach is to enlist real customers in the surveillance of frontline workers. While ostensibly to do with customer feedback, this approach turns all customers into supervisors. In Fuller and Smith's research, the feedback was frequently concerned to identify how well the individual who served the customer performed but with some firms it was at a more general level.[53] Some of the feedback questions that the researchers present as examples of the kinds of questions asked were very much to do with issues that were the focus of the previous chapter, such as whether the employee greeted the customer graciously, the nature of the employee's appearance, and whether the employee was cheerful. Feedback about particular employees would often be entered into their files to form a part of subsequent performance appraisals. Negative feedback also often resulted in discussions with management and formed the springboard for the first stages of disciplinary action. The use of customers in this way is consistent with the customer is king philosophy that is the *raison d'être* of many service organizations, but it extends the mystery shopper approach to surveillance into a context in which frontline service workers are increasingly governed by their customers as much as by their managers and supervisors.

The fourth approach is to use hardware in the monitoring of service workers. Call centre workers have been identified as especially affected by this form of surveillance. Precisely because their work is conducted by telephone and can therefore be easily monitored, it is particularly easy for managements to deploy technology as a means of surveillance. Even two researchers who argued that forms of resistance to control in call centres should not be overestimated conceded that:

> workers' output and performance can potentially be measured and monitored to an unprecedented degree. Additionally, workers may have the expression and intonation of their speech assessed according to a range of subjective criteria. This performance of emotional labour contributes further to the intensity of the work.[54]

Indeed, customers who telephone call centres are often forewarned that the call may be monitored for 'training' or other purposes. A firm studied by Bain and Taylor, which was briefly described in the previous chapter, also used mystery shopper surveillance.[55] In the firm studied by Callaghan and Thompson (2002), monitoring of calls was undertaken by a 'Research Department' which carried out random checks and also responded to customer complaints.[56] In addition, team leaders listened to calls. The main focus of monitoring was on reducing the amount of time an employee spent on calls if his or her typical time was above average. This suggests that many call centre staff are caught between a rock and a hard place, in that they must exhibit the correct approach in terms of emotional labour but not take too long over it. The fact that they are increasingly required not to be slaves to scripts but to be themselves and vary their approach to dealing with customers means that a further dilemma is built into their work in connection with its surveillance.[57]

A further way in which hardware can be employed for monitoring of service workers is through CCTV. This hardware is usually installed in order to detect shoplifters and other external miscreants but is frequently also introduced to watch staff. Pilferage is one reason for watching staff but some firms extend this watching brief to include the monitoring of customer service. This is an example of the 'leaky container' phenomenon, whereby surveillance used for one purpose is gradually extended to include other goals and targets.[58] A study of the use of CCTV in firms in a northern British town found that in the retail stores that were in the sample, this hardware was often employed to scrutinize customer service standards among staff. One security manager in a store claimed that he found CCTV useful for ensuring 'that the staff are being polite, friendly and are smiling'.[59] At another retailer, the researchers were told that it was used to check on 'customer care': 'It's how you are with the customer. You know, your eye contact and things like that.'[60]

The four different forms of surveillance sometimes overlap, for example, when bogus shoppers are captured on CCTV in interaction with a targeted service worker. However, they are analytically distinct and point to a powerful armoury of methods at the disposal of service firms.

Resistance

As I signalled at the outset of this chapter, it is important not to generate an unduly deterministic account of the significance of control and surveillance under Disneyization. Both customers and workers can hit back if they so choose, perhaps sometimes unconsciously. The examples that I provide are ones that occur during what might be thought of as the micropolitics of interaction, but resistance is also possible at a more macropolitical level. The case of the failure of the Disney's America theme park to get off the ground, in spite of the company's continued protestations that it would not back down (see Chapter 1), is an illustration of the way in which Disneyization – in the form of its tendency both to bring nature to heel and to provide a bowdlerized version of history – can be resisted.

A similar macropolitical example relates to McDonald's which, insofar as it is a Disneyized organization as I have tried to argue in the relevant sections in Chapters 2 to 5, serves as a further example of resistance to Disneyization. This example relates to the building in 1994 of a McDonald's at what is known as 'Golani Junction' in Israel. Like the case of Disney's America, the building was close to hallowed ground, namely, the site of a ferocious battle in 1948 and which also attracted around 60,000 visitors per year. Unlike the case of Disney's America, the McDonald's was constructed and the controversy raged after it had been built (whereas Disney's America was not built), so that the representatives of the bereaved were dealing with a *fait accompli*.[61] McDonald's were persuaded to carry out some changes, such as making the signs less obtrusive, installing filters to reduce smells, closing the restaurant when memorial ceremonies were taking place at the site, and planting trees so that visitors did not have direct eye contact with the outlet. A further example of resistance to Disneyization at a macropolitical level can be seen in the case of the attempt to 'Disneyfy' Seattle's civic centre, which was referred to in Chapter 1. In this case, 'Seattle residents in the end were able to appropriate what they liked from the Disney city and discard what they did not like through political channels.'[62]

Resistance at the Disney theme parks

Visitor resistance

Resistance is not easy for visitors at Disney theme parks. For one thing, outright resistance will often result in censure, not just from security guards, but also from fellow guests who have come to the happiest place on Earth to have a good time à la Disney. Kuenz has written: 'It's easy to spot those who come to Disney World just to make a point of their alienation from it. There aren't many but they are there.'[63] The fact there 'aren't many' suggests that Disney have successfully persuaded most of us that if you go to Disney theme parks you go there to have a good time. Those who are truly alienated simply do not go or do not go again. One way of expressing Disney disdain, according to Willis is to wear merchandise associated with Disney villains,[64] although since it involves the purchase of precisely what is scorned, as a form of resistance it is more symbolic than practical. Moreover, those visitors who resist Disney instructions, for example, when being loaded onto rides risk getting their comeuppance through informal retribution from ride operators, about which more will be said below. One form of resistance to the barrage of ways of making the guest conform occurs in attractions in theatres, such as *Honey, I Shrunk the Audience*, a 3-D film with special effects. Visitors are always being instructed to 'move *aaaaaaall* the way down the row'. Of course, some ignore the pleas and sit wherever they want. Even then there is a Disney response to resistance – a Disney cast member will give permission for guests to trample over them.[65] Interestingly, in Disneyland Paris, where such attractions are more chaotic than in the US, no such instructions are given.

One form of resistance to control over the visitor's movement is to use one of the unofficial guides to the Disney theme parks as a means of circumventing the directions that are implied by Disney landscaping in order to avoid long lines. However, this is a strategy that is doomed to failure since the advice is widely available and often accessible on the internet, resulting in large numbers of visitors employing precisely the same tactics and still ending up in long lines.

There are also unsavoury forms of resistance. Characters in costumes are often attacked. For example:

> the wolf from *Pinocchio* was strolling through the park when a group of teenage girls asked him to pose for a picture. They carefully positioned him, with a nearby wall as a backdrop, a girl under each arm and two kneeling in front of him. The camerawoman announced, 'Ready … set …' But just as she was about to snap the photo, the girls at the wolf's sides swung around and pinned his arms against the wall and the other two reached up and fondled him. Then she quickly took the shot.[66]

One wonders whether the girls had thought about the gender of the inhabitant of the costume. In addition, Snow White's breasts are sometimes fondled,[67] as are Minnie Mouse's, while two Snow Whites have reportedly been raped.[68] In Disneyland Paris, there have been reports of children attacking costumed characters.[69] In Disneyland, Plutos frequently get bloody noses as a result of being punched by children[70] and a Brer Bear has been stabbed.[71]

In addition, consumption of drugs and alcohol among teenagers and young adults is occasionally encountered,[72] while occasional queue jumping sometimes occurs too. Whether these various infractions of Disney rules and the law represent resistance to Disney as such is open to debate but together they point to a variety of ways in which resistance by visitors is not only possible but occurs with some frequency. Disney control of them is not total.

Worker resistance

Worker resistance in the Disney theme parks can take several different forms which to a certain extent are affected by the kind of job under consideration. One response is to 'switch off'. According to Van Maanen, when feeling too tired to smile but still having to, ride operators simply switch off.[73] Various names are given to this sensation: automatic pilot; going robot; can't feel a thing; lapse into a dream; go into a trance; checking out. He describes these as passive forms of resistance – ways of preserving an element of individuality and of retaining self-respect. However, more active forms of resistance are also in evidence. One is to become difficult or overbearingly polite. The latter essentially entails exaggerating emotional labour with the clear implication that the worker clearly does not mean it. As an example of the latter, a cast member may respond to a difficult visitor by saying in an exaggeratedly Disney voice 'It's been our pleasure to serve you.'[74]

A good example of being difficult while simultaneously not transgressing Disney rules or ways of doing things is the following remark from a cast member:

> We have to smile at a guest no matter what he does. It's really a way of controlling what you're really feeling. That smile has to be there. But it's also the one way we can fight back. For instance, if someone's really snotty with a credit card you can take all the time in the world because their signature doesn't match. 'Oh, gee, I'm going to have to see some kind of ID.' You know.[75]

More outright forms of resistance occur when cast members take direct action against visitors for their misbehaviour. Van Maanen lists several forms of retribution meted out by ride operators:

- the seatbelt squeeze – tightening a seatbelt excessively;
- the seatbelt slap – the seatbelt is used to give the rider a sharp slap;
- the break-up-the-party gambit – members of a party are separated at the last moment so that they ride on different cars;
- the hatch-cover ploy – used by submarine pilots (this attraction no longer exists) to ensure difficult visitors are drenched when they travel under a waterfall;
- the-sorry-I-didn't-see-your-hand (foot, finger, arm, leg, etc.) tactic – 'bringing a piece of Disney property to bear on the appendage'.[76]

At Disneyland Paris, worker resistance seems in large part to have been a resistance to conforming to Disney ideals:

> Some employees delighted in refusing, in subtle – or not so subtle – ways, to become 'Disneyfied'. One French cast member bragged about exacting revenge on 'demanding' guests by cutting off their heads in group photographs he was asked to take. Others, stationed outside attractions as 'greeters', capitalized on the confused expectations of visitors by charging an entrance fee of 20 francs … before admitting them.[77]

In fact, a further aspect of worker resistance at Disneyland Paris is in the sense that it is often remarked that many of its cast members distance themselves from the Disney style of service delivery. Lainsbury quotes an American journalist at the park's opening weekend: 'They are acting like real people instead of "Disney" people'.[78] Similarly, an American journalist commented positively in connection with a visit to the park in 2001 that staff at his hotel were 'cheerful' rather than 'cloying'.[79] It is very clear then that resistance to control at the Disney theme parks is possible, though its prevalence and significance are difficult to gauge from the anecdotes that various authorities provide. The key point, however, would seem to be that, as with resistance among visitors, control at the Disney theme parks is not total.

Resistance to Disneyization

As with resistance at the Disney theme parks, it is useful to distinguish between visitor (or in this case *consumer*) and worker resistance.

Consumer resistance

In a sense, consumer resistance is an odd notion in this connection because to a very large extent Disneyization is underpinned by a philosophy of the customer is king, so customers have a lot to gain from many aspects of Disneyization. Therefore, it is not obvious what their resistance might be *against*, although it could be that they sometimes rail against the sense of being manipulated by malls and other Disneyized forms into spending more time and money than they had originally intended. Nonetheless, it is occasionally found and the shopping mall again provides some useful pointers to its existence.

Because security staff frequently target groups of teenagers for surveillance, young people visiting malls have responded by tactics to make them appear legitimate. At West Edmonton Mall in the 1980s, young people had to avoid clothing that might have attracted the unwanted interest of security guards who were an ingredient of the Mall's strategy of ensuring that only those who are fully able to participate in consumption – basically the middle class and the wealthier working-class strata – were present so that they were not distracted by concerns about personal safety or otherwise made to feel uneasy.[80] Accordingly, clothing that might have led to eviction had to be substituted with more conservative garb. At Mall of America, Goss writes that in spite of the transparent operation of surveillance, he witnessed the 'problems of unchaperoned teenagers, disrupting tenants and shoppers and being disrespectful to security guards'.[81]

In addition, Shields observes that loitering is discouraged in the West Edmonton Mall so that young people, as well as others who might otherwise be a focus for security, must always appear as though they are about to buy and so need to be on the move.[82] This kind of slow-moving idling away of time is not restricted to teenagers seeking to avoid the watchful eye of security personnel. Visiting the mall to while away time, often with little intention of buying anything, is a not uncommon activity to which several commentators on malls have drawn attention[83] and is itself indicative of resistance to the aspirations of malls and their designers. Moreover, the fact that it is possible to distinguish several distinct categories of shopper in malls strongly implies that shoppers are capable of putting malls to a variety of uses and therefore to resist, at least to some degree, the designers' ploys. A study of mall visitors distinguished four types of shopper – mall enthusiasts, traditionalists, grazers and minimalists – on a declining scale of participation in mall activities, in particular shopping.[84] The grazers, for example, tended to browse but are susceptible to impulse buying. This classification of types of mall visitor implies that some groups succeed in resisting the malls' attempts to seduce them to buy. These various indications of resistance imply that control and surveillance in consumption venues like malls are rarely total in their effects.

Worker resistance

Like Disney theme park employees, resistance among frontline service employees can take a relatively passive form of trying to distance themselves from the task of or the person performing emotional labour. This frequently involves surface acting when deep acting is encouraged, if not required. This process of distancing can be seen in the words of one of the customer service representatives at a call centre:

> My way of handling it is coming in and saying to myself, 'I do this shift from 2 to 10, it's not a career, it's a job. I answer the phone and that's it'. By not looking for anything more than that, that's my way of handling it. When I first came in, I thought it was maybe just me, but speaking to other people it's the same.[85]

Such strategies allow workers to establish some distance between the roles they have to play and their true selves.

More active forms of resistance exist too. Leidner notes that at the McDonald's where she conducted her research she encountered some employees who would not smile and others who did not include in their scripted interactions those portions that they felt frequently annoyed customers.[86] Among the insurance agents she studied, there were those who also omitted parts of scripts that they disliked. At one large American hotel, the introduction of a mystery shopper system resulted in a 'smile strike'.[87] An almost opposite form of resistance is described by a coffee shop waitress in Harford, Connecticut, who claimed to adopt the tactic of dealing with customers who were acting as though they were superior by becoming overbearingly polite: 'Treat them overly politely, without being too obnoxious ... give them a big, big smile ... they know you're play acting but can't really say anything because you're being nice.'[88] A waitress in an upmarket restaurant in the same area claimed that she reacted to diners who treated her badly by displaying an exaggerated deference.

One less obvious form of resistance that is related to emotional labour is the display of philanthropic emotional labour, which was referred to in the previous chapter.[89] Sometimes such emotional labour is not a form of resistance because it is consistent with management imperatives, even if it goes somewhat beyond them. In some contexts, however, it can be depicted as a form of resistance. At the call centre studied by Callaghan and Thompson, where there was a management preoccupation with the duration of the average call, customer service representatives would sometimes go beyond the emotional labour demands the company made of them. This tendency was particularly apparent in interaction with older people and with regular customers, who frequently called for a friendly chat.[90]

Conclusion

In this chapter, I have demonstrated that control and surveillance are central to Disneyization and not just to McDonaldization. Control is a key feature of the

Disney theme parks in a variety of ways: in the way in which the behaviour, imagination and experience of visitors are controlled; as a recurring motif; in terms of control over the behaviour of employees; and in its control over its own destiny. These facets of control are not found in other Disneyized institutions to the same degree, but that is not to say that control is unimportant in them. Control is crucial to consumption because prospective consumers have to be placed in positions that are likely to maximize their inclination to consume, so it is not surprising that one of the chief contexts within which control in relation to Disneyization was discussed in this chapter was the shopping mall. This is also a major site for surveillance which is designed to ensure that consumers feel safe and that undesirable elements are kept out as far as possible. Under Disneyization, service workers too are controlled in ways that are common to most jobs – that is, control involves a mixture of technical, supervisory, bureaucratic and cultural approaches – but in addition they are frequently subject to surveillance to ensure that they conform to the customer service norms that are so important to service sector firms.

However, resistance is also possible and there has been a discussion of forms of resistance that are specific responses to the demands of Disneyized work, that is, work that requires the service worker to engage with customers in a warm and accommodating manner. In addition, consumers sometimes resist the implied requirements of being in a mall. That such forms of resistance exist provides an important corrective to any implication of excessive determinism that might be inferred from an emphasis on control but it also represents a less pessimistic standpoint.

Control and surveillance have been presented as enabling factors. They help Disneyization to be realized rather than being a dimension of it. They are a means of smoothing the progress of the four dimensions outlined in the previous four chapters. Moreover, when dealing with control over service workers, I have been less interested in covering the whole gamut of approaches, most of which have been addressed in the concept of McDonaldization.[91] Instead, I have been concerned with aspects of the control of employees that are directly relevant to Disneyization, namely, the requirement to display emotional labour and the growing use of procedures to check on whether service employees conform to this requirement. Disneyization needs control and surveillance to operate effectively, which means that they are required to enhance the capacity and propensity of consumers to spend.

Notes

1 Ritzer (1993).
2 Bryman (1995: 123–4, 1999a).
3 Bryman (1995: 99–117); Wasko (2001: 166–70).
4 Shearing and Stenning (1984: 345).
5 Hiaasen (1998: 35).
6 Quoted in Raz (1999: 188).
7 Walt used this term to refer to visual lures that enticed the visitor in a certain direction.
8 Sayers (1965).
9 Bryman (1995: 105).

10 Beardsworth and Bryman (2001).
11 Van Maanen and Kunda (1989).
12 Foglesong (2001: 5).
13 Frantz and Collins (1999: 230).
14 Lainsbury (2000: 31).
15 Giddens (1990: 59).
16 Trafford Centre Information Pack, p. 6.
17 Sterne (1997).
18 Bryman (1999b).
19 Quoted in Buckingham (2001: 289).
20 Willis (1995a: 1).
21 Wasko (2001: 218).
22 Shields (1989: 158).
23 Barker (1996: 3).
24 Russell and Tyler (2002: 627).
25 Quoted in Russell and Tyler (2002: 628).
26 Beardsworth and Bryman (2001).
27 Trafford Centre Information Pack, p. 6.
28 MacCannell (1976).
29 Frantz and Collins (1999); Ross (1999).
30 Frantz and Collins (1999).
31 Gephart (2001).
32 Hubbard (2002).
33 Willis (1995b: 181).
34 Graham (1998: 97).
35 Goss (1993); Shields (1989).
36 Goss (1993); Sterne (1997).
37 Miller et al. (1998).
38 Goss (1993).
39 Dyckhoff (2003: 17).
40 Barker (1996: 3).
41 Hopkins (1990: 14).
42 Wooden (1995).
43 Lyon (2001: 59).
44 Fainstein and Judd (1999).
45 Judd (1999).
46 Van Maanen (1991).
47 Quoted in Kuenz (1995a: 124).
48 Disney Institute (2001: 87).
49 Quoted in Ogbonna and Wilkinson (1990: 11). Note the assumption here that the smiling checkout operator is always female.
50 Tolich (1993: 367).
51 Ogbonna and Wilkinson (1990: 13).
52 Fuller and Smith (1991).
53 Fuller and Smith (1991).
54 Bain and Taylor (2000: 17).
55 Bain and Taylor (2000).
56 Callaghan and Thompson (2002).
57 Frenkel et al. (1999).
58 Lyon (2001).
59 Quoted in McCahill and Norris (1999: 220–1).
60 Quoted in McCahill and Norris (1999: 221).
61 Azaryahu (1999).
62 Warren (1994: 105).
63 Kuenz (1995b: 57).
64 Willis (1995b: 191).
65 Bryman (1999a).
66 Koenig (1994: 102).
67 Letts (1996).
68 Warren (1996).
69 Burchill (1998).
70 Koenig (1994: 103).
71 Koenig (1999: 141).
72 Koenig (1999: 109, 135).
73 Van Maanen (1991).
74 Kuenz (1995a: 153).
75 Kuenz (1995a: 152–3).
76 Van Maanen (1991: 72)).
77 Lainsbury (2000: 106–7).
78 Quoted in Lainsbury (2000: 106).
79 Margolis (2001).
80 Shields (1989).
81 Goss (1999: 67).
82 Shields (1989).
83 For example, Goss (1993); Langman (1992).
84 Bloch et al. (1994).
85 Quoted in Callaghan and Thompson (2002: 249).
86 Leidner (1999: 91).
87 Fuller and Smith (1991: 12).
88 Quoted in Hall (1993: 463).
89 Bolton (2000).
90 Callaghan and Thompson (2002: 249–50).
91 Ritzer (1993).

Chapter Seven

Implications of Disneyization

Mini Contents

In this chapter, I reflect on some of the broader ramifications of Disneyization. The discussion entails spelling out some issues and themes that have been implicit in the book thus far. Two areas of particular concern in this chapter are the interconnections between Disneyization and both consumption and globalization. The latter two concepts are themselves connected, of course, since globalization is frequently motivated by pressures to spread the canon of consumerism and to provide an infrastructure for it, along with the goods and services themselves. As noted in earlier chapters, consumption lies at the heart of Disneyization and will therefore be a recurring motif in these final reflections. Consumption provides the rationale and context for the mechanisms of Disneyization that have been explored.

The affinity with consumption is a feature that Disneyization shares with McDonaldization.[1] Like McDonaldization, Disneyization is a large-scale social process that is made up of a number of analytically separate components. Some institutions may be described as *both* Disneyized and McDonaldized. Shopping malls, McDonald's itself, and theme parks are prominent examples, in that they reveal elements of both processes. However, although Disneyization and McDonaldization may sometimes overlap with respect to certain institutions, they are distinctively different processes. Disneyization should not be viewed as an implied critique of the concept of McDonaldization. If there is a critical element in the concept of Disneyization when juxtaposed with McDonaldization, it is to suggest that McDonaldization does not fully capture some of the changes that are occurring in the service and consumption spheres in modern society – changes that are the subject of the preceding chapters – and that the concept of Disneyization does address these transformations. Equally, Disneyization leaves the door open for other narratives of large-scale change that, along with McDonaldization, provide useful accounts of what is going on in the modern economy and its culture.

Consumption also connects with another major theme in this chapter, namely, globalization. Disneyization is depicted as a globalizing force in that it is spreading in various ways and degrees to different parts of the globe. The link between consumption and globalization is not a coincidence, of course. What Sklair calls 'the culture-ideology of consumerism' is one of the main factors in the spread of global capitalism today.[2] Consumption provides both the rationale and the motor for much of what we see as denoting globalization. In treating Disneyization in this chapter as linked to both consumption and globalization, it is being depicted as a potent means of increasing the consumption of services and goods that is spreading across the globe.

Disneyization as Systemscape

One way in which Disneyization and McDonaldization can be viewed as parallel processes is that both can be viewed as signals of globalization, the sense that the world is becoming one place in which national boundaries become less significant than in earlier times. Ritzer makes this point in relation to McDonaldization in his more recent work,[3] and it is apparent that the dimensions of Disneyization outlined previously are similarly spreading globally, the implications of which are given further attention below. But what is striking about Disneyization and McDonaldization is that they are not to do with the global diffusion of *products*. Much of the writing on globalization is full of hyperbole about the global spread and recognizability of prominent brands: Nike, Coca-Cola, Pepsi, Pizza Hut, Starbucks, KFC, Benetton, Body Shop and so on. And, of course, one could hardly disregard Mickey's ears and Walt's signature or the golden arches of McDonald's as symbols involved in the global travels of brand names.

But the spread of well-known brand names is *not* what Disneyization (and McDonaldization) are about: they are concerned essentially with the diffusion of *modes of delivery* of goods and services. McDonaldization relates primarily to a mode of delivery in the sense of the *production* of goods and services. It is a means of providing an efficient and highly predictable product and service in a manner that would have met with the approval of Henry Ford and Frederick Winslow

Taylor as the founders of the assembly-line and scientific management respectively. It belongs to an era of mass consumption that is by no means disappearing but whose emphases are becoming less central with the passage of time to what we take to be late modern society. Disneyization is a mode of delivery in the sense of the *staging* of goods and services for consumption. It provides a framework for increasing the allure of goods and services. Disneyization seeks to increase the appeal of goods and services that might otherwise appear mundane and uninteresting. For example, theming in restaurants increases the attractiveness of food that is often unexceptional; placing the restaurants in environments in which other consumption opportunities are on offer (such as going to the cinema) enhances the likelihood that consumers will visit them; situating the restaurants in relation to other consumption avenues means that they form part of a destination that is more likely to be visited; placing their logos onto t-shirts and other merchandise makes otherwise ordinary goods interesting; and encouraging the display of emotions on the part of serving staff helps to differentiate restaurants, increase the likelihood that diners will return, and improve the chances that they will purchase merchandise.

Indeed, it may be that one of the reasons for the growing use of theming in the form of external narratives in some McDonald's restaurants is associated at least in part with the limitations of McDonaldization itself. McDonaldization's emphasis on standardization sits uneasily in an increasingly post-Fordist era of choice and variety. Theming becomes a means of reducing the sense of sameness and thereby enhancing the appeal of its products.

Disneyization is therefore integrally associated with consumption and in particular with what might be thought of consumerism and consumer culture – the pressure on consumers to buy more than they need and often want and consumers' frequent willing compliance, a compliance associated with the conviction among many consumers that goods bestow meaning and are a source of identity. Consumerism and consumer culture have been with us for a long time, but there is a clear feeling among many commentators that in recent times there has been a sea change. With this transformation, the emphasis on inducing consumers to purchase considerably beyond their needs and consumers' reasonably willing participation in the new order has attained new levels. Disneyization is a set of mechanisms for encouraging consumers to spend more than they would have done otherwise. That is not to say that the blandishments that make up Disneyization are always successful, since consumers are well aware that they are under attack to part company with their money and are familiar with the signs for doing so. Writers like Twitchell argue that consumers well know what is happening in shops, malls, restaurants, and so on to make them consume, and are active seekers of meaning rather than passive dupes.[4] For example, he suggests that consumers 'are not duped by advertising, packaging, branding, fashion, or merchandising. They actively seek and enjoy what surrounds the object, especially when they are young'.[5] However, he also recognizes that the manipulation is sometimes successful when he writes: 'Does the audience manipulate things to make meaning, or do other people use things to manipulate them?... both points of view are supportable. Let's split the difference and be done with it.'[6] In other words, there is no point debating whether consumers are duped and therefore successfully manoeuvred by corporations or are active resistors of their machinations, frequently making their own uses and interpretations of these corporate plots: both processes occur in relation to most people some of the time. What Disneyization describes is a set of strategies for 'manipulating' consumers into parting company with their money. Some of the time it is successful, but consumers are often aware of what is going on and that is why organizations often seek to create a ludic ambience with which to shroud consumption and to mask its commercialism. Encouraging a ludic atmosphere may persuade consumers to lower their guard, although consumers are frequently likely to be aware of that too.

Whether consumerism is a positive or negative development is a very moot point. Consumerism as a process of going beyond mere need clearly has many negative consequences for individuals; for many of them, it may encourage debt, for example. On the other hand, there is little doubt that consumption has become a major focus for many people and families, which obviously has been encouraged by the agents of capitalism. One problem with the association of consumerism with going beyond mere need is that it assumes the status of a moral position rather than providing a platform for a search of its adverse effects. My preference here has been to treat the term and its meaning in a more neutral way in order to understand its operation, while simultaneously recognizing its adverse consequences for individuals and the environment. The crucial issue then becomes one of seeking to uncover the ways in which Disneyization as a process reinforces consumerism, which is a major emphasis of the rest of this section, while the discussion of 'anti-Disneyization' below deals with some of its adverse effects.

One implication of suggesting that Disneyization and McDonaldization are modes of delivery of goods and services is that it is crucial to appreciate that Disneyization and McDonaldization are both *systems*, that is, they are ways of presenting or producing goods and services. One of the problems with tying the names of these systems to well-know icons of popular culture – Disney and McDonald's – is that it is easy to make the mistake of lapsing into a discussion of just Disney theme parks and McDonald's. This is an error because the two companies are merely *emblems* of the underlying processes associated with their respective systems.

By emphasizing the processes associated with Disneyization and McDonaldization as systems, it is possible to get away from the shrill but not always revealing accounts of the global reach of prominent brands. It can hardly be doubted that there is a clutch of high-profile brands that have spread through much of the globe, but systems like Disneyization and McDonaldization are in a sense more significant than that. For one thing, they are not tied to particular companies so that their influence and diffusion are less immediately obvious and less high profile than the arrival of prominent brand names and the goods and services they offer. While the arrival on foreign shores of a new theme park like Disneyland Paris, or McDonald's restaurants, or Starbucks coffee shops is sometimes greeted with an outcry, it is hard to imagine a similar chorus of disapproval greeting the arrival of the principles of Disneyization. Focusing on products obscures the more fundamental issue of the diffusion of underlying principles through which goods and services are produced and then put into people's mouths, onto their bodies, and into their homes. McDonald's restaurants have been the focus of anti-globalization campaigners and Disney was given a decidedly gallic cold shoulder among intellectuals in France when Disneyland Paris was in the planning stage, occasioning the famous 'cultural Chernobyl' comment. However, the spread of the fundamental principles that can be deduced from an examination of what the Disney theme parks and McDonald's exemplify is much less frequently, and perhaps less likely to be, a focus of comment.

When considered in this way, it is striking how poorly Disneyization and McDonaldization fit into Appadurai's influential delineation of different forms of '-scape', that is contexts for the flow of goods, people, finance, and other items around the globe. Appadurai distinguished between five scapes: ethnoscapes (the movement of people); technoscapes (the movement of technology in the form of hardware and software); financescapes (the movement of capital); mediascapes (the movement of information); and ideoscapes (the movement of ideas and ideals).[7] Waters has argued that 'McDonaldization infiltrates several of these flows'.[8] However, such a view does not do justice to the significance of McDonaldization and by implication Disneyization. In a sense, we need a new conceptual term for them, which we might call *systemscape* to refer to the flow of contexts for the production and display of goods and services. While they incorporate elements of the five 'scapes', as Waters suggests, Disneyization and McDonaldization are somewhat more than this. They represent important templates for the production of goods and services and their exhibition for sale. In the case of Disneyization, it is a non-machine technology for the delivery of goods and services, a technology that can be transferred across the globe.

Disneyization and Globalization

In describing Disneyization as a globalizing force, there is a risk of a simplistic globalization or Americanization thesis that depicts symbols of American culture spreading by design across the globe and riding roughshod over local conditions and practices, creating an homogenized world in their wake. As writers on globalization who prefer to emphasize the accommodations that global tendencies have to make to local contexts and conditions observe, the principles underlying apparently global forces do not necessarily spread without adaptation. Notions like 'glocalization',[9] 'creolization',[10] and 'hybridization',[11] while different from each other in certain respects and also serving somewhat different functions for the authors concerned, have been devised as ways of coming to terms with the varied ways in which global forces have to run the gauntlet of local cultural conditions and preferences. Globalization is a strange mixture of apparently contradictory forces: similarity and homogenization on the one hand, the assertion and imposition of difference and uniqueness, which might be called 'heterogenization', on the other.[12] Viewed in this way, a concept such as glocalization, Robertson's adaptation of business discussions which plays on the words 'global' and 'local', is in a sense what globalization is all about. As Robertson puts it: 'the insistence on heterogeneity and variety in an increasingly globalized world is integral to globalization theory'.[13] Thus, glocalization is not a separate process from globalization because all globalization is ultimately a process of glocalization, since the forces of globalization will almost always have to be moulded by the local. Patterns of such glocalization are likely to differ in connection with the relative significance of the forces for homogeneity and those for heterogeneity. Some global impulses may be stronger than others, or more covert, or allow fewer alternative interpretations or uses. Similarly, some local contexts may be more resistant or compliant than others. Thus, the forms that glocalization or hybridization assume may vary not just in surface appearance but also in the relative significance of the global and the local or the vigour of the pressure for homogeneity against that for heterogeneity. Such a view means that it is necessary to view with caution not just naive views of globalization as creating cultural homogeneity, but also arguments that suggest that everything global is up for grabs and infinitely alterable or resistible when it hits foreign shores. Parenthetically, nations are also likely to be influential in what turns up at their shores in the first place, since 'reference societies' are likely to vary considerably over time and between countries.[14] The notion that globalization or glocalization is associated with the west and America is itself widely seen as flawed nowadays.

Although the following distinction is crude, globalization can be said to meet the forces of the local in several ways but two basic forms seem to stand out. First, there is *anticipatory localization*, whereby firms adapt the principles of Disneyization (or indeed any globalizing force) to local conditions in anticipation of how they are likely to be received. Thus, when entering a new market, based on their knowledge of local conditions and customs, a service firm anticipates the likely receptiveness to its services and how they are to be delivered by fine-tuning them to the host culture. Secondly, there is *responsive localization*, whereby as a result of its contact with local conditions and culture, a firm feels compelled or inclined to adapt its services and how they are to be delivered. The firm may have engaged in anticipatory localization, but perhaps feels that it has not gone far enough or feels it has misread the local culture.

The Disney theme parks encounter the local

We can see the operation of these two levels of the assertion of the local in connection with the Disney theme parks, though this is not to suggest that this is the same as Disneyization, since the former serve merely as markers of the latter. This brief discussion also brings out the difficult balancing act that global companies must engage in when taking their goods and services abroad.

The Disney theme parks have themselves been forced to adapt to foreign sensibilities when they have been transported abroad to Tokyo and Paris (the Hong Kong park will be interesting to look at in these terms when it opens). In many ways, the designers of the two foreign Disney theme parks have been caught in a pincer movement between, on the one hand recognizing that visitors are likely to be attracted to a piece of Americana in their own countries and therefore not wanting to adapt too much, and on the other hand realizing that the American parks cannot be transplanted wholesale and without consideration of overseas customs and feelings.

In the case of Tokyo Disneyland, Eisner asserts that Disney were under pressure not to Japanize the park,[15] so a clear sense of wanting to give visitors the impression of visiting a park that was clearly American was retained. Similarly, a spokesperson told one writer on the park: 'We really tried to avoid creating a Japanese version of Disneyland. We wanted the Japanese visitors to feel they were taking a foreign vacation by coming here'.[16] More and more of such 'foreign' lands within Japan have been built in the wake of Disneyland.[17] However, although this sense of taking an American vacation without leaving Japan is often conveyed in publicity and in public statements about the park (as in Eisner's and the spokesperson's remarks quoted above), there are grounds for thinking that more adaptation has taken place than such statements acknowledge.

Certain attractions were altered in anticipation of Japanese needs and preoccupations. For example, the Hall of Presidents was dropped because of its extreme foreignness, but the case for dropping others is less obvious; for example, Main Street, USA was replaced by World Bazaar. Raz observes that, although Tokyo Disneyland is invariably claimed to be a copy of the American original, it has in fact been Japanized. Thus, the Mystery Tour in the castle in Tokyo Disneyland is a Disney version of the Japanese ghost-house. The Meet the World show is described by Raz as 'a show about and for the Japanese'.[18] Changes such as these would seem to be token anticipatory localization but in addition responsive localization has taken place. This is particularly apparent in connection with food, with the opening of a Japanese restaurant catering for local tastes and allowing visitors to have picnics in the park, something very much in tune with Japanese lifestyle but unimaginable in the American parks where importing one's own food is discouraged. Also, Brannen notes that ride operators' commentaries are translations of the American originals but are invariably peppered with modifications in the form of 'Japan-specific puns, jokes, and creative explanations'.[19] In addition, Raz argues that the hiring, orientation and training of regular employees are very different from in the US (but not of part-time employees for whom these three phases of becoming a cast member are the same as in the US).[20] For example, there is less emphasis in training on Disney traditions and on learning about and imbibing the Disney corporate culture; instead, there tends to be greater emphasis at Tokyo Disneyland on helping the trainee to become accustomed to his or her work area.

In Disneyland Paris, Disney were keen to keep an essentially American format and ambience. Michael Eisner has written: 'for the most part we were determined to make [Disneyland Paris] every bit as American as Tokyo Disneyland and our domestic parks'.[21] The comment is interesting in part because of the conviction that it was important not to surrender the parks' sense of America, but also because it depicts the Tokyo park as American. Eisner notes that the American qualities are particularly apparent with the Paris park's hotels, all of which are themed on American places or symbols of American culture.

However, local adaptation can be seen in Disneyland Paris, where after a disappointing beginning, the company was forced to adapt the park to European tastes.[22] Anticipatory localization was not a prominent feature of the park. The Jungle Cruise was dropped, perhaps in part because of its potential to offend in post-colonial times and the more American attractions, such as Hall of Presidents, were also not included. Responsive localization was more in evidence though this also demonstrates the difficult balancing act that firms like Disney are engaged in. The alcohol ban, in particular, was soon dropped. There is some evidence that the company does not seek to insist on emotional labour among cast members to the degree that occurs in the US.[23] But in fact, it has been difficult to fine tune the balance of the American and the European. A year after it opened, the then new chairman of the Park was quoted as saying:

> Each time we tried to Europeanise the product we found it didn't work. Europeans want America and they want Disney, whether French intellectuals like it or not.[24]

This quotation brings out the dilemmas that globalizing firms are involved in when they seek to engage in both anticipatory and responsive localization.

Disneyization and local conditions

However, while reassuring, these indications of the continued relevance of the local for the Disney theme parks should not blind us to the fact that while Tokyo

Disneyland and Disneyland Paris have adapted many attractions and other aspects of the parks to local sensibilities, this is not what Disneyization is about. As previously argued, it is about *principles* to do with the production and delivery of goods and services. In a sense, Disneyization could be regarded as more worrying for the critics of the notion of globalization as an homogenizing force than the transplanting of Disney theme parks abroad. It is potentially more worrying because Disneyization, like McDonaldization, is a more insidious process: it is less conspicuous in its emergence than the appearance of magic kingdoms (and the various other symbols of globalization, such as McDonald's, Starbucks coffee shops, Coca-Cola, and so on) on nations' doorsteps. In other words, finding adaptations and local uses of Disney theme parks should not lead us to think that they denote or necessarily entail adaptations to and local uses of Disneyization.

None of what has been said previously should be taken to imply that there are likely to be no processes of local adaptation or resistance or culturally-specific uses in relation to Disneyization. Emotional labour has been a particularly prominent site for resistance, as studies of the local reception of McDonald's restaurants demonstrate. During the early period of the restaurant's arrival in Moscow, people standing in queues had to be given information about such things as how to order.[25] In addition, they had to be told: 'the employees inside will smile at you. This does not mean that they are laughing at you. We smile because we are happy to serve you'. Watson remarks on the basis of his fieldwork in Hong Kong that people who are overly congenial are regarded with suspicion, so that a smile is not necessarily regarded as a positive feature.[26] Also, consumers did not display any interest in the displays of friendliness from crew personnel. It is not surprising, therefore, that the display of emotional labour is not a significant feature of the behaviour and demeanour of counter staff in McDonald's in Hong Kong. Watson says that: 'Instead, they project qualities that are admired in the local culture: competence, directness, and unflappability. ... Workers who smile on the job are assumed to be enjoying themselves at the consumer's (and the management's) expense.'[27]

Similarly, in her research on fast-food restaurants in New York, Talwar found that the requirement to express emotions was often a problem for managers of the outlets in immigrant areas. For example, she was told by a Malaysian manager of a restaurant in New York's Chinatown:

> If you are smiling to them [Chinese customers], first of all they think what is it that you want since you are smiling? Every day you are smiling to them [customers] and he or she is trying to smile with you but the first time you are smiling at them they are so shocked, they [customers] are thinking, why is this lady smiling? I receive a lot of letters. One letter asked why they [employees] are smiling here.[28]

Among the Inuit of Greenland, it appears that there is no tradition of smiling, so that services are frequently administered with a scowl rather than a smile. According to one journalist, staff at a chain of co-operative shops are being sent to train in North American sales service, of which learning to engage in pleasantries and smiling are a key component.[29] Service quality began to improve quite quickly, although some assistants found it difficult to adapt. Interestingly, the chain's main competitor also began smiling and customer service lessons. Also, the suggestion that the insistence on emotional labour in Disneyland Paris has not been as pronounced as in the American parks (see above) is relevant to Disneyization and local adaptations to it and suggests that this aspect of Disneyization could not be easily introduced in the park. These various fragments suggest that emotional labour may face constraints and even resistance among customers and staff when it is transplanted into some national contexts.

A somewhat different slant is provided by Fantasia's account of the reception of McDonald's in France.[30] There, the attraction of McDonald's for young people was what he calls the 'American ambience'. Insofar as the display of emotional labour is an ingredient of this ambience, it may be that it is not that the French enthusiasts respond positively to emotional labour *per se*, but that in the context of McDonald's they respond positively to the total package, of which smiling counter staff is a component. In other words, as the writers who emphasize local adaptations to global processes point out, local consumers frequently make their own culturally bespoke uses of globalizing forces like Disneyization.

Clearly, while it is being suggested that Disneyization is a set of principles that is spreading outwards across the globe, it is also apparent that, as the case of emotional labour shows, the principles are not allowed to travel without hindrance. On the other hand, evidence to suggest that there are local forms of or responses to the other three dimensions of Disneyization is sparse. The evidence with regard to emotional labour suggests that they may be adapted, but since this is only one of four dimensions of Disneyization, further evidence is needed to establish a tendency towards glocalization or hybridization. Indeed, as the previously cited evidence concerning emotional labour implies, we need to take into account the ways such global influences are working their way into and are being incorporated into local cultures. At the same time, the process of local adaptation helps to bring into sharper relief the significance of cultures. At precisely the same time that the world is frequently viewed as becoming more homogeneous, our awareness of the nature and significance of local cultures seems to become better defined.

Disneyization is a less visible process than the arrival of brand names on foreign shores. It is a set of processes designed to maximize consumers' willingness to purchase goods and services that in many cases they might not otherwise have been prompted to buy or that they might have bought from a competitor. Theming provides the consumer with a narrative that acts as a draw by providing an experience that lessens the sense of an economic transaction and increases the likelihood of purchasing merchandise. Hybrid consumption is meant to give the consumer as many opportunities as possible to make purchases and therefore to keep them as long as possible in the theme park, mall, or whatever. Emotional labour is the oil of the whole process in many ways: in differentiating otherwise identical goods and services, as an enactment of theming, and as a means for increasing the inclination to purchase merchandise.

Structures of similarity

The direction that these reflections are pointing is to suggest that systemscapes like Disneyization and McDonaldization constitute templates for the way goods and services are presented and delivered in modern society. When exported abroad they are capable of being adapted to local conditions, circumstances and culture in numerous ways by both corporations and consumers. They do not determine the forms that institutions will assume. Instead, they provide templates that allow variation in the concrete forms that institutions can take on. However, there is a crucial difference here between Disneyization and McDonaldization. While there is evidence from studies of the export of McDonald's abroad and its reception among overseas consumers to suggest that McDonaldization should not automatically be associated with homogeneity of appearance and reaction,[31] it also needs to be recognized that McDonaldization is considerably more prone to creating a sense of homogeneity than Disneyization. In fact, one of the dimensions of McDonaldization – predictability – is very much associated with the drift towards standardization. As Ritzer puts it:

> Rationalization involves the increasing effort to ensure predictability from one time or place to another. In a rational society people prefer to know what to expect in all settings and at all times. They neither want nor expect surprises. … In order to ensure such predictability over time and place, a rational society emphasizes such things as discipline, order, systematization, formalization, routine, consistency, and methodical operation.[32]

In other words, homogeneity and standardization lie at the heart of McDonaldization. While McDonald's restaurants frequently adapt their overseas menus slightly or adjust to local uses of their restaurants, such as the practice of treating them as leisure centres in parts of East Asia,[33] the basic features of a McDonald's restaurant are usually intact and highly predictable in terms of the food and the manner of its presentation. Thus, as a systemscape, McDonaldization is capable of some adaptation to local conditions, but the emphasis on predictability tends to propel it towards homogeneity and standardization.

Beck, for example, has linked McDonaldization with homogenization. He writes:

> The keyword here has become *McDonaldization*. According to this view, there is an ever greater uniformity of lifestyles, cultural symbols and transnational modes of behaviour. In the villages of

Lower Bavaria, just as in Calcutta, Singapore or the *favelas* of Rio de Janeiro, people watch *Dallas* on TV, wear blue jeans and smoke Marlboro as a sign of 'free, untouched nature'. In short, a global culture industry increasingly signifies the *convergence* of cultural symbols and ways of life.[34]

Disneyization, however, works differently. It is a systemscape that encourages variety and differentiation. It is a mechanism for delivering goods and services that emphasizes distinguishing the delivery of services and goods from other providers. The template for the delivery of goods and services associated with a systemscape like Disneyization creates *structures of similarity* within which commercial and other organizations and institutions can take on a wide variety of forms. For example, theming permits various styles and intensities in the application of narratives. It can therefore assume a host of different kinds or patterns. These can and will vary greatly within nation states as well as across them. Therefore, while Disneyization may be deemed to imply a logic of homogeneity in our culture and its institutions, no such commonality is likely to arise. Within the structures of similarity that Disneyization creates, wide variations in practice are possible and likely to be expected, as Disneyization runs the gauntlet of local conditions. Disneyization creates structures of similarity that enable considerable variation in outward appearance rather than homogeneous forms.

Of course, it could be argued that many of the carriers of Disneyization are in fact global brands and chains that bring Disneyization in their wake. A thoroughly Disneyized operation like Hard Rock Cafe, for example, is both a deliverer of a globally recognized service and goods and a carrier of Disneyization. To that extent, it might be argued that Disneyization is associated with cultural homogenization. However, the point about Disneyization and the suggestion that it creates structures of similarity is that it is not simply being exported by prominent globally recognized brands and organizations. Two points are relevant here. First, when something such as a themed restaurant reaches an overseas market it is likely to undergo a process of localization of the kind previously discussed. Second, and more importantly, Disneyization is also imported by local entrepreneurs and businesses who mould it into culturally modified forms. Consequently, we should not think of the underlying principles of Disneyization as creating uniformity, in that they may be both *exported* by transnational firms and *imported* by local businesses as part of a process of emulation. When the latter occurs, the character of the business concerned is likely to be shaped to local preferences while keeping the underlying principles of Disneyization broadly intact. For example, Ritzer refers to the interesting case of the Rock in Rio Cafe in Latin America which has clearly been influenced by themed restaurants in the US but has placed in its own stamp on the format. Guests enter by monorail, images are projected onto the walls so that the décor constantly changes, and there are indoor fireworks each night. The developer of the chain asks: 'Why import something American when we can do better ourselves.'[35] In a case such as this, the principle of theming has been imported but a distinctive imprint has been placed on it so that there is far less of a sense of the *déjà vu* that is associated with standardization.

Anti-Disneyization

It might be imagined that Disneyization is less likely than other globalizing tendencies to give rise to the displeasure of anti-globalization writers. For one thing, it is not a homogenizing force and as such is less vulnerable to the charge of creating a bland world of sameness. In addition, it is much less directly associated with specific companies than the flow of prominent brand names and institutions. It is precisely the companies that are deeply associated with such brands (such as, McDonald's, Starbucks, Nike, Burger King, Coca-Cola) that are the typical targets of their ire.[36] Disneyization may be directly associated with companies that export its principles, albeit in localized formats, but it is also adopted abroad by local companies, as the discussion at the end of the last section suggested. Thus, Disneyization's lack of direct connection with specific companies renders it less visible and at least to some extent, perhaps, less objectionable.

That Disneyization is less likely to engender such criticism than transnational companies and their brands does not render it immune to ideological criticism. It is vulnerable on several fronts. The following have been touched on in earlier chapters:

- *Distortion of history and place.* The widespread use through theming of historical periods and events as the foundation for commercial activity has been criticized for the frequently sanitized and bowdlerized images that are served up as capsule accounts of the past. The distortions that are heaped on the past in such locations as South Street Seaport in New York and The Rocks in Sydney are examples of the way in which the past is ransacked and then purged of the realities of labour, exploitation and poverty. These representations have been highly contentious for many writers, some of whom were mentioned in Chapter 2. Similarly, images of place are prone to distortion and frequently produce patronising representations sometimes with colonial overtones. Relatedly, it may be worth observing that the large sums of money that can be invested in making such representations compelling in the name of 'education' may make it more difficult for hard-pressed public educational organizations to compete in terms of both the mechanisms for getting pedagogical messages across and the subversion of simplistic versions of time and place.

- *Manipulation of children.* Disneyization is strongly associated with the manipulation of children. As we saw in Chapters 3 and 4, the use of such techniques as giving toys away with meals and the widespread merchandising directed at children are blatant marketing appeals to get children to spend money via their parents. Because children are seen as more vulnerable to such appeals, some commentators, such as the Archbishop of Canterbury, see these techniques as reprehensible for their priming of the young for consumerism.[37]

- *Manipulation of consumers.* The use of various tactics for getting consumers to stay longer, to purchase items they had not intended to buy by positioning outlets strategically, using theming to create a ludic atmosphere to make them more likely to spend, and directing their movements towards the purchase of merchandise are all features of Disneyization that might be criticized. Of course, as noted in the previous chapter, we should not presume that consumers are pliant dupes who succumb to these strategies, but the frequency with which they are employed nowadays suggests that they must be successful at least some of the time.

- *Manipulation of workers' emotions.* The extensive use of emotional labour as a means of differentiating services means that workers are increasingly being expected to display certain emotions but to suppress others. This manipulation of how workers feel about both themselves and their work situation may be deeply alienating for some of them and there is some evidence that its effects on their well-being are sometimes negative. On the other hand, while this is a possible source of criticism, like the previous point, it should not be assumed that people are passive in the face of organizations' exhortations. They are frequently capable of reacting to these requirements and of fighting back in their own ways.

These and other similar sources of criticism of Disneyization have been implicit in the previous chapters. However, the possible grounds for an ideological critique of Disneyization do not end there and the following additional points are worthy of consideration.

Sweated labour

Much of the apparently benign merchandise that is sold in theme parks, themed restaurants, and similar outlets is often likely to be the product of sweated labour. In August 1996, Tracy participated in a market survey of merchandise licensed by Disney for *The Hunchback of Notre Dame* in various retail outlets in Tucson, Arizona.[38] The survey entailed noting the place of manufacture and the price and type of item. It was found that 47% of the products were from what he calls 'dependent countries'. Of these products, 16% were made in countries where the average wage per worker was just under $4,000. These items are often produced in working conditions that are extremely unpleasant and at wage rates that are very low. Even in China, which is one of the dependent countries (though not among the 16% previously mentioned), he cites a 1999 study that reported extremely poor working conditions in Chinese factories making Disney merchandise. Apparently, working days of 16 hours were not uncommon at peak times.

Moreover, even the merchandise produced in the United States, which formed 48% of all *Hunchback* merchandise, is frequently manufactured under sweatshop conditions. This is particularly the case with clothing items, which, Tracy suggests, are frequently manufactured in sweatshops regardless of the country of origin. These factories do not pay the minimum wage or overtime in the US. The owners of these factories frequently take advantage of the fact that the workers do not have proper immigration status and are therefore less likely to complain. He argues that because Disney charge so much for licensing agreements, contractors are compelled to find the least expensive manufacturers possible and it is this pressure that results in the frequent use of sweated labour. Klein's assault on the use of sweated labour for the manufacture of branded goods has similarly implicated Disney merchandise in her purview.[39] While it is difficult to establish the prevalence of sweatshops to produce merchandise of the kind discussed in Chapter 4, the case of Disney film-related goods suggests that they are also likely to be involved in the manufacture of these other kinds of merchandise.

Destruction of land and natural habitats

Disneyization frequently requires large-scale building projects that are extremely destructive as land and the natural habitats of animals are brought to heel by bulldozers. This is especially likely to be the case with theme parks and large themed malls. Certainly the Disney theme parks themselves serve as a reminder of this undesirable aspect of Disneyization which is likely to be at least partly generalizable to other large-scale projects underpinned by its principles. Disney World serves as a reminder of the environmental hazards involved. When the Assistant Editor of *National Geographic* visited the region he was told by a conservationist that the development of Orlando was likely to result in the 'probably death, by thirst, of southern Florida'.[40] While that viewpoint was viewed as unduly pessimistic by other commentators cited in Judge's article, it is important to bear in mind that it was voiced within just a year or so of the opening of the Magic Kingdom in Orlando and therefore well before the opening of the other Disney theme parks, the non-Disney theme parks and various other Disneyized attractions in the region. In other words, since those words were uttered, over 30 years of development have occurred in the region and have therefore wrought their impacts on the region's ecology. The tinge of guilt about the impact of Disneyland on the local environment is palpable in the following passage written by the founder of the University of Disneyland:

> Those of us working on the Disneyland project felt that we were bringing 'progress' to a farming community. In the name of progress we replaced the fragrance of orange groves with the smell of smog, two-lane roads with freeways and comfortable homes with motels, shopping centres and fast-food restaurants.[41]

Relatedly, the expansion of massive developments of the kind that Disneyization frequently entails can create a situation in which the state becomes preoccupied with assisting theme parks and entertainment-cum-retail projects to the exclusion and ultimately neglect of natural or indigenous attractions. Cartier has shown how in the small Malaysian state of Melaka a tendency to encourage *faux* leisurescapes has led to an abandonment of authentic attractions of both historical and natural interest in favour of these more high profile projects.[42] Not only has this resulted in a distortion of the nature of tourism in the region but it has also created problems for the local ecology.

Running down of cities

The growth of out of town shopping- and entertainment-based destinations has often led to a deterioration in the fabric of many cities. As noted in the previous chapter, cities have often come to be seen as dangerous areas and Disneyized developments such as these have capitalized on these fears to create the impression of safety. As a result, many downtowns have suffered as they have come to be seen as dangerous 'no go' areas.[43] Orlando again acts as a salutary reminder. When a British journalist visited downtown Orlando, he reported: 'Downtown … is now downbeat. Derelict shops, homeless people sleeping on benches, police signs warning "TV surveillance is in operation", piles of litter'.[44]

Some cities have reacted to fears about downtown areas by creating upmarket shopping and eating sites for tourists and wealthier locals with a strong surveillance presence.[45] As Zukin puts it, such developments 'make the waterfront of older cities into a consumers' playground, far safer for tourists and cultural consumers than the closed worlds of wholesale fish and vegetable dealers and longshoremen'.[46] However, this strategy only shifts the location of the problem since it leaves the city areas outside such tourist bubbles with struggling businesses and with fears about personal security. While there are several factors that contribute to the decline of city downtown areas, of which Disneyization is merely one, it nonetheless constitutes an important factor, especially in terms of its contribution to the perception of downtowns as dangerous and to be avoided.

Creation of partial citizens

It was argued at the outset of this chapter that Disneyization is driven by consumption and by consumerism in particular. It is the *raison d'être* of Disneyization. Citizenship under Disneyization almost comes to be defined in terms of one's capacity to consume. Consequently, as we saw in the last chapter, those without the capacity to consume or who are deemed to have a limited capacity to do so, or those who might hinder the consumption inclinations of consumers are either excluded or are kept under the watchful gaze of security cameras and guards.

One of the problems with an emphasis on consumerism is that it is easy to get carried away with the view that the world out there is replete with discerning, credit-card toting consumers rushing around fulfilling their life projects by developing, and enveloping themselves in, distinctive lifestyles. Such behaviour may occur, but we must bear in mind that many people on low incomes or those who endure a disability that interferes with the consumerist quest are in a very real sense alienated from, or at least unable to participate meaningfully in, this consumer culture. How humdrum, boring and dull their lives appear from the vantage point of writings about consumerism. In much the same way that, as observers of the Disney theme parks have long noticed, it is largely the middle class and the more affluent sections of the working class who enter the parks' gates, so it is with consumerism in general.

Bauman is one writer on consumerism and the consumer society to take poverty seriously.[47] He argues that essentially the poor in consumer society are not normal. They cannot participate as fully fledged members because they do not have the means to succumb to the blandishments of the suppliers of goods and services. They are therefore, as he puts it, 'flawed consumers'.[48] In a consumer society, the crucial point is *not* that the poor do not work, or that their work is irregular or meagrely paid, but that they do not consume, or more precisely, they do not consume in the manner that consumer society expects and that Disneyization is designed to encourage.

Bauman's discussion reminds us that in our fascination with the discovery of consumerism, we should not ignore the poor simply because they do not fit the general picture. He reminds us that a significant number of people are disenfranchised from consumerism and by implication from what Disneyization has to offer. In a sense, they are only capable of what I would call *limited consumption*, that is consumption that is limited relative to the supposed criteria of a consumer society. But from the position of Disneyization it is not just that the poor are flawed consumers that is striking, but that they are *limited citizens*. Their ability to enter the temples of Disneyization is limited not just by their capacity to purchase its offerings but also because they are heavily guarded and under surveillance. This issue, like the others that I have suggested in this section on 'anti-Disneyization', is an unsettling matter that may make Disneyization vulnerable to ideological criticism even though it is possibly less likely to attract the attentions of anti-globalization campaigners and writers.

The Economic Meets the Cultural

Disneyization provides a striking illustration of a process to which many writers have drawn attention, namely, the growing interpenetration of the economic and the cultural. Although the two spheres have always been linked, as Lash and Urry have argued: 'the economy is increasingly culturally inflected and ... culture is more and more economically inflected. Thus, the boundaries between the two become more and more blurred...'[49] The former process is evident in the way in which commercial organizations draw on well-known cultural notions in terms of time, place and ethnicity in order to theme commercial environments. That these cultural idioms are representations that often contain distortions that have built up over decades is not the key point in this connection. They serve as emblems that are widely acknowledged in our culture and that are then commercially appropriated. Commercially appropriated thematic narratives feed back into culture and are reinforced by enterprise.

Equally, culture becomes more and more economically inflected when commercial organizations create idioms that find their way into culture. These cultural elements are representations that frequently sanitize and distort. Nowhere is distortion more apparent than in the frequent appeals to feelings of nostalgia concerning a lost but revered time when life was supposedly more exotic, simpler or more varied. As was noted in Chapter 2, such developments as the widespread use in waterfront developments of images drawn from a partly constructed past of mercantile and maritime adventure are an illustration of this trend. The fabricated nostalgia that is commercially appropriated is one that occludes unpleasantness and as such is with some justification referred to as 'memory with the pain removed'.[50] However, the fact that these cultural idioms are distortions is not the main point for the present discussion, the more salient issue is that they are fabrications that are given form and which feed into our culture as representations of what different times or places were like. They therefore add to our cultural stock of misunderstanding.

A further aspect of the way in which culture becomes increasingly economically inflected occurs in connection with merchandising, where items bearing commercial logos come to infiltrate culture's sense of what a souvenir is. Also, hybrid consumption sites come to influence our sense of what constitutes a destination so that destinations are increasingly seen as associated with shopping and eating.

In addition, we find that the very notion of culture has come to have a prominent economic component. In Chapter 5, it was noted that one way in which many management consultants and organizations have sought to enhance the organizational commitment of their employees has been to 'manage' their organizational cultures. In fact, this was only one rationale for the clarion call for corporate cultural change in the 1980s and 1990s but it was a prominent one. The notion that 'companies with a record of outstanding financial performance often have powerful corporate cultures'[51] led to a fashion for managing cultures to make them more distinctive that received a further boost from the growing use of TQM initiatives where cultural change is a key ingredient.[52] Some writers have expressed doubts about how far managed cultural change really makes an impact on employees' values and beliefs, as against their behaviour.[53] However, the more crucial point is that the culture movement of the 1980s, which, because of its affinities with TQM, has by no means disappeared, conveyed an image of 'culture' as something that has economic implications and which can be managed.

Culture thus became central to the business sphere as something that can be enlisted for commercial ends and indeed almost inseparable from it. Such a view radically alters our perception of what cultures are, where they come from and how they arise, but most importantly they revise our understanding of them by investing them with an economic aspect.

Conclusion

In this final chapter, I have sought to outline some of the broader ramifications of Disneyization and some of the wider theoretical issues with which I see it as being entangled. In a sense, it becomes a useful lens through which to view a number of issues that are of concern in contemporary social sciences, such as globalization and the fusion of the economic and the cultural. More fundamentally, I have sought to outline how I perceive Disneyization, namely, as a set of processes that are circling the globe and which are to do with the provision of a framework for making goods, and in particular services, desirable and therefore more likely to be bought. It is not in any sense an alternative to the concept of McDonaldization and is in many ways to do with increasing the appeal of goods and services in the face of the growing standardization that is associated with McDonaldization.

Disneyization has almost certainly not infiltrated modern economies and cultures to the degree that McDonaldization has. In particular, relatively few institutions are fully Disneyized in terms of all four dimensions. In this connection, it is worth recalling the distinction introduced in Chapter 1 between structural and transferred Disneyization. The success of the Disney theme parks and the growing contact that people from different corners of the globe have with them (either through overseas visits or through the arrival of Disney theme parks abroad) enhance people's awareness of the commercial and other advantages of Disneyization. In other words, the growing awareness of the parks is likely to result in transferred Disneyization, though structural Disneyization is also likely to continue apace. In previous chapters, particularly Chapter 5, I have shown that such a process of transferred Disneyization has almost certainly been taking place.

There is a growing recognition that the Disney theme parks are widely held up as models that are directly copied and the dimensions of Disneyization articulated in this book are likely to be deeply implicated in this process of emulation. As one writer has put it:

Disney has been so successful in promoting a new type of resort that Disneyland and particularly Disney World have become not just product leaders but yardsticks against which an ever wider range of facilities dealing directly with the general public are measured, whether by developers [or] the public. These range from shopping malls to a new generation of world fairs and convention centres via galleries and museums. ... Every mall, not just every amusement park developer, has to recognise that Disney has set the standards for large integrated site developments, just as Henry Ford once set standards for factory-based manufacturing.[54]

Mills's reference to world fairs is striking in the light of the growing influence of the Disney theme parks on these institutions. Roche quotes the director of Expo 86 as saying in response to a question about Disneyland in relation to his plans for the fair: 'when you ask me about Disneyland I have to say that it's one of the highest quality theme park experiences around, and what we'd like to see is that kind of operational quality applied to the product of a world's fair. ... We are committed to high quality education and entertainment'.[55] In a similar manner to Mills, Zukin writes:

> Disney World is not only important because it confirms and consolidates the significance of cultural power – the power to impose a vision – for social control. It is important because it offers a model of privatization and globalization; it manages social diversity; it imposes a frame of meaning on the city, a frame that earlier in history came from other forms of public culture.[56]

And another writes:

> Whether we see Disneyland as the great spore bed of tastelessness and corporate control or as a seedbed of flamboyance and folk creativity, it has reshaped American and global landscapes in the form of theme parks, shopping malls, fast food places, sports centers, museums, resorts, and planned communities.[57]

Davis suggests that 'urban planners and shopping mall designers draw heavily from theme park technique'.[58] In other words, for various commentators the Disney theme parks provide *models* for cities, malls, museums and a host of other institutions and forms of organization. Taking the point slightly further, Zukin describes 'Disney's consumption regime' as one which 'creates a safe, clean, public space in which strangers apparently trust each other and just "have fun". The appeal of this accomplishment is universal'.[59] This regime is depicted as a major influence on the modern city and its consumption settings. Sometimes the process of emulation is fairly direct. Judd has remarked that it was James Rouse, the architect behind the much-copied Faneuil Hall in Boston, who extolled the virtues of Disney's impact on urban planning 13 years before the marketplace opened.[60] Also, it is likely that the imagineers and executives who have been associated with Disney and its theme parks and who have moved on have provided a pool of talent that other companies in the entertainment industries and beyond have been able to draw upon. And of course, Disney's management training programmes are themselves likely to influence work and human resource management practices in many organizations (see Chapter 5). This is recognized by Zukin when she writes that 'Disney World's control over its labor force and their interaction with consumers have been taken as models for other service firms'.[61]

What we see in these various viewpoints is the suggestion that the Disney theme parks frequently serve as models for a variety of social institutions. They imply that a process of transferred Disneyization is taking place, but the references are in general terms that signal a feeling that the Disney theme parks are providing models without delineating in more precise terms what the nature of the impact might be. It is this issue that I have sought to address in this book. While these various commentators suggest that transferred Disneyization is increasing, structural Disneyization has also been occurring and is likely to continue to do so. Together these two processes will contribute to the growing Disneyization of society.

Notes

1 Ritzer (1993).
2 Sklair (2002).
3 For example, Ritzer (1998).
4 Twitchell (1999).
5 Twitchell (1999: 22).
6 Twitchell (1999: 272).
7 Appadurai (1990).
8 Waters (2002: 216).
9 Robertson (1992).
10 Hannerz (1987).
11 Pieterse (1994).
12 Kellner (2002).
13 Robertson (1992: 131).
14 Robertson (2001).
15 Eisner (1998: 270).
16 Quoted in Brannen (1992: 216).
17 Hendry (2000).
18 Raz (1999: 52).
19 Brannen (1992: 226).
20 Raz (1999).
21 Eisner (1998: 270).
22 Lainsbury (2000: 133).
23 Warren (1999: 119–20).
24 Quoted in Skapinker and Rawsthorn (1993: 18).
25 Watson (1997a: 27–8).
26 Watson (1997b).
27 Watson (1997b: 91).
28 Quoted in Talwar (2002:103).
29 Jones (1999).
30 Fantasia (1995).
31 Fantasia (1995); Watson (1997a).
32 Ritzer (1993: 83).
33 Watson (1997a).
34 Beck (2000: 42 emphases in original).
35 Ritzer (1999: 49).
36 For example, Klein (2000).
37 See Helgadottir (2003) for another outburst about merchandising for children.
38 Tracy (1999). See also the discussion in Chapter 4 of the same survey in connection with Pecora and Meehan (2001).
39 Klein (2000: 328, 353).
40 Quoted in Judge (1973: 596).
41 France (1991: 19).
42 Cartier (1998).
43 Hubbard (2002, 2003).
44 Chesshyre (2002b: 2).
45 Coleman and Sim (1998); Fainstein and Judd (1999).
46 Zukin (1995: 19).
47 Bauman (1998).
48 Bauman (1998: 38, 90).
49 Lash and Urry (1994: 64).
50 Lowenthal (1985: 8).
51 Uttal (1983: 66).
52 Powell (1995).
53 For example, Thompson and Findlay (1999).
54 Mills (1998: 5).
55 Quoted in Roche (2000: 127).
56 Zukin (1995: 77).
57 Steiner (1998: 8).
58 Davis (1997: 23).
59 Zukin (1998: 832).
60 Judd (1999).
61 Zukin (1995: 55).

Bibliography

Adams, J.A. (1991) *The American Amusement Park Industry: A History of Technology and Thrills*, Boston: Twayne Publishers.

Akwagyiram, A. (2001) 'Potter-mania boost for sock business', *Nottingham Evening Post*, November 23: 3.

Alexander, G. (1993) 'Takeover titans fight to control Marvel', *Sunday Times* (Business section), March 25: 3.7.

Anderson, K. (1995) 'Culture and nature at the Adelaide Zoo: at the frontiers of "human" geography', *Transactions of the Institute of British Geographers*, 20: 275–94.

Anon. (1932) 'Mickey Mouse's fourth birthday', *Motion Picture Herald*, October 1: 42–3, 51.

Anon. (1948) 'The mighty mouse', *Time*, October 25: 33.

Anon. (2001) 'McAtlas shrugged', *Foreign Policy*, May/June: 26–37.

Appadurai, A. (1990) 'Disjuncture and difference in the global political economy', in M. Featherstone (ed.), *Global Culture: Nationalism, Globalization and Modernity*, London: Sage.

Armstrong, P. (2000) 'Phantom takes it out of Character', *The Times*, May 31: 32.

Armstrong, S. (1999) 'How to make a killing', *Sunday Times* (Culture section), January 24: 10.

Ashworth, J. (2000) 'Diana fund seeks to build new brand', *The Times*, June 21: 31.

Ashworth, J. (2002) 'New chapter after Star Wars fiasco', *The Times*, March 5: 30.

Augé, M. (1995) *Non-places: Introduction to an Anthropology of Supermodernity*, London: Verso.

Azaryahu, M. (1999) 'McDonald's or Golani junction? A case of a contested place in Israel', *Professional Geographer*, 51: 481–92.

Bagli, C.V. (1998) 'Novelty gone, themed restaurants are tumbling', *New York Times*, December 27 (consulted online).

Bagli, C.V. (2001) 'Toy store is leading retail shuffle in Times Sq', *New York Times*, December 15 (consulted online).

Bailey, A. (1982) *Walt Disney's World of Fantasy*, New York: Everest House.

Bain, P. and Taylor, P. (2000) 'Entrapped by the "electronic panopticon"? Worker resistance in a call centre', *New Technology, Work and Employment*, 15: 2–18.

Baldwin, D. (2002) 'Main Street as memory lane', *New York Times*, January 10 (consulted online).

Bale, J. (1998) 'Princess fund sues over US "Diana doll"', *The Times*, May 19: 11.

Ball, E. (1991) 'Theme player: Disneyland is our land', *Village Voice*, August 6: 81.

Barber, B.R. (1995) *Jihad vs. McWorld: How Globalism and Tribalism are Shaping the World*, New York: Times Books.

Barboza, D. (1999) 'The Markets: Market place–pluralism under golden arches; from abroad, McDonald's finds value in local control', *New York Times*, February 12.

Barker, P. (1996) 'Living on the edge', *Guardian*, October 8: 2–3.

Bates, W. (1997) 'Distributors of adult materials sue over handbill ban', *Las Vegas Review-Journal*, February 4. www.reviewjournal.com/lvrj_home/1997/Feb-04-Tue-1997/news/4798395.html

Bauman, Z. (1998) *Work, Consumerism and the New Poor*, Buckingham: Open University Press.

Beardsworth, A. and Bryman, A. (1999) 'Late modernity and the dynamics of quasification: the case of the themed restaurant', *Sociological Review*, 47: 228–57.

Beardsworth, A. and Bryman, A. (2001) 'The wild animal in late modernity: the case of the Disneyization of zoos', *Tourist Studies*, 1: 83–104.

Beck, U. (2000) *What is Globalization?* Cambridge: Polity Press.

Bellas, M.L. (1999) 'Emotional labor in academia: the case of professors', *The Annals of the American Academy of Political and Social Science*, 561: 96–110.

Bitner, M.J. (1992) 'Servicescapes: the impact of physical surroundings on customers and employees', *Journal of Marketing*, 56: 57–71.

Bitner, M.J., Booms, B.H. and Tetreault, M.S. (1990) 'The service encounter: diagnosing favorable and unfavorable incidents', *Journal of Marketing*, 54: 71–84.

Bloch, P.H., Ridgway, N.M. and Dawson, S.A. (1994) 'The shopping mall as consumer habitat', *Journal of Retailing*, 70: 23–42.

Blocklyn, P.L. (1988) 'Making magic: the Disney approach to people management', *Personnel*, 65 (December): 28–35.

Bolton, S.C. (2000) 'Emotion here, emotion there, emotional organisations everywhere', *Critical Perspectives on Accounting*, 11: 155–71.

Bolton, S.C. and Boyd, C. (2003) 'Trolley dolly or skilled emotion manager? Moving on from Hochschild's Managed Heart', *Work, Employment and Society*, 17: 289–308.

Bone, J. (2001). 'Diners are back on the US menu', *The Times*, June 25: 9.

Boyer, M.C. (1992) 'Cities for sale: merchandising history at South Street Seaport', in M. Sorkin (ed.), *Variations on a Theme Park: The New American City and the End of Public Space*, New York: Noonday.

Boztas, S. (2003) 'Rowling could win £10m at quidditch', *Sunday Times*, May 4: 1.13.

Brannen, M.Y. (1992) ' "Bwana Mickey": constructing cultural consumption at Tokyo Disneyland', in J.J. Tobin (ed.), *Re-Made in Japan: Everyday Life and Consumer Taste in a Changing Society*, New Haven, CT: Yale University Press.

Bright, R. (1987) *Disneyland: Inside Story*, New York: Harry N. Abrams.

Brodie, I. (1996) 'Gambling on a modern Marvel', *The Times*, November 18: 46.

Bryman, A. (1995) *Disney and his Worlds*, London: Routledge.

Bryman, A. (1997) 'Animating the pioneer versus late entrant debate: an historical case study', *Journal of Management Studies*, 34: 415–38.

Bryman, A. (1999a) 'Theme parks and McDonaldization', in B. Smart (ed.), *Resisting McDonaldization*, London: Sage.

Bryman, A. (1999b) 'Global Disney', in D. Slater and P.J. Taylor (eds), *The American Century*, Oxford, Blackwell.

Buckingham, D. (2001) 'United Kingdom: Disney dialectics: debating the politics of children's media culture', in J. Wasko, M. Phillips, and E.R. Meehan (eds), *Dazzled by Disney: The Global Disney Audiences Project*, London: Leicester University Press.

Buescher, D.T. and Ono, K.A. (1996) 'Civilized colonialism: *Pocahontas* as neo-colonial rhetoric', *Women's Studies in Communication*, 19: 127–53.

Burchill, J. (1998) 'Taking the Mickey', *The Guardian* (Travel section), October 10.

Butler, S.R. and Snizek, W.E. (1976) 'The waitress-diner relationship', *Sociology of Work and Occupations*, 3: 209–22.

Byrne, C. (1997) 'Terror tourists queue for trips to war zones', *Sunday Times*, March 16.

Cain, L.P. and Merritt, D.A. (1998) 'The growing commercialism of zoos and aquariums', *Journal of Policy Analysis and Management*, 17: 298–312.

Callaghan, G. and Thompson, P. (2002) ' "We recruit attitude": the selection and shaping of routine call centre labour', *Journal of Management Studies*, 39: 233–54.

Canemaker, J. (1991) *Felix: the Twisted Tale of the World's Most Famous Cat*, New York: Pantheon.

Cartler, C. (1998) 'Megadevelopment in Malaysia: from heritage landscapes to "leisurescapes" in Melaka's tourism sector', *Singapore Journal of Tropical Geography*, 19: 151–76.

Chaney, D. (1983) 'The department store as a cultural form', *Theory, Culture and Society*, 1: 22–31.

Chaney, D. (1990) 'Subtopia in Gateshead: the MetroCentre as a cultural form', *Theory, Culture and Society*, 7: 49–68.

Chesshyre, T. (2002a) 'Viva the sleazy side of Vegas', *The Times* (Travel section), March 30: 4.

Chesshyre, T. (2002b) 'Under threat: the real face of Florida', *The Times* (Travel section), May 25: 1–2.

Chittenden, M. and Winnett, R. (2001) 'Rowling could be first billionaire writer', *Sunday Times*, November 25: 24.

Chua, B-H. (1998) 'World cities, globalisation and the spread of consumerism: a view from Singapore', *Urban Studies*, 35: 981–1000.

Churchill, D. (1998) 'Beware, it's a jungle out there', *The Times* (Weekend section), March 28: 3.

Coe, J.C. (1996) 'Future vision: the twenty-first century zoo', in M. Nichols (ed.), *Keepers of the Kingdom: The New American Zoo*, New York: Thomasson-Grant & Lickle.

Cohen, S. (1997) 'More than the Beatles: popular music, tourism and urban regeneration', in S. Abram, J. Waldren and D.V.L. Macleod (eds), *Tourists and Tourism: Identifying with People and Places*, Oxford: Berg.

Cohn, N. (1996) 'Talking shop', *Sunday Times* (Travel section), January 21: 1.

Coleman, R. and Sim, J. (1998) 'From the dockyards to the Disney Store: surveillance, risk and security in Liverpool city centre', *International Review of Law Computers and Technology*, 12: 27–44.

Connellan, T. (1996) *Inside the Magic Kingdom: Seven Keys to Disney's Success*, Austin, TX: Bard.

Conway, W. (1996) 'From zoos to conservation parks', in M. Nichols (ed.), *Keepers of the Kingdom: The New American Zoo*, New York: Thomasson-Grant & Lickle: 27–34.

Cowley, J. (1998) 'Can the stiff upper lip survive?', *The Times*, July 7: 17.

Crang, P. (1994) 'It's showtime: on the workplace geographies of display in a restaurant in south-east England', *Environment and Planning D: Society and Space*, 12: 675–704.

Crawford, M. (1992) 'The world in a shopping mall', in M. Sorkin (ed.), *Variations on a Theme Park: The New American City and the End of Public Space*, New York: Noonday.

Croke, V. (1997) *The Modern Ark*, New York: Scribner.

Cunningham, J. (2001) 'Potty about Harry', *The Times*, October 20: 3.

Davis, S.G. (1996) 'The theme park: global industry and cultural form', *Media, Culture and Society*, 18: 399–422.

Davis, S.G. (1997) *Spectacular Nature: Corporate Culture and the Sea World Experience*, Berkeley, CA: University of California Press.

Davis, S.G. (1999) 'Space Jam: Media conglomerates build the entertainment city', *European Journal of Communication*, 14: 435–59.

deCordova, R. (1994) 'The Mickey in Macy's window: childhood, consumerism, and Disney animation', in E. Smoodin (ed.), *Disney Discourse*, New York: Routledge.

Dedman, B. (1998) 'Chicago – for fans of the blues, it's no heartbreak hotel', *New York Times*, December 6 (consulted online).

Desmond, J.C. (1999) *Staging Tourism: Bodies on Display from Waikiki to Sea World*, Chicago: University of Chicago Press.

Dibb, S. (1995) 'Understanding the level of marketing activity in the leisure sector', *Service Industries Journal*, 15: 257–75.

Disney Institute (2001) *Be Our Guest: Perfecting the Art of Customer Service*, New York: Disney Editions.

Doss, E. (1997) 'Making imagination safe in the 1950s: Disneyland's fantasy art and architecture', in K.A. Marling (ed.), *Designing Disney's Theme Parks: The Architecture of Reassurance*, Paris: Flammarion.

du Gay, P. (1996) *Consumption and Identity at Work*, London: Sage.

du Gay, P. and Salaman, G. (1992) 'The cult(ure) of the customer', *Journal of Management Studies*, 29: 195–213.

Durrett, R. (2003) 'Cowboys wait for a selling star: without a big name, whose jersey will fans buy?', *Dallas Morning News*, July 25 (consulted online).

Dutka, E. (1997) 'No Herculean gross: why?', *Los Angeles Times*, July 19: F1.

Dyckhoff, T. (2003) 'Theme park city', *The Times* (T2 section) April 29: 17.

Eco, U. (1986) *Travels in Hyperreality*, London: Pan.

Edensor, T. (2001) 'Performing tourism, staging tourism: (re)producing tourist space and practice', *Tourist Studies*, 1: 59–81.

Edgerton, G. and Jackson, K.M. (1996) 'Redesigning *Pocahontas*: Disney, the "white man's Indian," and the marketing of dreams', *Journal of Popular Film and Television*, 24: 90–8.

Edwards, R. (1979) *Contested Terrain: The Transformation of the Workplace in the Twentieth Century*, London: Heinemann.

Eisman, R. (1993) 'Disney magic', *Incentive*, September: 45–56.

Eisner, M.D. (1998) *Work in Progress*, London: Penguin.

Elliott, S. (1998) 'Marketing Diana, Princess of brand names', *New York Times*, August 26: D1, D3.

Ellwood, W. (1998) 'Service with a smile', *New Internationalist*, 308, (December): 17.

Fainstein, S.S. and Judd, D.R. (1999) 'Global forces, local strategies, and urban tourism', in D.R. Judd and S.S. Fainstein (eds), *The Tourist City*, New Haven, CT: Yale University Press.

Falconer Al-Hindi, K. and Staddon, C. (1997) 'The hidden histories and geographies of traditional town planning: the case of Seaside, Florida', *Environment and Planning D: Society and Space*, 15: 349–72.

Falconer Al-Hindi, K. and Till, K.E. (2001) '(Re)placing the New Urbanism debates: toward an interdisciplinary research agenda', *Urban Geography*, 22: 189–201.

Fantasia, R. (1995) 'Fast food in France', *Theory and Society*, 24: 201–43.

Fessier, M. (1977) 'Legacy of a last tycoon', *Los Angeles Times West*, November 12: 16–23.

Findlay, J.M. (1992) *Magic Lands: Western Cityscapes and American Culture After 1940*, Berkeley, CA: University of California Press.

Fjellman, S.M. (1992) *Vinyl Leaves: Walt Disney World and America*, Boulder, CO: Westview Press.

Foglesong, R.E. (2001) *Married to the Mouse: Walt Disney World and Orlando*, New Haven, CT: Yale University Press.

Forgacs, D. (1992) 'Disney animation and the business of childhood', *Screen*, 33: 361–74.

Fox, N. (1996) 'Cartoon heroes are drawn into a money machine', *Sunday Times* (Business section), February 4: 9.

France, V.A. (1991) *Window on Main Street*, Nashua, NH: Laughter Publications.

Frantz, D. and Collins, C. (1999) *Celebration, U.S.A.: Living in Disney's Brave New Town*, New York: Henry Holt.

Frenkel, S.J., Korczynksi, M., Shire, K.A. and Tam, M. (1999) *On the Front Line: Organization of Work in the Information Economy*, Ithaca, NY: ILR Press.

Fresco, A. (2001) 'Football club profits hit as fans rip off replica shirts', *The Times*, April 3: 9.

Fuller, L. and Smith, V. (1991) 'Consumers' reports: management by customers in a changing economy', *Work, Employment and Society*, 5: 1–16.

Gephardt, R.P. (2001) 'Safe risk in Las Vegas', *M@n@gement*, 4: 141–58.

Giddens, A. (1990) *The Consequences of Modernity*, California: Stanford University Press.

Gill, B. (1991) 'Disneyitis', *The New Yorker*, April 19: 113–17.

Giroux, H. (1999) *The Mouse that Roared: Disney and the End of Innocence*, Lanham, ML: Rowman & Littlefield.

Gledhill, R. (2002) 'Archbishop fires opening shot at Disney', *The Times*, July 23: 1.

Goldberger, P. (1972) 'Mickey Mouse teaches the architects', *New York Times Magazine*, October 22: 40–1, 92–9.

Goldberger, P. (1997a) 'The store strikes back', *New York Times*, April 6 (consulted online).

Goldberger, P. (1997b) 'The sameness of things', *New York Times*, April 6 (consulted online).

Goodman, M. (2002) 'Star Wars: the menace of merchandise overkill', *Sunday Times* (Business section), May 5: 3.9.

Goodwin, C. (1995) 'Toys 'R' Disney', *Sunday Times*, December 3: 10.7.

Goodwin, C. (2002) 'The King: dead and forgotten', *The Times* (T2 section), April 29: 6.

Gordon, M. (1958) 'Walt's profit formula: dream, diversify – and never miss an angle', *Wall Street Journal*, February 4: 1, 12.

Gordon, P.H. and Meunier, S. (2001). *The French challenge: Adapting to Globalization*, Washington, D.C.: Brookings Institution Press.

Goss, J. (1993a) 'The "magic of the mall": an analysis of form, function, and meaning in the contemporary retail built environment', *Annals of the Association of American Geographers*, 83: 18–47.

Goss, J. (1993b) 'Placing the market and marketing place: tourist advertising of the Hawaiian Islands, 1972–92', *Environment and Planning D: Society and Space*, 11: 663–88.

Goss, J. (1996) 'Disquiet on the waterfront: reflections on nostalgia and utopia in the urban archetypes of festival marketplaces', *Urban Geography*, 17: 221–47.

Goss, J. (1999) 'Once-upon-a-time in the commodity world: an unofficial guide to Mall of America', *Annals of the Association of American Geographers*, 89: 45–75.

Gottdiener, M. (1997) *The Theming of America: Dreams, Visions and Commercial Spaces*. Boulder, CO: Westview.

Gottdiener, M. (2001) *The Theming of America: American Dreams, Media Fantasies, and Themed Environments*, second edition, Boulder, CO: Westview.

Gottdiener, M., Collins, C.C. and Dickens, D.R. (1999) *Las Vegas: The Social Production of an All-American City* Malden, MA: Blackwell.

Gould, S.J. (1979) 'Mickey Mouse meets Konrad Lorenz', *Natural History*, 88: 30–6.

Graham, S. (1998) 'Towards the fifth utility? On the extension and normalisation of public CCTV', in C. Norris, J. Moran, and G. Armstrong (eds), *Surveillance, Closed Circuit Television and Social Control*, Aldershot: Ashgate.

Grover, R. (2001) 'Now Disneyland won't seem so Mickey Mouse', *Business Week*: January 29 (consulted online).

Guerrier, Y. and Adib, A. S. (2000) '"No, we don't provide that service": the harassment of hotel employees', *Work, Employment and Society*, 14: 689–705.

Gwynne, S.C. (1997) 'Love me legal tender', *Time*, August 11: 46–9.

Haas, R. (1995) 'Disney goes Dutch: *Billy Bathgate* and the Disneyfication of the gangster genre', in E. Bell, L. Haas, and L. Sells (eds), *From Mouse to Mermaid: The Politics of Film, Gender and Culture*, Bloomington: Indiana University Press.

Halewood, C. and Hannan, K. (2001) 'Viking heritage tourism: authenticity and commodification', *Annals of Tourism Research*, 28: 565–80.

Hall, E.J. (1993) 'Smiling, deferring, and flirting: doing gender by giving "good service"', *Work and Occupations*, 20: 452–71.

Hamel, G. and Prahalad, C.K. (1994) *Competing for the Future*, Boston, MA: Harvard Business School Press.

Hamilton, A. (1999) 'Queen joins zoo's beetle drive', *The Times*, June 4: 4.

Hamilton, A. (2002) 'Princess is alive but fading fast in cyberspace', *The Times*, August 31: 11.

Hamilton, K. (1999) 'Wal*Smart', *Sunday Times* (Business Section), June 10: 3.5.

Hamilton, K. and Harlow, J. (1995) 'Retailers fly in to exploit airport shopping boom', *Sunday Times* (Business section), May 14: 2.

Hamilton, M. (2000) 'The latest malling of America: Mills Corp. draws crowds to unusual shopping environments', *Washington Post*, July 22: E1.

Handler, R. and Gable, E. (1997) *The New History in an Old Museum: Creating the Past at Colonial Williamsburg*, Durham, NC: Duke University Press.

Handy, B. (1996) '101 movie tie-ins', *Time*, December 16: 54–6.

Hannerz, U. (1987) 'The world in creolization', *Africa*, 57: 546–59.

Hannigan, J. (1998) *Fantasy City: Pleasure and Profit in the Postmodern Metropolis*, London: Routledge.

Harley, E. (2002) 'Sack the Ripper', *The Business (Financial Times Weekend Magazine)*, January 26: 14.

Harris, N. (1997) 'Expository expositions: preparing for the theme parks', in K.A. Marling (ed.), *Designing Disney's Theme Parks: The Architecture of Reassurance*, Paris: Flammarion.

Heide, R. and Gilman, J. (1997) *The Mickey Mouse Watch: From the Beginning of Time*, New York: Hyperion.

Heise, S. (1994) 'Disney approach to managing', *Executive Excellence*, October: 18–19.

Helgadottir, B. (2003) 'Tinies: ripe for plucking', *The Times* (Weekend section), May 24: 6.

Hendry, J. (2000) *The Orient Strikes Back: A Global View of Cultural Display*, Oxford: Berg.

Henkoff, R. (1994) 'Finding, training and keeping the best service workers', *Fortune*, October 3: 52–8.

Hiaasen, C. (1998) *Team Rodent: How Disney Devours the World*, New York: Ballantine.

Hachschild, A.R. (1983) *The Managed Heart*, Berkeley, CA: University of California Press.

Hollister, P. (1940) 'Genius at work: Walt Disney', *Atlantic Monthly*, December: 689–701.

Holson, L.M. and Lyman, R. (2002) 'In Warner Brothers' strategy, a movie is now a product line', *New York Times*, February 11 (consulted online).

Hopkins, J.S.P. (1990) 'West Edmonton mall: landscape of myths and elsewhereness', *The Canadian Geographer*, 34: 2–17.

Hopkins, N. (2002) 'HIT talks to rival Gullane on £215 million offer', *The Times*, May 28: 25.

Hubbard, P. (2002) 'Screen-shifting: consumption, "riskless risks" and the changing geographies of cinema', *Environment and Planning A*, 34: 1239–58.

Hubbard, P. (2003) 'A good night out? Multiplex cinemas as sites of embodied leisure', *Leisure Studies*, 22: 1–18.

Hughes, K.D. and Tadic, V. (1998) '"Something to deal with": customer sexual harassment and women's retail service work in Canada', *Gender, Work and Organization*, 5: 207–19.

Huxtable, A.L. (1997) *The Unreal America: Architecture and Illusion*, New York: New Press.

Jamieson, D. (1995) 'Zoos revisited', in B.G. Norton, M. Hutchins, E.F. Stevens, and T.L. Maple (eds), *Ethics on the Ark: Zoos, Animal Welfare, and Wildlife Conservation*, Washington, D.C: Smithsonian Institute.

Jenkins, R. (1998) 'The last word in shopping', *The Times*, September 5: 20.

Jones, A. (1999) 'Vatican stores to sell treasures on earth', *The Times*, June 10: 27.

Jones, L. (1999) 'Smiling lessons end service with a scowl in Greenland', *The Guardian*, October 23 (consulted online).

Judd, D.R. (1999) 'Constructing the tourist bubble', in D.R. Judd and S.S. Fainstein (eds), *The Tourist City*, New Haven, CT: Yale University Press.

Judge, J. (1973) 'Florida's booming – and beleaguered – heartland', *National Geographic*, 144: 585–621.

Kasson, J.F. (1978) *Amusing the Million: Coney Island at the Turn of the Century*, New York: Hill & Wang.

Keily, D. (1991) 'Body Shop blues', *Sunday Times (Style section)*, December 8: 3.4.

Kellner, D. (2002) 'Theorizing globalization', *Sociological Theory*, 20: 285–305.

Kenny, J.T. and Zimmerman, J. (2004) 'Constructing the "genuine American city": neo-traditionalism', New Urbanism and neo-liberalism in the remaking of downtown Milwaukee', *Cultural Geographies*, 11: 74–98.

Kincheloe, J.L. (2002) *The Sign of the Burger: McDonald's and the Culture of Power*, Philadelphia, PA: Temple University Press.

King, A. (2002) *The End of the Terraces: The Transformation of English Football in the 1990s*, revised edition, London: Leicester University Press.

King, M. (1991) 'The theme park experience: what museums can learn from Mickey Mouse', *The Futurist*, November-December: 24–31.

Kirshenblatt-Gimblett, B. (1998) *Destination Culture: Tourism, Museums, and Heritage*, Berkeley, CA: University of California Press.

Klein, N. (2000) *No Logo*, London: Flamingo.

Klein, N.M. (1993) *Seven Minutes: The Life and Death of the American Animated Cartoon*, London: Verso.

Kline, S. (1993) *Out of the Garden: Toys and Children's Culture in the Age of TV Marketing*, New York: Verso.

Koenig, D. (1994) *Mouse Tales: A Behind-the-Ears Look at Disneyland*, Irvine, CA: Bonaventure Press.

Koenig, D. (1999) *More Mouse Tales: A Closer Peek Backstage at Disneyland*, Irvine, CA: Bonaventure Press.

Koenig, R. (1996) 'The toys are back in town', *Sunday Times Magazine*, September 1: 40–2.

Korczynski, M. (2002) *Human Resource Management in Service Work*, Basingstoke: Palgrave.

Koster, O. (2001) 'Harry Potter and the not-so-wizard Coca-Cola wheeze', *Daily Mail*, October 18: 21.

Kozinets, R.V., Sherry, J.F. Jr., DeBerry-Spence, B., Duhachek, A., Nuttavuthisit, K. and Storm, D. (2002) 'Themed flagship brand stores in the new millennium: theory, practice, prospects', *Journal of Retailing*, 78: 17–29.

Kroc, R. (1987 [1977]) *Grinding it Out: The Making of McDonald's*, New York: St Martin's.

Kuenz, J. (1995a) 'Working at the rat', in The Project on Disney, *Inside the Mouse: Work and Play at Disney World*, Durham, NC: Duke University Press.

Kuenz, J. (1995b) 'It's a small world after all', in The Project on Disney, *Inside the Mouse: Work and Play at Disney World*, Durham, NC: Duke University Press.

Kuper, A. (1996) 'Dutch football looks to its future – and sees custard', *Financial Times*, March 16: 2.

Lainsbury, A. (2000) *Once Upon an American Dream: The Story of EuroDisneyland*, Lawrence, KA: University of Kansas Press.

Lanfant, M.-F. (1995) 'International tourism, internationalisation and the challenge to identity', in M.-F. Lanfant, J.B. Allcock and E.M. Bruner (eds), *International Tourism: Identity and Change*, London: Sage.

Langman, L. (1992) 'Neon cages: shopping for subjectivity', in R. Shields (ed.), *Lifestyle Shopping: The Subject of Consumption*, London: Routledge.

Larson, A. (2003) 'Re-drawing the bottom line', in C.A. Stabile and M. Harrison (eds), *Prime Time Animation: Television Animation and American Culture*, London: Routledge.

Lash, S. and Urry, J. (1994) *Economies of Signs and Space*, London: Sage.

Lauro, P.W. (2002) 'New York police and firefighter merchandise tests the market at the 2002 licensing exposition', *New York Times*, June 10: C 11.

Legge, K. (1995) *Human Resource Management: Rhetorics and Realities*, Basingstoke: Macmillan.

Leidner, R. (1993) *Fast Food, Fast Talk: Service Work and the Routinization of Everyday Life*, Berkeley, CA: University of California Press.

Leidner, R. (1999) 'Emotional labor in service work', *The Annals of the American Academy of Political and Social Science*, 561: 81–95.

Leong, S.T. (2001a) '…And then there was shopping', in *Harvard Design School Guide to Shopping*, Köln: Taschen.

Leong, S.T. (2001b) 'Captive', in *Harvard Design School Guide to Shopping*, Köln: Taschen.

Letts, S. (1996) 'Snow White gets mini-camera to keep bodice pure', *The Times*, October 7.

Linstead, S. (1995) 'Averting the gaze: gender and power on the perfumed picket line', *Gender, Work and Organization*, 2: 192–206.

Lipsitz, G. (1993) 'The making of Disneyland', in W. Graebner (ed.), *True Stories from America's Past*, New York: McGraw-Hill.

Litman, J. (1994) 'Mickey Mouse emeritus: character protection and the public domain', *University of Miami Entertainment and Sports Law Review*, 11: 429–35.

Longmore, A. (1996) 'Roll up, roll up and sell the game', *The Times*, May 22: 46.

Lowenthal, D. (1985) *The Past is a Foreign Country*, Cambridge: Cambridge University Press.

Ludlow, M. (2002) 'Police put their money under their helmet with merchandising deal', *Sunday Times*, November 3: 1.10.

Lutz, C.A. and Collins, J.L. (1993) *Reading National Geographic*, Chicago: University of Chicago Press.

Lyon, D. (2001) *Surveillance Society: Monitoring Everyday Life*, Buckingham: Open University Press.

MacCannell, D. (1976) *The Tourist: A New Theory of the Leisure Class*, New York: Schocken.

Macdonald, S. (1996) 'Introduction', in S. Macdonald and G. Fyfe (eds), *Theorizing Museums: Representing Identity and Diversity in a Changing World*, Oxford: Blackwell/The Sociological Review.

Maguire, J.S. (2001) 'Fit and flexible: the fitness industry, personal trainers and emotional service labor', *Sociology of Sport Journal*, 18: 379–402.

Malamud, R. (1998) *Reading Zoos: Representations of Animals and Captivity*, New York: New York University Press.

Manning, P.K. and Callum-Swan, B. (1994) 'Narrative, content, and semiotic analysis', in N.K. Denzin and Y.S. Lincoln (eds), *Handbook of Qualitative Research*, Thousand Oaks, CA: Sage.

Maple, T. and Archibald, E. (1993) *Zoo Man: Inside the Zoo Revolution*, Atlanta, GA: Longstreet.

Margolis, S. (2001) 'The old world's new world', *New York Times*, July 15 (consulted online).

Marling, K.A. (1994) *As Seen on TV: The Visual Culture of Everyday Life in the 1950s*, Cambridge, MA: Harvard University Press.

Marling, K.A. (1997) 'Imagineering the "Disney theme parks"', in K.A. Marling (ed.), *Designing Disney's Theme Parks: The Architecture of Reassurance*, Paris: Flammarion.

Martin, J., Knopoff, K. and Beckman, C. (1998) 'An alternative to bureaucratic impersonality and emotional labor: bounded emotionality at The Body Shop', *Administrative Science Quarterly*, 43: 429–69.

Masters, K. (2000) *The Keys to the Kingdom: How Michael Eisner Lost His Grip*, New York: William Morrow.

McCahill, M. and Norris, C. (1999) 'Watching the workers: crime, CCTV and the workplace', in P. Davies, P. Francis, and V. Jupp (eds), *Invisible Crimes: Their Victims and Their Regulation*, London: Macmillan.

Mccalla, J. (1999a) 'Hypertheme restaurants: hyped out', *Philadelphia Business Journal*, January 25. http://philadelphia.bcentral.com/philadelphia/stories/1999/01/25/story3.html

Mccalla. J. (1999b) 'Daroff's advice: turn it up', *Philadelphia Business Journal*, January 25. http://philadelphia.bcentral.com/philadelphia/stories/1999/01/25/story4.html

McGill, D.C. (1989) 'A 'Mickey Mouse' class – for real', *New York Times*, August 27: 4.

Merritt, R. and Kaufman, J.B. (1992) *Walt in Wonderland: The Silent Films of Walt Disney*, Perdenone: Edizioni Biblioteca dell'Imagine.

Midgley, C. (1999) 'Tubbies land fat profits of £32 million in one year', *The Times*, June 23: 7.

Miller, D., Jackson, P., Thrift, N., Holbrook, B. and Rowlands, M. (1998) *Shopping, Place and Identity*, London: Routledge.

Mills, S. (1998) 'American theme parks and the landscapes of mass culture', *American Studies Today Online* www.americansc.org.uk/online/disney.htm

Milne, S., Grekin, J. and Woodley, S. (1998) 'Tourism and the construction of place in Canada's eastern Arctic', in G. Ringer (ed.), *Destinations: Cultural Landscapes of Tourism*, London: Routledge.

Mintz, L. (1998) 'Simulated tourism at Busch Gardens: The Old Country and Disney's World Showcase, Epcot Center', *Journal of Popular Culture*, 32: 47–58.

Mordue, T. (2001) 'Performing and directing resident/tourist cultures in *Heartbeat* country', *Tourist Studies*, 1: 233–52.

Moretti, F. (2001) 'Planet Hollywood', *New Left Review*, number 9: 90–101.

Mosley, L. (1986) *Disney's World*, Briarcliff Manor, NY: Stein and Day.

Mullan, B. and Marvin, G. (1999) *Zoo Culture*, second edition, Urbana, IL: University of Illinois Press.

Nel, P. (2003) 'The Disneyfication of Dr Seuss: faithful to profit, one hundred percent?', *Cultural Studies*, 17: 579–614.

Nelson, S. (1986) 'Walt Disney's EPCOT and the world's fair performance tradition', *Drama Review*, 30: 106–46.

Nickson, D., Warhurst, C., Witz, A. and Cullen A.-M. (2001) 'The importance of being aesthetic: work, employment and service organisation', in A. Sturdy, I. Grugulis, and H. Willmott (eds), *Customer Service: Empowerment and Entrapment*, Basingstoke: Palgrave.

Nicolas, R. (2002) 'Man Utd "at risk" of a branding own goal', *The Times*, June 10: 34.

Norton, A. (1996) 'Experiencing nature: the reproduction of environmental discourse through safari tourism in East Africa', *Geoforum*, 27: 355–73.

Nuttall, M. (1997) 'Packaging the wild: tourism development in Alaska', in S. Abram, J. Waldren and D.V.L. Macleod (eds), *Tourists and Tourism: Identifying with People and Places*, Oxford: Berg.

O'Brien, P.C. (1996) 'The happiest films on earth: Walt Disney's *Cinderella* and *The Little Mermaid*', *Women's Studies in Communication*, 19: 155–83.

O'Donnell, J. (2002) 'Galleon recruits PC Pepper for TV', *Sunday Times* (Business section), January 6: 3.3.

Ogbonna, E. and Wilkinson, B. (1990) 'Corporate strategy and corporate culture: the view from the checkout', *Personnel Review*, 19: 9–15.

Pecora, N. and Meehan, E.R. (2001) 'United States: A Disney dialectic: A tale of two American cities', in J. Wasko, M. Phillips, and E.R. Meehan (eds), *Dazzled by Disney: The Global Disney Audiences Project*, London: Leicester University Press.

Peñaloza, L. (1999) 'Just doing it: a visual ethnographic study of spectacular consumption behavior at Niketown', *Consumption, Markets and Culture*, 2: 337–400.

Pereira, J. (1995) 'Toy Sellers wish that Pocahontas were a lion', *Wall Street Journal*, July 24: B1, B7.

Peters, T. and Austin, N. (1985) *A Passion for Excellence*, New York: Random House.

Peters, T. and Waterman, R. (1982) *In Search of Excellence: Lessons from America's Best-Run Companies*, New York: Harper & Row.

Pieterse, J.N. (1994) 'Globalisation as hybridisation', *International Sociology*, 9: 161–84.

Pine, B.J. and Gilmore, J.H. (1999) *The Experience Economy: Work is Theatre and Every Business a Stage*, Boston, MA: Harvard Business School Press.

Pollan, M. (1997) 'Town-building is no Mickey Mouse operation', *New York Times*, December 14 (consulted online).

Powell, T.C. (1995) 'Total quality management as competitive advantage: a review and empirical study', *Strategic Management Journal*, 16: 15–37.

Pretes, M. (1995) 'Postmodern tourism: the Santa Claus industry', *Annals of Tourism Research*, 22: 1–13.

Rafaeli, A. and Sutton, R. (1989) 'The expression of emotion in organizational life', *Research in Organizational Behavior*, 11: 1–42.

Raz, A.E. (1999) *Riding the Black Ship: Japan and Tokyo Disneyland*, Cambridge, MA: Harvard University Press.

Reid, T. and Peek, L. (2001) 'Potter playtime is a Muggle's game at £350 a time', *The Times*, November 6: 11.

Reiter, E. (1996) *Making Fast Food: From the Frying Pan into the Fryer*, second edition, Montreal & Kingston: McGill-Queen's University Press.

Ritzer, G. (1993) *The McDonaldization of Society*, Thousand Oaks, CA: Pine Forge.

Ritzer, G. (1998) *The McDonaldization Thesis*, London: Sage.

Ritzer, G. (1999) *Enchanting a Disenchanted World: Revolutionizing the Means of Consumption*, Thousand Oaks, CA: Pine Forge.

Ritzer, G. (2004) *The Globalization of Nothing*, Thousand Oaks, CA: Pine Forge.

Ritzer, G. and Liska, A. (1997) ' "McDisneyization" and "post-tourism": complementary perspectives on contemporary tourism', in C. Rojek and J. Urry (eds), *Touring Cultures: Transformations of Travel and Theory*, London: Routledge.

Ritzer, G. and Stillman, T. (2001a) 'The modern Las Vegas casino-hotel: the paradigmatic new means of consumption', *M@n@gement*, 4: 83–99.

Ritzer, G. and Stillman, T. (2001b) 'The postmodern ballpark as a leisure setting: enchantment and simulated de-McDonaldization', *Leisure Sciences*, 23: 99–113.

Robbins, T. (2002) 'Tourists to invade Kabul on "axis of evil" holidays', *Sunday Times*, July 28.

Robertson, R. (1992) *Globalization: Social Theory and Global Culture*, London: Sage.

Robertson, R. (2001) 'Globalization theory 2000+: major problematics', in G. Ritzer and B. Smart (eds), *Handbook of Social Theory*, London: Sage.

Robinson, M.B. (2003) 'The Mouse who would rule the world! How American criminal justice reflects the themes of Disneyization', *Journal of Criminal Justice and Popular Culture*, 10: 69–86.

Roche, M. (2000) *Mega-events and Modernity: Olympics and Expos in the Growth of Global Culture*, London: Routledge.

Rosenthal, P., Hill, S. and Peccei, R. (1997) 'Checking out service: evaluating excellence, HRM and TQM in retailing', *Work, Employment and Society*, 11: 481–503.

Ross, A. (1999) *The Celebration Chronicles: Life, Liberty, and the Pursuit of Property Value in Disney's New Town*, New York: Ballantine.

Royle, T. (2000) *Working for McDonald's in Europe: The Unequal Struggle*, London: Routledge.

Rugoff, R. (1999) 'Shopping mall with social ambitions', *Financial Times* (Weekend section), March 6: VII.

Rushe, D. (2003) 'Is the world fed up with McDonald's?' *Sunday Times* (Business section), April 6: 3.8.

Russell, R. and Tyler, M. (2002) 'Thank heaven for little girls: "Girl Heaven" and the commercial context of feminine childhood', *Sociology*, 36: 619–37.

Sandicki, O. and Holt, D.B. (1998) 'Malling society: mall consumption practices and the future of public space', in J.F. Sherry, Jr. (ed.), *ServiceScapes: The Concept of Place in Contemporary Markets*, Lincolnwood, IL: NTC Business Books.

Sayers, F.C. (1965) 'Walt Disney accused', *Horn Book*, December: 602–11.

Schickel, R. (1986) *The Disney Version: The Life, Times, Art, and Commerce of Walt Disney*, revised edition, London: Pavilion.

Schlossberg, H. (1996) *Sports Marketing*, Cambridge, MA: Blackwell.

Schlosser, E. (2001) *Fast Food Nation: The Dark Side of the All-American Meal*, Boston: Houghton Mifflin.

Schmitt, B. and Simonson, A. (1997) *Marketing Aesthetics: The Strategic Management of Brands, Identity, and Image*, New York: Free Press.

Schueller, J. (2000) 'Customer service through leadership: the Disney way', *Training and Development*, 54 (October): 26–31.

Sharma, U. and Black, P. (2001) 'Look good, feel better: beauty therapy as emotional labour', *Sociology*, 35: 913–31.

Shearing, C.D. and Stenning, P.C. (1984) 'From the panopticon to Disney World: the development of discipline', in A.N. Doob and E.L. Greenspan (eds), *Perspectives in Criminal Law*, Aurora, Ontario: Criminal Law Books.

Sherman, J. (2001) 'Pharaoh's riches for Golden Mile', *The Times*, July 18.

Sherry, J.F. Jr. (1998) 'The soul of the company store: Nike Town Chicago and the emplaced brandscape', in J.F. Sherry, Jr. (ed.), *ServiceScapes: The Concept of Place in Contemporary Markets*, Lincolnwood, IL: NTC Business Books.

Sherry, J.F. Jr., Kozinets, R.V., Storm, D., Duhachek, A., Nuttavuthisit, K. and DeBerry-Spence, B. (2001) 'Being in the Zone: staging retail theater at ESPN Zone Chicago', *Journal of Contemporary Ethnography*, 30: 465–510.

Sherwin, A. (2001) 'Tourism rivals fight for Middle Earth', *The Times*, December 11.

Sherwin, T. (2002) 'Monsters Inc makes sure Fairy Liquid cleans up', *The Times*, February 16: 11.

Shields, R. (1989) 'Social spatialization and the built environment: the West Edmonton mall', *Environment and Planning D: Society and Space*, 7: 147–64.

Shoval, N. (2000) 'Commodification and theming of the sacred: changing patterns of tourist consumption in the "Holy Land"', in M. Gottdiener (ed.), *New Forms of Consumption: Consumers, Culture, and Commodification*, Lanham, Maryland: Rowman & Littlefield.

Simensky, L. (1998) 'Selling Bugs Bunny: Warner Bros. and character merchandising in the nineties', in K.S. Sandler (ed.), *Reading the Rabbit: Explorations in Warner Bros. Animation*, New Brunswick, NJ: Rutgers University Press.

Skapinker, M. and Rawsthorn, A. (1993) 'An older, wiser Mickey Mouse', *Financial Times*, April 10: 18.

Sklair, L. (2002) *Globalization: Capitalism and its Alternatives*, Oxford: Oxford University Press.

Solomon, M.R. (1998) 'Dressing for the part: the role of costume in the staging of the servicescape', in J.F. Sherry, Jr. (ed.), *ServiceScapes: The Concept of Place in Contemporary Markets*, Lincolnwood, IL: NTC Business Books.

Sorkin, M. (1992) 'Introduction: variations on a theme park', in M. Sorkin (ed.), *Variations on a Theme Park: The New American City and the End of Public Space*, New York: Noonday.

Sparks, C. (1998) *From the Hundred Aker Wood to The Magic Kingdom*, Inaugural Lecture, School of Communication, Design and Media, University of Westminster, 14 October 1998 www.wmin.ac.uk/events/sparks.htm

Spellmeyer, A.W. (1993) 'Mall of America: confounding the skeptics', *Urban Land*, 52: 43–6, 81–3.

Squire, S.J. (1993) 'The cultural values of literary tourism', *Annals of Tourism Research*, 20: 103–20.

Steiner, M. (1998) 'Frontierland as Tomorrowland: Walt Disney and the architectural packaging of the mythic west', *Montana – The Magazine of Western History*, 48: 2–17.

Steiner, R. (2002) 'Teletubbies' tubby profits tumble', *Sunday Times* (Business section), February 24: 3.2.

Steinhauer, J. (1998) 'It's a mall … It's an airport … It's both: The latest trend in terminals', *New York Times*: D1.

Sterne, J. (1997) 'Sounds like the Mall of America: programmed music and the architectonics of commercial space', *Ethnomusicology*, 41: 22–50.

Studd, H. (2002) 'Toy sellers are not so wild about Harry', *The Times*, January 28: 9.

Sturdy, A. (2001) 'The global diffusion of customer service: a critique of cultural and institutional perspectives', *Asia Pacific Business Review*, 7: 75–89.

Sutton, R.I. and Rafaeli, A. (1988) 'Untangling the relationship between displayed emotions and organizational sales: the case of convenience stores', *Academy of Management Journal*, 31: 461–87.

Swanton, O. (1996) 'Pocahontas, eat your heart out', *Guardian* (Higher education section), February 25: vi.

Synnott, M.G. (1995) 'Disney's America: whose patrimony, whose profits, whose past?', *The Public Historian*, 17: 43–59.

Talwar, J.P. (2002) *Fast Food, Fast Track: Immigrants, Big Business, and the American Dream*, Boulder, CO: Westview.

Tarpy, C. (1993) 'New zoos – taking down the bars', *National Geographic*, July: 2–37.

Taylor, C.R. and Wheatley-Lovoy, C. (1998) 'Leadership: lessons from the Magic Kingdom', *Training and Development*, July: 22–5.

Taylor, S. (1998) 'Emotional labour and the new workplace', in P. Thompson and C. Warhurst (eds), *Workplaces of the Future*, London: Macmillan.

Taylor, S. and Tyler, M. (2000) 'Emotional labour and sexual difference in the airline industry', *Work, Employment and Society*, 14: 77–95.

Thomas, B. (1976) *Walt Disney: An American Original*, New York: Simon and Schuster.

Thompson, P. and Findlay, P. (1999) 'Changing the people: social engineering in the contemporary workplace', in L. Ray and A. Sayer (eds), *Culture and Economy after the Cultural Turn*, London: Sage.

Tolich, M.B. (1993) 'Alienating and liberating emotions at work: supermarket clerks' performance of customer service', *Journal of Contemporary Ethnography*, 22: 361–81.

Tomkins, R. (1998) 'Fair game for a gentle savaging', *Financial Times*, April 25: 9.

Tracy, J.F. (1999) 'Whistle while you work: The Disney Company and the global division of labor', *Journal of Communication Inquiry*, 23: 374–89.

Tucker, H. (2002) 'Welcome to Flintstones-Land: contesting place and identity in Goreme, Central Turkey', in S. Coleman and M. Crang (eds), *Tourism: Between Place and Performance*, New York: Berghahn Books.

Tumbusch, T. (1989) *Tomart's Illustrated Disneyana Catalog and Price Guide*, Radnor, PA: Wallace-Homestead.

Turner, S. (2001) 'In bed with McDonald's', *The Times* (Travel section), March 24.

Twitchell, J.B. (1999) *Lead Us Into Temptation: The Triumph of American Materialism*, New York: Columbia University Press.

Urry, J. (1990) *The Tourist Gaze*, London: Sage.

Urry, J. (2002) *The Tourist Gaze*, second edition, London: Sage.

Uttal, B. (1983) 'The corporate culture vultures', *Fortune*, October 17: 66–72.

Van Maanen, J. (1991) 'The smile factory: work at Disneyland', in P.J. Frost, L.F. Moore, M.L. Louis, C.C. Lundberg, and J. Martin (eds), *Reframing Organizational Culture*, Newbury Park, CA: Sage.

Van Maanen, J. and Kunda, G. (1989) '"Real feelings": emotional expression and organizational culture', *Research in Organizational Behavior*, 11: 43–103.

Voyle, S. (2001) 'Harry Potter tops list of wizard stocking filler ideas', *Financial Times*, November 17: 3.

Waitt, G. (2000) 'Consuming heritage: perceived historical authenticity', *Annals of Tourism Research*, 27: 835–62.

Walker, S. (1997) 'Hair salons, hot tubs and … oh yeah, baseball', *Wall Street Journal*, March 27: W1, W6.

Wallendorf, M., Lindsey-Mullikin, J., and Pimentel, R. (1998) 'Gorilla marketing: customer animation and regional embeddedness of a toy store servicescape', in J.F. Sherry, Jr. (ed.), *ServiceScapes: The Concept of Place in Contemporary Markets*, Lincolnwood, IL: NTC Business Books.

Walton, R. (1985) 'From control to commitment in the workplace', *Harvard Business Review*, 63: 77–84.

Walz, G. (1998) 'Charlie Thorson and the temporary Disneyfication of Warner Bros. cartoons', in K.S. Sandler (ed.), *Reading the Rabbit: Explorations in Warner Bros. Animation*, New Brunswick, NJ: Rutgers University Press.

Waples, J. (1997) 'City reaps riches on the road to Toytown', *Sunday Times* (Business section), May 18: 3.4.

Waples, J. (2003) 'Dome boss makes running in sporting fun', *Sunday Times*, (Business Section), April 13: 3.11.

Warren, S. (1994) 'Disneyfication of the Metropolis: popular resistance in Seattle', *Journal of Urban Affairs*, 16: 89–107.

Warren, S. (1996) 'Popular cultural practices in the "postmodern city"', *Urban Geography*, 17: 545–67.

Warren, S. (1999) 'Cultural contestation at Disneyland Paris', in D. Crouch (ed.), *Leisure/Tourism Geographies: Practices and Geographical Knowledge*, London: Routledge.

Wasko, J. (2001) *Understanding Disney: The Manufacture of Fantasy*, Cambridge: Polity.

Waters, M. (2002) 'McDonaldization and the global culture of consumption', in G. Ritzer (ed.), *McDonaldization: The Reader*, Thousand Oaks, CA: Pine Forge.

Watson, J.L. (1997a) 'Introduction: transnationalism, localization, and fast foods in East Asia', in J.L. Watson (ed.), *Golden Arches East: McDonald's in East Asia*, Stanford, CA: Stanford University Press.

Watson, J.L. (1997b) 'McDonald's in Hong Kong: consumerism, dietary change, and the rise of a children's culture', in J.L. Watson (ed.), *Golden Arches East: McDonald's in East Asia*, Stanford, CA: Stanford University Press.

Watts, S. (1997) *The Magic Kingdom: Walt Disney and the American Way of Life*, Boston: Houghton Mifflin.

Weatherford, M. (1998) 'Fantasy lands', *Las Vegas Review-Journal*, February 26 (consulted online).

Weatherford, M. (2000) 'Branding of Las Vegas', *Las Vegas Review-Journal*, August 20 (consulted online).

Weinstein, R.M. (1992) 'Disneyland and Coney Island: reflections in the evolution of the modern amusement park', *Journal of Popular Culture*, 26: 131–64.

Wharton, A.S. (1993) 'The affective consequences of service work', *Work and Occupations*, 20: 205–32.

Wharton, A.S. (1999) 'The psychosocial consequences of emotional labor', *The Annals of the American Academy of Political and Social Science*, 561: 158–76.

Whittell, G. (1999) 'Earth moves for fans of "Star Wars"', *The Times*, January 16: 14.

Wickers, D. (1999) 'The mouse boat', *Sunday Times* (Travel section), June 27: 6.

Wiley, K.W. (1999–2000) 'How do they stay so nice?', *Disney Magazine*, Winter: 54–8, 101.

Willis, S. (1995a) 'The problem with pleasure', in The Project on Disney, *Inside the Mouse: Work and Play at Disney World*, Durham, NC: Duke University Press.

Willis, S. (1995b) 'Private use/public state', in The Project on Disney, *Inside the Mouse: Work and Play at Disney World*, Durham, NC: Duke University Press.

Witz, A., Warhurst, C. and Nickson, D. (2003) 'The labour of aesthetics and the aesthetics of organization', *Organization*, 10: 33–54.

Wolf, M.J. (1999) *The Entertainment Economy: How Mega-Media Forces are Transforming our Lives*, New York: Times Books.

Wood, R.E. (2000) 'Caribbean cruise tourism: globalization at sea', *Annals of Tourism Research*, 27: 345–70.

Wooden, W. (1995) *Renegade Kids, Suburban Outlaws: From Youth Culture to Delinquency*, Belmont: Wadsworth.

Wouters, C. (1989) 'The sociology of emotions and flight attendants: Hochschild's *Managed Heart*', *Theory, Culture and Society*, 6: 95–123.

Yan, Y. (1997) 'McDonald's in Beijing: the localization of Americana', in J.L. Watson (ed.), *Golden Arches East: McDonald's in East Asia*, Stanford, CA: Stanford University Press.

Young, R. (1998) 'Baghdad package tour is a hostage to fortune', *The Times*, February 10.

Zehnder, L.E. (1975) *Florida's Disney World*, Tallahassee, FL: Peninsular Press Publishing.

Zemke, R. (1989) *The Service Edge: 101 Companies That Profit from Customer Care*, New York: New American Library.

Zibart, E. (1997) *The Unofficial Disney Companion*, New York: Macmillan.

Zukin, S. (1991) *Landscapes of Power: From Detroit to Disney World*, Berkeley, CA: University of California Press.

Zukin, S. (1995) *The Cultures of Cities*, Cambridge, MA: Blackwell.

Zukin, S. (1998) 'Urban lifestyles: diversity and standardisation in spaces of consumption', *Urban Studies*, 35: 825–39.

Author Index

Subject Index